A HISTORY OF THE

AUSTRALIAN
MILITARY

From the First Fleet to the Modern Day

A HISTORY OF THE
AUSTRALIAN MILITARY

From the First Fleet to the Modern Day

JONATHAN J. MOORE

Thank you to my family Jacinta, Jamie, Christopher and Caitlin who have helped with my never ending search for military, medical and criminal history. Also thanks to all in the Living History and War Gaming fraternities who have contributed so much knowledge over the years and make the field so enjoyable.

CONTENTS

INTRODUCTION

Australia is a remote nation, tucked away in the Southern Hemisphere, with a tiny population compared to their densely populated neighbours to the North. Despite this, over several hundred years the Australian military has always punched well above its weight, earning a reputation for bravery and efficiency unrivalled in the modern world.

In 1789 the First Fleet under Captain Phillip moored in Botany Bay. The first to land on the shore were Marines – representatives of hundreds of years of the British military. These elite troops, with their excellent discipline and state-of-the-art weaponry, were the blueprint for more than 200 years of the Australian Army.

The Marines were the backbone of the infant colony, and even in the two difficult years when supplies were scarce and starvation was a very real threat they remained a disciplined force, keeping the colony safe.

The Marines had signed on for a limited amount of time and they were replaced by the New South Wales Corps. This unit was recruited as a garrison regiment to sail to the colony, where they were required to defend from both external aggressors and to maintain the peace with the fractious convicts. This unit, best known as the 'Rum Corps', now has something of a mixed reputation. Nevertheless, when a disciplined force was called for to put down a potentially calamitous convict uprising a small detachment marched to Parramatta and, combined with some locally raised militia, was able to deliver a volley of lead that broke the back of the rebellion in less than five minutes.

The New South Wales Corps was replaced by a succession of regiments sent from Britain. These were sent to all corners of the continent in large and small detachments. Their duties were innumerable and fraught with danger. Guarding convicts, protecting the colonies from foreign invasion and hunting down ferocious bushrangers were all duties that the redcoats were expected to fulfil. These regiments were the cream of the British Empire and had seen action in the wilds of North America and on the fierce battlefields of the Napoleonic wars. Many saw service on the horrifically violent frontiers of the subcontinent where capture by Afghan tribesmen or rebelling Indian sepoys had but one outcome – a long and painful death. No quarter was given in these fierce battles for empire, and when redcoats were asked to put down the insurrection at Ballarat they destroyed it with one violent bayonet assault.

In 1870 the redcoats were withdrawn. It was up to the colonies to provide their own armed forces. The disparate colonies vied with each other to form the most colourful and flamboyant militia units possible. Prestige could be gained by parading lancers, mounted rifles and even some kilted infantry. Behind the fine uniforms and love of display the colonial units took their business seriously and when the call went out to help the British Empire, thousands of volunteers flocked to fight Britain's enemies. Whether they were fierce tribesmen in New Zealand or the Sudan, or canny Boer farmers defending the veldt, Australian volunteers proved that they were doughty fighters – true sons of empire.

When the call went out from the British Empire to help subdue the wily Boers, fighting men from all of the colonies and territories flocked to the colours. Landing in Cape town, conventional training and formations were abandoned and the bush wise Australians proved to be perfectly suited to tracking down and destroying the elusive Boer fighters.

When fanatical Chinese nationalists began massacring Europeans in the Boxer Rebellion, Australia was able to contribute to the coalition's forces some state-of-the-art naval technology with the pride of the South Australian fleet – the heavy cruiser *Protector*. A well equipped naval brigade drawn from NSW and Victoria steamed North to partake in the fighting at the major Chinese ports. When they steamed back through the heads to Sydney in 1901 they found that they were not only Victorians or New South Welshmen, but were first and foremost Australians. In their absence the colonies had voted to federate. Disparate forces from the colonies were organised under a unified command and they began to move towards coherent drills discipline and unified equipment. The seeds of a superior professional force were sown.

The Kaiser's forces swept through Belgium on 4 August 1914. The British government had not been cowed by German sabre rattling and honoured her agreement to fight if the Germans violated Belgium's neutrality. The German military planners ignored geopolitical reality and, for the sake of a tactical advantage on a limited front, invited the British to declare war.

This one act brought the massive resources of the British Empire into play. The Triple Alliance powers of Germany, Turkey and Austria-Hungary had cause to rue the day the Australians poured into recruiting stations around our vast continent. After the initial setbacks at Gallipoli, the Anzacs proved to be the difference between victory and defeat in both the Eastern Theatre of Palestine and the Western Theatre on the Somme.

Despite the traumatic battle of Fromelles on the Western Front, where the Australians suffered horrendous casualties from outdated tactics, the ANZAC divisions soon learned how to fight and defeat the Hun. Epic fights such as the defence of Amiens in 1918 proved that the Australians were capable of taking on the best of the Kaiser's formations in their last desperate attempts to win the war. Sir John Monash rose from a Melbourne militia commander to be the most innovative and effective commander on the Western Front. He proved his worth when, in the battle of Hamel, combined arms tactics smashed through the German lines. His remarkable victory paved the way for what we now describe as modern warfare – offensive battles based on combined arms and rapid movement. His tactics were adopted by allied commanders, helping to burst through the Hindenburg line and bring the Kaiser's army to its knees. His innovative tactics set the stage for the fantastic sweeping battles of the Second World War. In the Middle East, the heroic charge of the light horse at Beersheba was one of many actions taken by the Australians to help the British General Allenby crack the Turkish lines and sweep the Ottomans out of territories that they had held for centuries.

Australia was one of the few participants in the First World War with an entirely volunteer force which was formed without recourse to conscription.

Despite this the AIF had the highest ratio of casualties than any other nation – a high price indeed of Australian blood spilled on foreign fields.

The astounding successes of the First World War were almost exceeded by the next generation's participation fighting the most dangerous aggressors in the 20th Century. German panzer divisions had ridden roughshod over Poland, France, the Balkans and much of North Africa. No army had managed to stand for any strategically significant amount of time against the combined armour of the Wehrmacht and the terror weapons of the Luftwaffe. That was until one understrength and poorly equipped Australian division, holed up in a tiny desert port called Tobruk, stopped Hitler's golden boy general Erwin Rommel's famed Africa Korps. The Axis timetable was thrown out and Nazi schemes to push through Egypt and the Middle East to link up with Germans in the Caucasus oil fields – guaranteeing limitless supplies of fuel – was halted for ever. Although the soldiers of the AIF (Australian Imperial Forces) were mauled in Greece and Crete, they were instrumental in Montgomery's attacks at Alamein that resulted in the Germans being thrown out of North Africa.

In the Pacific the story was much the same. The Japanese Imperial onslaught had swept aside any organised opposition. Millions of people from China to Timor were groaning under savage Japanese oppression in the optimistically named 'Greater East Asia Co-Prosperity sphere'. In reality this was an empire that extorted resources by subjugating indigenous populations with a brutality not seen since the Dark Ages. It seemed nothing could stop the elite jungle formations descending on Australia. At Milne Bay – one of the wettest places on Earth – dug in Australian troops resisted fanatical charges of Japanese infantry backed by tanks. Such were the casualties inflicted on the aggressor that the Japanese had to evacuate the shattered remnants of their assault forces.

These Japanese troops were lucky. Another thrust by the seemingly unstoppable Japanese, over the Owen Stanley Ranges to capture the strategic prize of Port Moresby, was impeded by the Australians, who flung them back over Papua's backbone. The once invincible soldiers of Nippon retreated in a nightmare of starvation, suicide and cannibalism.

The Axis advance had been stopped. Many years of hard fighting remained but the forces of a tiny nation in the Pacific had altered world history through bravery alone.

After World War II a new threat emerged. Cloaked in the promise of a socialist utopia, a communist juggernaut sought to extinguish freedom. The Iron Curtain descended over Europe. Not content with capturing all of Eastern Europe, Stalin cast his covetous eye over France, Italy and Greece. While the communist menace was quickly dealt with in these countries, in Asia it was an entirely different matter.

A massive invasion from Soviet North Korea into its southern neighbour drew an immediate response from UN troops. Australian forces were soon engaged in merciless hand-to-hand combat in the frozen hills above the 38th parallel. Many heroic deeds were performed in this conflict, but a war weary public barely took notice, making Korea Australia's forgotten war.

Other threats emerged. In Malaya, insurgents tried to establish a communist state. The RAAF and Australian Infantry were instrumental in bringing this conflict to an end and guaranteeing the freedom of one of the most populous nations in South-East Asia. When conflict broke out with the unbalanced Indonesian dictator Sukarno's forces, Australians once again used sophisticated tactics to dominate the rough jungle expanses found on the island of Borneo.

The Malayan emergency and the Indonesian 'Konfrontation' allowed the Australian military to develop effective counterinsurgency tactics. These would provide invaluable when the 8,000 strong Task Force was committed to Phuoc Tuy Province in South Vietnam. Professional Australian soldiers combined with National Service recruits came to dominate the terrain to such an extent that the North Vietnamese High Command ceased almost all military actions in the province. Battles such as those at Long Tan and Firebase Balmoral proved that no matter what the enemy threw at them, the Australian military would not take a step backwards.

While this book cannot cover all of the events of Australian military history, it can throw light on many of the crucial events of all who have fought in Australia and for Australia. Whether they were Aboriginal warriors, marines, soldiers of the crown, men of the Army or RAAF or RAN; all have contributed to a proud military tradition – proving that Australians were, and ever will be, the cutting edge.

CHAPTER 1

ABORIGINAL WARRIORS

When the First Fleet arrived in Port Jackson in 1788, the British under Governor Phillip claimed the Great Southern Land as the latest acquisition of the immense British Empire. He was operating under the principle that Australia was *Terra Nullius*. This can be roughly translated as 'land without owners.' The European settlers presumed that since no roads, fences, borders, crops or buildings were evident that the indigenous peoples roamed the land, hunting and gathering wherever they chose.

Nothing could have been further from the truth. The original Australians had deep and significant ties with the land that they drew sustenance from. Even the most insignificant landmark, to European eyes, often had a huge cultural significance to the inhabitants of a territory. They could only leave their tribal territories under certain strict protocols or in pursuit of warfare.

It was these intimate ties with their land that led the Aboriginals to defend it so desperately from the white colonists.

TRIBAL WARFARE

Aboriginals were divided into tribes that were further subdivided into clans. Each tribe had their own territory, which they roamed throughout the year in pursuit of seasonal bounties. Most of the time they were separated into smaller clans but on occasion the whole tribe would get together. This was for celebrations but also for war! One of the best eyewitness reports of Aboriginal battles comes from William Buckley.

William Buckley's story is fascinating and unique. He lived among Aboriginal peoples in the Port Phillip district for thirty years before their lifestyle was impacted by European settlement. He left a detailed record of his experiences in an autobiography, and this has vivid descriptions of warfare as practiced by the Aboriginals.

The British Government decided that it was important to establish a settlement in what is now known as Port Phillip Bay, near the Heads, in order to ensure that any hostile nation such as France or Russia could not seize land or establish a colony. Settling one kilometre from modern day Sorrento, the new settlement was to be called Sullivan Bay. The convicts and military who arrived in 1803 found that there was no fresh water and no timber appropriate for building a camp. Although some fresh water was obtained by sinking barrels into the groundwater table, it was realised that the township settlement would not be viable and after three months they all returned to Hobart. Prior to the evacuation three convicts had escaped, but after several days heading around the Bay, two had surrendered to a search party. One man, William Buckley, continued on his way, ending up near Geelong in the Barwon district.

Buckley's previous occupation was in the British Army and he had seen service in the Low Countries as an infantryman. Only the toughest men survived these malarial campaigns fighting against the Revolutionary French government, and this no doubt accounts for his resilience when his companions gave way. Buckley was immensely tall for the time, well over 6 feet, with bright red hair and very pale skin. This was a stroke of luck for him because as soon as the local tribe discovered him, they presumed he was a ghost of a dead clan member rather than a man and did not immediately spear him. Buckley made his own luck too. Just before coming upon members of the tribe he removed a spear from a mound that marked the grave of a recently deceased warrior. Seeing the spear, the Aboriginals considered him one of their own. The Aboriginals believed that the true colour of all dead people was white.

Buckley gives vivid and detailed narratives of the many conflicts he experienced when living among the Barwon tribes. He frequently witnessed battles, ranging from small scale skirmishes between one or two small clans, to large incursions where whole tribes would unite to attack another group. The battles were not concerned with acquiring land or resources, as tribal boundaries were well defined. They were more concerned with settling scores and resolving conflicts that usually involved women. Battles often began with champions calling one another out and finished with free for all melees.

Buckley recounted the first battle that he witnessed, soon after being adopted by his tribe:

> After a little time, and a great deal of challenging bluster, the two tribes commenced fighting in reality. When my relations…saw what was going on, they led me a short distance off, where they remained with me, looking at the conflict. It was anything but play work – it was evidently earnest. One man was speared through the thigh, and removed into the bush, where the spear was drawn. A woman of the tribe to which I had become attached, was also speared under the arm, and she died immediately.
>
> *The Life and Adventures of William Buckley [1854] Reverend John Morgan*

Small skirmishes often broke out. They resembled guerilla warfare.

> The next day we all started together to meet another tribe; but on joining, from some cause or other, they quarreled, commenced fighting, and two boys were killed. I could not then understand what all these quarrels were about, but afterwards understood that they were occasioned by the women having been taken away from one tribe by another; which was of frequent occurrence. At other times they were caused by the women willingly leaving their husbands, and joining other men, which the natives consider very bad.
>
> When these fights occurred, I was always kept in the rear. After the skirmish just mentioned was over, the tribe to whom the boys belonged retired farther into the bush, when we made our huts, as I have described,

with boughs and bark. Suddenly in the night, the others came upon our party and drove us away. The bodies of the two boys who were killed were laying in one of the huts, so they cut off their legs and thighs, carrying them away; the remains of their bodies our people burned in the usual manner.

Other battles resembled conventional warfare, with large tribes engaged in continued melees.

Before we left this place, we were unexpectedly intruded upon by a very numerous tribe, about three hundred. Their appearance, coming across the plain, occasioned great alarm, as they were seen to be the Waarengbadawá, with whom my tribe was at enmity. On their approach, our men retreated into the lake, and smeared their bodies all over with clay, preparatory to a fight. The women ran with their children into the bush, and hid themselves, and being a living dead man, as they supposed, I was told to accompany them. On the hostile tribe coming near, I saw they were all men, no women being amongst them. They were smeared all over with red and white clay, and were by far the most hideous looking savages I had seen. In a very short time the fight began, by a shower of spears from the contending parties. One of our men advanced singly, as a sort of champion; he then began to dance and sing, and beat himself about with his war implements; presently they all sat down, and he seated himself also. For a few minutes all was silent; then our champion stood up, and commenced dancing and singing again. Seven or eight of the savages—for so I must call them—our opponents, then got up also, and threw their spears at him; but, with great dexterity, he warded them off, or broke them every one, so that he did not receive a single wound. They then threw their boomerangs at him, but he warded them off also, with ease. After this, one man advanced, as a sort of champion from their party, to within three yards of him, and threw his boomerang, but the other avoided the blow by falling on his hands and knees, and instantly jumping up again he shook himself like a dog coming out of the water. At seeing this, the enemy shouted out in their language 'enough,' and the two men went and embraced each other.

After this, the same two beat their own heads until the blood ran down in streams over their shoulders.

A general fight now commenced, of which all this had been the prelude, spears and boomerangs flying in all directions. The sight was very terrific, and their yells and shouts of defiance very horrible. At length one of our tribe had a spear sent right through his body, and he fell. On this, our fellows raised a war cry; on hearing which, the women threw off their rugs, and each armed with a short club, flew to the assistance of their husbands and brothers; I being peremptorily ordered to stay where I was: my supposed brother's wife remaining with me. Even with this augmentation, our tribe fought to great disadvantage, the enemy being all men, and much more numerous.

As I have said in the early part of this narrative, I had seen skirmishing and fighting in Holland; and knew something therefore, of what is done when men are knocking one another about with powder and shot, in real earnest, but the scene now before me was much more frightful – both parties looking like so many devils turned loose from Tartarus. Men and women were fighting furiously, and indiscriminately, covered with blood; two of the latter were killed in this affair, which lasted without intermission for two hours; the Waarengbadawás then retreated a short distance, apparently to recover themselves. After this, several messages were sent from one tribe to the other, and long conversations were held – I suppose on the matters in dispute.

Night approaching, we retired to our huts, the women making the most pitiable lamentations over the mangled remains of their deceased friends. Soon after dark the hostile tribe left the neighborhood; and, on discovering this retreat from the battle ground, ours determined on following them immediately, leaving the women and myself where we were. On approaching the enemy's quarters, they laid themselves down in ambush until all was quiet, and finding most of them asleep, laying about in groups, our party rushed upon them, killing three on the spot, and wounding several others. The enemy fled precipitately, leaving their war implements in the hands of their assailants and their wounded to be beaten to death by boomerangs, three loud shouts closing the victors' triumph.

For a soldier who was familiar with the horrible effects of black powder weapons to call the Aboriginal battles 'much more frightful' attests to the violent nature of this hand-to-hand combat. Napoleonic musket balls would flatten out on impact, causing hideous injuries to the man hit, and often his neighbour as bits of bone and kit were blown off the original soldier. Cannon balls could knock men down like ninepins, eviscerate horses and vaporise heads. Napoleonic battles rarely degenerated into hand-to-hand combat, especially with the infantry, so maybe Buckley was shocked by the close combat techniques displayed by the indigenous warriors.

Buckley was not the only observer of the good discipline displayed by clan warriors. Watkin Tench was an officer of the marines on the First Fleet, and was present at the earliest contacts between Aboriginals and the settlers. Generally, relations between the two peoples were good in the early years of settlement, but he had no doubt that Aboriginal warriors were fierce and effective fighters. He wrote in one of his journals:

> From circumstances which have been observed, we have sometimes been inclined to believe these people at war with each other. They have more than once been seen assembled, as if bent on an expedition. An officer one day met fourteen of them marching along in a regular Indian file through the woods, each man armed with a spear in his right hand, and a large stone in his left: at their head appeared a chief, who was distinguished by being painted. Though in the proportion of five to one of our people they passed peaceably on.
>
> *A Complete Account of the Settlement at Port Jackson [1793] Watkin Tench*

ABORIGINAL WEAPONS

The Aboriginal weapons had been developed over tens of thousands of years and were finely honed for their purpose. Each tribe knew which timber was best for a specific weapon, and many were multipurpose tools that could be used for the gathering and preparation of foodstuffs as well as for killing other tribespeople.

Although Aboriginal societies had probably encountered the bow and arrow, they did not utilise that technology. As an ex-soldier, Buckley was impressed with the lethal nature of the Aboriginal arsenal:

> At break of day, I heard a great noise and talking; at length I saw that a quarrel had ensued, for they began to flourish their spears as a token of hostilities. I should here observe, that these spears are very formidable weapons, about twelve feet long, sharp at one end; others are about half that length, being made of a kind of reed with pointed sticks joined to them; these are sharpened with hard cutting stones, or shells. The boomerang is another weapon of war, something like a half-moon. The throwing-stick is one made, or shaped, for flinging the spears.

Tench too had an intimate understanding of the Aboriginal weapons:

> On first setting foot in the country, we were inclined to hold the spears of the natives very cheap. Fatal experience has, however, convinced us, that the wound inflicted by this weapon is not a trivial one; and that the skill of the Indians in throwing it, is far from despicable. Besides more than a dozen convicts who have unaccountably disappeared, we know that two, who were employed as rush cutters up the harbor, were (from what cause we are yet ignorant) most dreadfully mangled and butchered by the natives. A spear had passed entirely through the thickest part of the body of one of them, though a very robust man, and the skull of the other was beaten in...We have found that these spears are not made invariably alike, some of them being barbed like a fish gig, and others simply pointed...Nor are their weapons of offence confined to the spear only, for they have besides long wooden swords, shaped like a sabre, capable of inflicting a mortal wound, and clubs of an immense size. Small targets, made of the bark of trees, are likewise now and then to be seen among them.
>
> *A Narrative of the Expedition to Botany Bay [1788] Watkin Tench*

The Spear

These were finely honed lengths of narrow wood with aerodynamic properties that allowed them to cut through the air. Their wooden points were often hardened in fire and sharpened by rubbing on stones. Some tribes utilised war spears which had microliths or sharpened seashells embedded along the spear point. Stone spearheads were attached with reeds hardened by using fat from the human liver.

Watkin Tench was present when two of the colonists were speared and saw the different wounds inflicted by the varied types of spear points. The first attack he witnessed was on Governor Phillip, who had gone with a large party to communicate with a group of natives who were feasting on a whale carcass at Manly Cove. It appears that the local Aboriginals had been joined by a warrior from another clan who was not used to the sight of the Europeans. The image of bewigged governor, complete with sword, red coat and powdered wig, must have been too much for the Aboriginal. As Phillip approached, the warrior 'instantly fixed his lance with his throwing-stick'. This was the aboriginal version of cocking a pistol and Phillip was suddenly aware of the danger he faced. He tried to calm the warrior. Tench wrote how Phillip:

> Therefore cried out to the man, Weeeree, Weeree, (bad; you are doing wrong) displaying at the same time, every token of amity and confidence. The words had, however, hardly gone forth, when the Indian, stepping back with one foot, aimed his lance with such force and dexterity, that striking the governor's right shoulder, just above the collar-bone, the point glancing downward, came out at his back, having made a wound of many inches long. The man was observed to keep his eye steadily fixed on the lance until it struck its object, when he directly dashed into the woods and was seen no more.

The Europeans rushed to their boat:

> A situation more distressing than that of the governor, during the time that this lasted, cannot readily be conceived: the pole of the spear, not less than ten feet in length, sticking out before him, and impeding his

flight, the butt frequently striking the ground, and lacerating the wound. In vain did Mr. Waterhouse try to break it; and the barb, which appeared on the other side, forbade extraction, until that could be performed. At length it was broken, and his excellency reached the boat, by which time the seamen with the muskets had got up, and were endeavoring to fire them, but one only would go off, and there is no room to believe that it was attended with any execution.

When the governor got home, the wound was examined. It had bled a good deal in the boat, and it was doubtful whether the subclavian artery might not be divided. On moving the spear, it was found, however, that it might be safely extracted, which was accordingly performed.

A Complete Account of the Settlement at Port Jackson [1793] Watkin Tench

The simple wooden barb on this spear had produced a clean wound and the governor soon recovered. Not so fortunate was the governor's gamekeeper, called McEntire. The Aboriginals were terrified of this man and, while on a hunting trip with some marines and two other convicts, he was speared in the side. The wound proved mortal. The spear was a composite spear, with pieces of shell and stone affixed to the shaft to cause the most damage. It was this that killed the gamekeeper. After his wounding he and the party returned to the colony, but few held out any hope. McEntire's condition worsened and it was decided to take drastic action:

On the 12th, the extraction of the spear was, however, judged practicable, and was accordingly performed. That part of it which had penetrated the body measured seven inches and a half long, having on it a wooden barb, and several smaller ones of stone, fastened on with yellow gum, most of which, owing to the force necessary in extraction, were torn off and lodged in the patient. The spear had passed between two ribs, and had wounded the left lobe of the lungs. He lingered until the 20th of January, and then expired. On opening the corpse, it was found that the left lung had perished from suppuration, its remains adhering to the ribs. Some pieces of stone, which had dropped from the spear were seen, but no barb of wood.

A Complete Account of the Settlement at Port Jackson [1793] Watkin Tench

Woomera

The Aboriginals never adopted the bow and arrow, and the reason could be because of the woomera. This spear thrower bestowed fantastic accuracy and velocity to the spear, making them lethal at 50 metres or more. Once the spears had been discharged the woomera doubled as a club.

Nulla-Nulla – War Club

These fearsome instruments could be used as throwing sticks to bring down prey, or for close-in melee. Hard timbers were usually chosen and often the root bulb was used to make the head of the club. Sea shells, stone and quartz could be embedded in the head to cause bloody wounds.

Boomerang

Aboriginals had multiple types of boomerangs. Light, curved boomerangs were perfect for knocking parrots out of the air. Heavy war boomerangs usually had a long handle with a sharp, axe like head. These were used for throwing at close range but also fulfilled the role of a sabre and could whip around a defender's shield to inflict a killing blow.

Shields

These were usually narrow pieces of carved timber with a grip built into the concave rear surface. They had to be light enough to allow a warrior to lift his spear and woomera but heavy enough to resist a spear.

Although excellent for hand-to-hand combat, the Aboriginal weapons were no match for the modern European weapons wielded by the mounted troopers that confronted them after 1825.

SKELETON REVEALS SAVAGE ATTACK

800 years ago a warrior was laid to rest near the banks of the Darling River in the north west of what is now called New South Wales. In 2014 his remains were excavated by local Aboriginals and archaeologists.

Named by his discoverers Kaakutja, (older brother) this man died sometime in his 20s from a series of wounds inflicted by a range of

Aboriginal weapons. It is likely that the large sharpened blade of a war boomerang brought the warrior down, allowing him to be finished off with spears and clubs.

Kaakutja was obviously no stranger to violence and he had two wounds from earlier fights, including one on his skull, which had healed.

The local peoples had a history of deploying clubs, which they called 'lil-lils', and fighting boomerangs called 'wonna' which were up to 18 inches long with a sharpened, axe-like projection on one end.

There were several wounds made just before Kaakutja died and the archaeologists pieced together a likely scenario. They suppose that during a melee the young man may have been holding a spear and shield to his front. There are no defensive marks on his arms. His opponent likely swung around the shield with his heavy boomerang, smashing Kaakutja's right brow and possibly taking out his eye. As the wounded warrior fell, several spear thrusts may have penetrated his chest wall and nicked his ribs. Any of these could have been killing blows and attest to the lethal nature of Aboriginal weapons.

WAR ON THE FRONTIERS

Despite the fact that the natives in the Sydney region lacked gunpowder, steel and muskets, they were able to use their superior bushcraft skills to hold their own against the early settlers when conflict over land arose. This was despite a devastating smallpox outbreak that decimated most of the tribes around Port Jackson and Botany Bay.

After the spearing of Phillip and McEntire, it was decided to send out a punitive expedition to catch the offending Aboriginals as well as to exact revenge on the local tribes in general. Lieutenant Watkin Tench was in command and he was issued ropes to tie captives together as well as sacks to place the heads of those warriors killed and decapitated by the marines. At 4a.m. on the morning of 14 December 1790, Tench set off with Captain Hill of the New South Wales Corps, two marine lieutenants, two surgeons, six non-commissioned officers and forty soldiers. They were also hauling three days of rations and the previously mentioned ropes, sacks and hatchets to chop off the head of the 'Indians'.

For several days they blundered around the Sydney region seeking to trap Aboriginals. They saw some people disappearing in the distance and came across many still smoking campfires, but the natives invariably made off with their weapons, making the entire expedition fruitless. At one stage it seemed the party might have been able to surround five young men fishing on a beach but in the words of Tench:

> We pursued; but a contest between heavy-armed Europeans, fettered by ligatures, and naked unencumbered Indians, was too unequal to last long. They darted into the wood and disappeared.

After several days of fruitless bush bashing, the punitive expedition returned to Sydney with nothing to reward them for their efforts but chafed thighs and torn uniforms.

Phillip was not ready to give up though, and he ordered Tench to lead another expedition; this time to the north arm of Botany Bay. They left on 22 December 1790, but instead of telegraphing their moves with an announcement they set off in the middle of the night, illuminated by the full moon. Tench became more savvy and instead of blundering around in full kit he instructed the thirty privates, six NCOs and the two accompanying officers to strip down to the bare essentials of rifle and cartridge box, while leaving their knapsacks and rations behind with the less athletic members of the party. Despite this, the group blundered into a tidal flat and only just managed to extract themselves without loss of life. Eventually Tench managed to lead his party towards an Aboriginal encampment.

Here, just before dawn, he divided his men into three parties and sent them to ambush the site from different directions and thus flush out and cut off any Aboriginals who tried to escape.

In this instance Tench was using methods that had been employed in British frontier wars against rebels during the American War of Independence and against Native Americans for several centuries. The three columns burst out of the bush into the Aborigine humpies in a perfectly timed attack, but sadly for the increasingly frustrated troopers the inhabitants were long gone.

Tench returned to the governor, once more empty-handed.

As the settlement moved beyond the confines of Sydney Harbour, they met an even less friendly reception from the natives. Colonists moved into the fertile grazing lands around the Hawkesbury and Nepean rivers around 1795, but by now the Aboriginals were aware that the settlers' one aim was to take over their ancestral lands.

They replied with economic warfare against the Europeans' assets. Crops were burnt just before harvesting; livestock was speared and left to rot, or else butchered and carried off. In some instances, whole herds of sheep were rustled and taken to a secluded gully. Here the Aboriginals would dislocate the rear legs of the sheep, preventing them from moving, and come back over several days to take tucker from these extemporised storage yards.

Settlers were targeted too. Farmsteads would be surrounded at the dead of night and attacked by concentric rows of warriors, or burnt to the ground with the inhabitants being speared as they tried to flee. The Darug, Darawal and Gandangara peoples proved to be resourceful and determined in their attempts to hold on to their sacred land. Fighting was common until 1809 when a truce was negotiated.

Pressure of settlement continued to grow, and in 1814 fighting broke out in the region around the Nepean River. Governor Macquarie sent troops from the Veteran Company. These troopers proved to be no match for the warriors of the Gandangara tribe, and on 7 May 1814 the two forces clashed. The redcoats managed to discharge their muskets, but before they could reload their Brown Besses the warriors were on them. Private Isaac Eustace was killed in the skirmish and was the first British soldier to die on the frontier. The fighting escalated and on 2 March 1815 seven settlers were ambushed while crossing the Nepean river. The Aboriginals seized their weapons and discharged them at the fleeing settlers. Three died and the rest fled.

It looked to Governor Macquarie that he was rapidly losing control of the frontier as colonists fled back towards the coast. He selected the Flank Companies from the 46th Regiment of Foot and sent them on excursions into the region with the aim of driving the hostile tribesmen into waiting ambushes. The three detachments were commanded by Captain Schaw, Captain Wallis and Lieutenant Dawe. They were composed of 68 soldiers from the Grenadier and Light Companies, as well as Aboriginal guides and armed settlers. Several concentric attacks were mounted over the month of April and two warriors, Durelle and Kanabygal, were killed. Captain Wallis had the bodies hung from trees on a prominent hill as a warning to other tribespeople.

In real terms this had no real effect and the foot detachments spent many fruitless hours blundering around the region. The Hawkesbury and Nepean regions stayed as very much no-man's-land for several years.

It was only in 1825 when the New South Wales Mounted Troopers were formed from infantry detachments that the settlers were able to combine mobility with fire power and wrest military superiority from their 'primitive' opponents.

CHAPTER 2

THE MARINES OF
THE FIRST FLEET

The decision to send a detachment of marines to help Governor Phillip to establish the new settlement at Botany Bay on the coast of New Holland was controversial. There was a good deal of rivalry between the marines, who can be loosely termed naval infantry, and the traditional land-based army. The marines were seen as very much the junior partner in the English Armed Forces.

Nevertheless, Lord Sydney made a sound decision. The companies sent with the fleet were composed of steady men, well disciplined and often well educated. Despite their fractious commander, Major Ross, the officers, non-coms and privates performed well with few breaches of discipline. Even in the famine year, before the arrival of the Second Fleet, discipline held – allowing the foundations of a new colony to arise in the vast and strange land of New Holland.

OUTWARD BOUND

In what could perhaps be a seen as a sign of what the new society was going to be like, the First Fleet almost didn't sail.

Just as the First Fleet had assembled at Portsmouth and was about to set off, the Marines went on strike and refused to sail until more 'grog' was laid in, to ensure that there would be plentiful supplies for their three-year posting.

The British authorities provided the required rum and the fleet sailed on 13 May 1787. Commanded by Captain Arthur Phillip, the fleet consisted of nine convict transports and two fleet escorts. The frigate *Sirius* was the chosen as the flagship. The fleet held 778 convicts, approximately 50 officials and 213 marines as its passengers, and it was their task to found a new colony in New Holland. The voyage that these 11 ships embarked upon would last for nine months, cover 24,000 kilometres and, when it finally reached Botany Bay, they were tasked with building a new nation from scratch.

The Marines would play a crucial role in protecting and creating the infant nation.

A marine is a soldier trained and equipped to fight at sea. During the Age of Sail, exceptional bravery was required by these men. In fleet actions, marines bore the brunt of much fighting when battleships clashed in bloody fleet actions. It was they who fought from elevated positions in the topgallant sails, lobbing grenades on enemy crewmen below or sniping at officers on an enemy forecastle. Marines armed with muskets and boarding pikes led assaults onto other ships when the order to board was given. It was these red coated soldiers who were asked to board flimsy rowing boats and lead amphibious assaults onto enemy-held coasts defended with muskets and cannon. What's more, the marines had to survive in the cramped conditions of a man-of-war for months on end while maintaining discipline and self-control.

As such, the Marines who set out on the First Fleet – the New South Wales Detachment – were seen as something of an elite force – especially since all had volunteered for the perilous duty.

The Marine Corps had been founded by King Charles II in October 1664 and was initially called the Duke of York and Albany's Maritime Regiment. In the years that followed they proved to be an exceptional fighting formation, instrumental in seizing many of Great Britain's overseas possessions, including Gibraltar. In the mid-18th Century, the Marines were placed under admiralty control and promotion based on merit became commonplace, rather than the army system which required large sums of money to advance up the hierarchy.

There was some antipathy between the army and the marines and it was seen as something of a feather in the admiralty's cap when the Secretary of State for Home affairs, Lord Sydney, decided to send a marine detachment on the Botany Bay expedition rather than a regular regiment. Admiralty was determined to reward the faith placed in them by Sydney and steps were made to ensure only the best possible men were included in the New South Wales Detachment. Four companies were formed for the expedition and each man was a volunteer. Two guineas were paid to each volunteer as a bounty and the usual request for life service was waived. Each man would be able to ask for discharge after the three-year mission was over. Officers were promised accelerated promotion. The generous pay scale, the excellent rations and the dashing Marine uniform were all further inducements to join.

As it was, more than enough marines volunteered and the four companies assigned to the expedition were made up of picked men. The OB (Order of Battle) of the four companies that mustered for the expedition was three sergeants, three corporals, two drummers and fifty privates. Each company had a captain as commander and a sprinkling of two or three subalterns (lieutenants). The detachment was commanded by Major Robert Ross.

Tough men were selected. Guarding convicts was no light work. As recently as 24 March 1786, convicts aboard a hulk moored in Plymouth had staged a violent revolt. During their attempt to escape eight had been shot dead and 36 were wounded before they surrendered.

Huge amounts of stores were laid in to meet the needs of the marines. One thousand muskets/carbines and ten thousand musket flints were sourced from the warehouses along the Thames (sadly no ammunition reserves were loaded). Marines were to be well fed during the nine months at sea. Their basic weekly rations were to include 3 kilos of bread, 2 kilos of beef, 1 kilo of pork, 1 litre of dried peas, 2 litres of oatmeal, 2 litres of rum, half a kilo of assorted dairy and some vinegar. This was supplemented throughout the voyage by plentiful supplies of oranges, onions and any greens that Phillip could source from the ports visited during the journey.

By the time the Fleet sailed, the Portsmouth locals were thoroughly sick of its presence and were keen to see them all disappear over the horizon. Sailors and marines were causing trouble in town with their drunken revelries, while as many as eight convict cadavers had been hoisted over the sides of the seven convict transports and had to be fished out of the bay. Each of the transports had approximately 100 to 150 convicts and 25 to 35 marines to keep them in line.

All breathed a sigh of relief when Captain Arthur Phillip finally set sail.

A routine was soon established on the outbound ships. Reveille was followed by rations and if the weather was suitable the marines would escort small parties of convicts onto the decks for daily exercise. The marines on the ships with female convicts got another kind of exercise. Even while at Portsmouth, holes had been bored into the cell's bulkheads and a shady trade in sexual favours was carried on. Rum and rations were frequently traded for a quick sexual encounter, and at one stage some sailors went on strike for an increased beef ration.

The trading of sexual favours was not the only thing distracting marines on the long journey to the new colony. There were remarkably few disciplinary reports for misbehaviour, but those that did eventuate were normally related to one thing – grog. The generous ration of grog given to each and every man, each and every day, was a privilege that marines and sailors alike depended on. In a notoriously hard service it was perhaps the one treat they could rely on. Many abused the system and were involved in violent altercations. Most of the marines and sailors who went on shore leave in Rio De Janeiro got blind drunk and many had to be released from the local lockups just before the fleet sailed on.

It was not only the enlisted men who got into strife. Several officers were rendered 'incapable of duty' by alcohol and only avoided a court-martial thanks to the consideration and tolerance of their fellow officers. The marines weren't the only ones who were disciplined by the restriction of rum rations; several of their wives soon gained a reputation for heavy drinking. Women received an equivalent ration amounting to three quarters of their husband's, so with a bit of scrimping and horse trading a real binge could be organised. On the outward journey a Sergeant Hume and his wife went on such a bender that her rum ration had to be stopped on 20 May. A week later the sergeant suffered the same fate – he had probably been passing it on to his wife. Private Michael Redman's wife was such a lush that his lieutenant put her on cold turkey for a month. There was obviously no concept of stopping drinking while pregnant and Martha Davis, the expectant wife of Private John Davis, caused such a scene that her ration was stopped for ten days. Once on shore things did not get much better and, from 26 February to 13 March 1788, no grog was issued to any female within the colony.

Despite these temptations and distractions, Phillip proved to be an excellent choice as commander. Thanks to his determination to provide high quality rations to all in the fleet, remarkably few died en route to Australia.

Only one marine died. After leaving the Cape of Good Hope, dysentery swept through some of the ships' companies. Private Daniel Creswell contracted it from some of the convicts in his charge and died 11 days later in acute agony. Presumably, like all of the others who died in the Royal Navy, he would have been wrapped in sail cloth with a cannon ball at his feet. The shroud would have been sewn together using a sail maker's needle and twine, with the last stitch going through poor Creswell's nose, just to make sure he was really dead. To the tune of the Lord's Prayer, the luckless marine was consigned to the deep, with the cannon ball dragging him down to the depths of the Atlantic Ocean.

Despite this loss, three fully manned companies of marines sailed into Botany Bay during January 1788. Apart from the occasional bruised head and ego, they were ready to carry out the traditional role of the marines – securing territory through force. More than two hundred well trained and equipped soldiers were the first known force of regular troops to land on the vast continental island of Australia. The red coats of the Marines would be followed by the red coats of different British regiments, and during the next 100 years these formations would spread English suzerainty throughout the new colonies and ward off any would-be aggressors.

THE MARINE REGIMENTS

The marines that looked out from the bows of the fleet as it sailed into Botany Bay were the first of many British troopers who were known as redcoats. The major empires of Europe had a distinctive coloured coatee that allowed their commanders to pick them out on the battlefield. Austrians were famed for their white coats, the Russians for their green and, during the revolutionary wars that would soon follow, the French adopted blue. Prussian troops were known for their almost black 'Prussian Blue'. The reason for the British adopting red as their national uniform did not have anything to do with arcane notions of heroism but was rather a cost cutting measure. During the English Civil War in 1645, the Parliamentarians sought to reform their troops into a disciplined regular force called the New Model Army. The cheapest die available was called 'Venetian Red', and the thrifty puritan Parliamentarians opted for this colour. These well trained regiments went on to smash the Royalists and win the civil war.

The first commitment of the redcoats off British soil was the Battle of the Dunes in 1658, when the Cromwellian forces and their French allies trounced a Spanish army near Dunkirk. It was the first overseas adventure of the British redcoats, who went on to establish a reputation of tough professionalism.

Some terms for the British infantry were not complimentary. They were also known as 'bloody backs' in recognition of the very common punishment of flogging. The American revolutionaries of the War of Independence referred to them as Lobsters.

This red coat was the basis of the Marine uniform. It was a red swallow tailed coat, with white cuffs, lapels and collar. They wore a white shirt, waistcoat and trousers, while black gaiters were buttoned up on the calves. A black leather stock and a black bicorn with white trim completed the ensemble. Two white cross belts held a cartridge box and a long bayonet. The troops were armed with a cut down sea service version of the famous Brown Bess musket. It was shorter to allow easier loading in the cramped confines of a ship and to reduce the chance that it might be ensnared in rigging. It also had a wooden ram rod as the standard metal ones corroded in the salt water environment of the sea.

Corporals wore a braided knot on their left shoulders while sergeants had a scarlet sash worn around the waist. Officers wore tailored uniforms, a magenta sash around their waist and silver bullion epaulettes on their shoulders. Officers were of course armed with a sword suspended from one cross belt.

It was in these uniforms, that represented hundreds of years of British military success, that the marines looked out upon what was hoped to be the newest addition to the British Empire.

ARRIVAL

Phillip had split the fleet into two elements when leaving Cape Town. The fastest group, which was led by *Supply*, entered Botany Bay at 2.15p.m. on Friday 18 January. The commander of the fleet, who would soon become the governor of the new territory, lost no time disembarking, and with a small escort of officers and marines landed on a beach on the north shore at 3.00p.m.

In the admiralty orders laying out Phillip's responsibilities, he was given strict instructions on how the indigenous peoples were to be treated. While establishing the rule of British law in the new colony Phillip was enjoined to try and coexist with the natives. In the original orders 'savages' had been written, but King George himself had scratched out that word and replaced it with 'natives.'

Phillip was a veteran of the American War of Independence and was known for both his efficiency and his humanity. He set out with good intentions and, despite beginning the process of depriving the Aboriginals of their land, he genuinely tried to establish good relations between the local tribes and the settlers. He told Major Ross that if threatened by the indigenous inhabitants the marines were to fire blank charges only.

This was no Terra Nullius (empty land) that the First Fleet was colonising. As Phillip's boat was rowed to his first landfall, there was a small group of bewildered Aboriginals there to observe this strange visitation. As Phillip and his escort disembarked, he made conciliatory gestures and approached the men. He offered colourful beads in his outstretched hands.

The Aboriginals retreated. It was a belief held among many Aboriginal peoples that ghosts of recently departed clan members often returned as tall pale figures. Trying to place Phillip, in his captain's coat and pomaded white wig, within any meaningful frame of reference must have been a challenging and confusing experience.

Phillip left the beads on the sand and retreated back to the boats. They were quickly gathered up by an Aboriginal and shown to his friends.

The Europeans returned to their ship – first contact had been made.

The next encounter was not so amicable.

Over the next few days, the rest of the fleet arrived and Botany Bay became a hub of activity. Marines soon settled into a routine of accompanying forage parties that went on shore to harvest grains for livestock. They also accompanied parties exploring the bay looking for resources such as fresh water. Each party that set out was accompanied by two or three armed marines.

On Sunday 20th, a group set out to explore the Georges River area on the southern part of Botany Bay. As the party crested a hill they were met by a group of warriors who made hostile gestures, urging the English to go away. Lieutenant King was aware that he only had three marines as escort and, leaving a small gift of beads, withdrew to his boat.

The Aboriginals were not placated and, as their band swelled with new arrivals, the warriors began to shout aggressively at the English. One warrior loaded his spear onto a woomera and hurled it into the midst of the landing party. King ordered a marine to discharge his musket. The blank charge had the desired effect and the men retreated in fear.

Phillip was leading another explorative party nearby and, when the two groups were reunited, they were led back to what became known as Lance Hill. Here Phillip restored harmony and gave gifts to the warriors. The group mingled in a friendly manner and such was their remorse at the offensive action of hurling a spear that the Aboriginals sought Phillip's approval to spear the thrower as a punishment. The warriors began preparing him for death when Phillip interceded and showed the Aboriginals that there were no hard feelings by giving the offender some beads.

A marine was soon called to deploy another kind of weapon. The Aboriginals were not familiar with clothes and wanted to identify the exact nature of the new arrivals. Lieutenant King ordered one of the marines to display his wedding tackle and it was greeted with a shout of admiration by the natives.

The new settlers considered all of the Aboriginals to be of one tribe. In fact, there were several groups occupying what is now known as Botany Bay and Sydney Harbor. It is estimated that 29 clan groups occupied what is now suburban Sydney. Collectively they are known as the Eora nation. The Darug thrived in the inland area from Parramatta to the Blue Mountains. The Darawal, who lived south of Botany Bay, would have welcomed the sight of the First Fleet sailing north to Port Jackson.

Botany Bay proved to be unsuitable for the new colony and, on Friday 25 January, the Fleet began the move to Sydney Cove, where fresh water had been found at a small inlet that is now known as Circular Quay. At 7p.m. the HMS *Supply*, with Phillip on board, moored off the inlet, with vital fresh water coming out of the newly named Tank Stream.

On 26 January, Phillip and a compact party of marines rowed to the cove and in a small clearing near Tank Stream erected a flag. A firing party was formed and, in between volleys, toasts were drunk to the Royal family. A new colony was founded.

Over the following two days, the rest of the fleet assembled and finally the convicts were disembarked. On the 30th the first Orders of the Day were issued. Setting a precedent for the next hundred years or so of British Army occupation, duties were assigned to different squads, mess times were determined and punishments laid down.

Relatively few marines were charged with disciplinary offences, but they did have to supervise the punishment of some convicts. Capital punishment was inflicted on convicts who stole rations. The first hanging that the detachment had to witness was that of Thomas Barrett on 27 February 1788. He, along with two companions, had been sentenced to death for stealing butter, pork and peas. At 5.00p.m. the assigned marine detachment formed up and marched at the quick to the execution sight. No gallows were built and the hanging was going to be of the most rudimentary form: a rope tossed over the limb of a large gum. At 5.15 the three condemned men arrived, and at 6.00p.m the marine commander Major Ross arrived.

With Ross came a stay of execution for two of the convicts, but the vile character Barrett was given no reprieve. The marines were to witness his fearfully mishandled execution. A convict had been 'volunteered' to carry out the execution and it was his role to get Barrett to mount a ladder, fling the rope over the limb, place the noose around the condemned criminal's neck and then 'turn him off.' Barrett seemed to be made of stern stuff until he mounted the ladder. He was observed to turn to water and to blanch. The hangman too had a failure of nerve and he could not place the noose around the criminal's neck.

The officials present tried to get him to perform his duty, but all to no avail. Major Ross even threatened that he would summon a squad of marines and fill the reluctant executioner's belly with lead balls. This threat had no effect and it fell to the Provost Marshall to place the noose around Barrett's neck and 'launch him into eternity.' No doubt the marines relished telling the tale to their comrades back at the settlement.

Most convicts were quite well behaved and the colony seemed to be muddling along despite food shortages and failed crops.

It is fortunate for the colony that the marines were present as a defence against the Aboriginals.

In the next couple of years the native warriors were keen to avoid confrontation with the marines. No doubt they recognised that the soldiers in their bright red coats with their state-of-the-art weaponry were not to be trifled with. In these early days of settlement, Surgeon George Wogan saw a warrior of the Iora people approach a marine and run his finger over the point of the soldier's bayonet. The native looked very serious and gave off a deep 'hmmmm.' While the indigenous Sydney peoples may not have previously had direct encounters with British military technology, native trading networks that ranged all across Australian waters and into the islands to the north would have communicated to them some inkling of the power of foreign weapons.

The Aboriginals were no doubt relieved when the fleet sailed out from Botany Bay. Perhaps they thought the same thing would happen in Port Jackson. Most Aboriginals were quite friendly to the parties that explored the many inlets and bays of what we now call Sydney Harbor. Phillip named Manly after the fine manly warriors whom he encountered there. The two parties mingled and Phillip served up some boiled bully-beef to the curious Aboriginals. On other occasions natives helped haul in fishing nets and even directed boats to good landing spots.

By February, the natives could not help but notice that land was being cleared around the settlement, and that women and children were evident in substantial numbers. They correctly deduced that the fleet was here to stay. On 4 February a large party of warriors gathered to threaten one of the exploratory parties. Rocks were hurled while the Englishmen were threatened with spears.

In March some convicts who left the safety of the settlement were set upon and murdered. Phillip and the Marines were respected by the Aboriginals. The strict discipline of the marines and their use of blank cartridges ensured that no atrocities were committed. The convicts were a different kettle of fish and no doubt, away from the authority of the governor, committed many crimes against the indigenous population. The Aboriginals began to make themselves scarce when convicts approached.

But not always. On 30 May 1788 two convicts had been detailed to cut rushes a short distance from the main settlement. William Okey and Samuel Davis camped overnight with a tent, but on the following morning they were both found dead. The Aboriginals had used their full arsenal against the men. Okey had three spears thrust through his chest, his brains were dashed out through a split in his head and an eye had been cut out with an axe. Davis had been bashed on the forehead, but he may have died of fright.

The next morning a party of about twenty marines and officers set out on a raid to net the culprits, but none could be found.

On October 4 one convict strayed a short distance from a party of marines who were collecting bush tucker. He was set upon by some warriors and his head was beaten to a pulp. In December 1788 one marine and several convicts went missing. A warband was reported to be gathering inland and a marine detachment chased them off.

In December 1790 Phillip decided that since 17 whites had been killed by Aboriginals an example was to be made of them. This was when Captain Tench was ordered to capture two warriors, kill ten others and return to Sydney Cove with their heads in hessian bags.

As described in Chapter One, these forays were easily defeated by the superior bushcraft of the Aboriginals.

One Aboriginal was killed by a marine. Soon after Trench's fruitless expeditions, two Aboriginals were detected taking food from a vegetable garden. In a pattern that would soon be repeated across the continent, Aboriginals whose traditional food sources were depleted by the new arrivals were forced to compensate by taking food from the settlers' farms. The colonists equated this with theft and would try to drive off the indigenous people with any means possible.

The marines set off in pursuit of the 'thieves' and, contrary to Phillip's orders, one of them loaded his musket with charge and ball and put a bullet into a warrior known as Bangai. The wound turned septic and two days later the Aboriginal died.

Marine detachments were sent to two new sites within the fledgling colony. On 2 March 1788 an exploratory party came across what is now known as Rose Hill, which had abundant, rich soil in contrast to Sydney Cove. A detachment set off in October 1788, consisting of three officers, four NCOs, a drummer and twenty marines. Seventy convicts accompanied the marines. By April 1790 a redoubt and barracks to sleep 100 men had been built. On 2 June 1791 Phillip renamed the town Parramatta.

Major Robert Ross was the commander of the Marine detachment and right from the start became a thorn in Phillip's side. He was sensitive to any slight and, being something of a pedant, he had refused the new governor's reasonable request that his detachment should help with the supervision of the convicts, citing a lack of instructions from admiralty. Ross created quite a few enemies among his subordinates, and it was no doubt with much relief that, in February 1790, Philip packed the Major off to take over the colony of Norfolk Island from Lieutenant King, who had been in command of this outpost since February 1788. Left to his own devices Ross made a fine fist of his task, and soon Norfolk Island was a successful, well built settlement. While the convicts and marines were near starving in the first difficult years in Sydney Cove, the marines on Norfolk Island were living off a tremendous natural bounty. One lieutenant caught 56 large snapper in one day, and in two weeks in May 1790 almost 2,000 large snapper were caught. Tens of thousands of muttonbirds were consumed.

Nevertheless, Ross's actions had not benefited his corps. Due to his intransigence Phillip requested that a regular regiment of troops should be sent to take over the new colony. The New South Wales Corps was born.

BUILT TO BATTLE BONAPARTE: THE FIRST PERMANENT FORTIFICATION BUILT ON AUSTRALIAN SOIL.

Sydney Cove proved to be a perfect embarkation point for the fledgling colony. It was sheltered from harsh winds. It was quite narrow and this was perfect from a defensive point of view. Phillip had been alarmed when he first encountered the two French ships in Port Jackson and once the colony seemed to be on a secure footing he decided to fortify the inlet. Two points thrust into the bay on either side of the harbour. We now know them as Dawes Point, which is covered by the Southern end of the Sydney Harbour Bridge, and Bennelong Point, where the Opera House now stands.

It seems that on arrival Phillip may have built a redoubt with two 6 pounder cannon, taken from *Sirius*, just below Bennelong Point. Rather than facing into the bay, these guns were trained on the convict encampment, a clear warning to any who might consider misbehaving.

Once the colony was on a more permanent footing it was decided that defences should be mounted to protect the town from seaborne assault. Dawes Point provided the perfect location for a battery as any ships approaching from the heads could be raked across the bow, and if they turned into the cove they would have their starboard flanks pounded by the land based artillery.

Lieutenant Dawes of the Marines had established an observatory on the headland and in 1789 Governor Phillip chose it as the location of the colony's gunpowder magazine. In 1791, in response to a British dispute with Spain, it was decided to build a permanent fortification. Eight more guns were commandeered from the First Fleet's flagship, *Sirius*. With the threat from France intensifying after 1798, Captain Edward Abbott of the New South Wales Corps was ordered to strengthen the Battery. In fact, the defences could have been sorely tested as in 1810 Emperor Napoleon Bonaparte ordered a fleet to attack Sydney, but the French Fleet's base at Mauritius was seized by the British before the plan could be put into action.

During the Napoleonic war, many French or Spanish ships that were captured in the Pacific were brought to Sydney as prizes and were met by a salute from the fort. It is likely that many cannon were taken from these prizes for use in the other fortifications springing up around the bay.

The cannon on Dawes Point performed one other vital function for the new nation. Every day at 1p.m. a blank was fired so that the good citizens of Sydney town could set their watches.

The fort was continually improved and upgraded and in 1856 an upper battery with five 42 pounders on traversing platforms was installed.

By the 1880s the principle harbour defences were located on the Heads of Sydney Harbour and the Dawes Point battery was decommissioned. It was largely destroyed when the foundations for the south tower of the Sydney Harbour Bridge was built in the 1920s.

MARINES – FIRST TO ARRIVE, LAST TO LEAVE

The Marine detachment that left Sydney Cove to return to England in 1792 was not the last to make a contribution to the new nation. Royal Navy ships surveyed the rest of the Australian coastline and were instrumental in founding new colonies. Wherever the ships put ashore it can be assumed that marines were there to protect the landing parties.

Not all of the endeavours were as successful as those carried out by Governor Phillip. In 1802, Lieutenant John Murray of the Royal Navy discovered Port Phillip Bay and claimed it for the British Empire. Matthew Flinders followed in Murray's footsteps, and the positive reports furnished by the two men prompted the British Government to found a new colony.

On 10 October 1803 a Marine detachment and 301 convicts landed just inside the South Heads and established a colony below the town that is now known as Sorrento. They named the new possession Sullivan Bay.

The need to keep the bay out of the grasping fingers of the French was the key motivation for the new settlement, and sadly this determined the chosen site of the new colony. While Sullivan Bay was close to the heads and enabled the British to control who entered the fine new bay, it was deficient in all of the resources needed to establish a new colony. There was no stone, timber, clay, arable land or fresh water. What's more, unlike the tools of the First Fleet, all of the farm implements and axes supplied to the marines were made of the worst standard of pig iron which broke without the slightest provocation from its user!

There were however many hostile natives who were keen to eject the new settlers. Scattering like blow flies, many convicts did a runner. Most were recaptured or died, the exception being Private Buckley (see Chapter One).

Captain Collins of the Marines saw the futility of the settlement, and on 30 January 1804 the first settlement of Port Phillip was abandoned. It took a syphilis ridden entrepreneur from convict stock, John Batman, to settle the colonial jewel that became known as Melbourne in 1832.

Royal Marines set up a garrison in the pestilential swamps of Port Essington, Northern Territory in 1838. This failed, not due to poor management but due to tropical disease, which ravaged the garrison until the settlement was abandoned in 1849.

Despite these setbacks, Royal Navy marines remained a continued presence on the shores of Australia. The last detachment was withdrawn from Sydney in 1913 when the Royal Navy Australia Squadron handed the responsibility for securing the new nation's waters to the Royal Australian Navy.

CHAPTER 3

THE NEW SOUTH WALES CORPS

When the New South Wales Regiment arrived at Sydney Cove they found a colony that was already humming along with a bustle of activity. The marines and convicts had already laid the sinews of the new society and the regiment was able to march up George Street to occupy the barracks built for their predecessors.

The corps has now got something of a ragged reputation, perhaps well deserved. Nevertheless, in the twenty years of their posting the personnel were able to perform a multiplicity of functions. Frontiers were expanded, new settlements were established in Van Diemen's Land and fractious convicts were kept in line.

When the 73rd relieved the NSW Corps, the two regiments were reviewed by the incoming governor – he found fault with neither.

A NEW REGIMENT OF THE CROWN

The Duke of Wellington famously said that the British Army was made up of 'the scum of the earth…fellows who have enlisted for drink. That is plain, they have all enlisted for drink.' British soldiers were well known for their propensity to get drunk.

Such a description may well have fitted the New South Wales Corps, who still to this day have a reputation for drunkenness and poor discipline. Nevertheless, during the crisis of Vinegar Hill a small detachment of less than 20 muskets managed to form line and deliver a succession of volleys that dispersed hundreds of menacing armed rebels. When the corps was relieved after 20 years of service in the new colony, there was not much to distinguish them from the newly arrived 73rd Regiment.

On 14 May 1789 a draft order from the Secretary of War decreed that the Marine detachment was to be replaced by a regular infantry regiment raised for the purpose. Major Francis Grose was empowered to raise a new formation, which would be given the title the 'New South Wales Corps.' He immediately began recruiting men from London, Chatham and Portsmouth and he and his officers received a bounty of more than 3 pounds for each recruit. But unlike the marine detachment, which had a surfeit of volunteers within two weeks, after three months Grose was still short of the required establishment for his new battalion. This was despite lax recruiting requirements – the men had to be 1.6 metres tall, but could be as young as sixteen.

Grose was forced to source the balance of his recruits from the Savoy. Not the Savoy Hotel but the Savoy Military Prison. This was full of deserters, miscreants and thieves, perhaps the dregs of the British military. Many willingly joined the new regiment to get out of the Savoy or to avoid sentences of up to a thousand lashes. There was some logic in Grose's decision – the men could not very well desert once they were in Sydney.

By hook or by crook Grose got his men and, with the arrival in Sydney of the Second Fleet in June 1790, the first detachment arrived. More arrived

44

on September 1791, and the balance in 1792. The recruits were joined by approximately 40 marines who decided to stay in the new colony.

In December 1791 the last of the marines left for England.

The British regimental system was different to that used by Continental armies. While in French, Russian and German regiments there could be two, three or four battalions, most British regiments consisted of one premier battalion. These were most often sent abroad on active service while the second battalion remained at home serving to recruit and train replacements for the first battalion. The pressures of the Napoleonic wars led to more and more regiments raising and sending second battalions to diverse theatres but it was rare for sister line battalions to serve together. The exceptions were the guard regiments, which usually had more than one battalion and were often deployed together in the same brigade.

As such, the New South Wales Corps was a battalion sized regiment and usually had an establishment of approximately 500 men. Most 'regiments' were composed of ten companies. Within this organisation were eight line companies and two flank companies; the grenadier company and the light company. The line companies had a white-over-red tuft above their hats. The grenadiers and light troops had an all-white and a green tuft respectively.

It appears that unlike the battalions that followed it, the New South Wales Corps did not have the flank battalions and was composed only of center companies. It seems the reason for this was because from its inception the regiment was a 'garrison' formation, rather than a front line fighting formation. One of the main complaints levelled against the marines was that they refused to act as overseers to the convicts. The New South Wales Corps was explicitly ordered to act as guards to the convicts and officers were to sit on juries to judge any miscreants.

Major Grose was not the best man to command such a fractious colony as Sydney Town. While Phillip was able to strike a balance between firmness and fairness with all of the tiny colony's residents, Grose was too easy-going and lacked ability. In the two years that he was in charge of the colony he allowed the Corps to become a law unto themselves.

Their discipline left much to be desired. A small party of 21 men and three officers coexisted with the Marine detachment on Norfolk Island for five months from May to October 1791. In that time, they had double the number of court martials than the marines, even though they were a much smaller detachment. When Governor Hunter arrived in Sydney he was shocked at the insubordination tolerated by the officers of the Corps.

A LAW UNTO THEMSELVES

Grose granted land parcels to his officers and men – 40 hectares of land for their own use. The convicts were then given to the soldiers to work these private holdings at the expense of building vital infrastructure. At the same time the commissary was opened up to the Corps, allowing them to help themselves to as many tools and supplies as they desired. Officers in particular bullied smaller freeholders off their land and accumulated large landholdings.

Grose even allowed his men to purchase the entire cargoes of visiting ships, store them in warehouses and then sell the goods on at exorbitant prices – a clear breach of regulations forbidding servicemen from indulging in trade.

As well as monopolising trade, neglecting the building of roads and public buildings, and controlling the courts, the regiment did one other thing that has earned them a place of infamy within the history of the British Army – they imported rum and sold it for profits of up to 1000%. Their 'battle honour' is to be called the 'Rum Corps'. For some reason the British government had not sent currency notes. The economy relied on barter, with rum as the main currency.

While the white-faced uniforms of the marines had earnt a deal of respect from settlers, emancipists (freed convicts) and convicts, the yellow facings of the Rum Corps were seen as symbols of tyranny. Successive governors tried to limit the powers of the regiment without success. In order to defend their corrupt entitlements, the New South Wales Corps even led an armed coup – the only time the military in Australia have overthrown a civilian government.

Governor Hunter arrived in 1795 and immediately tried to limit the Corps' privileges, with no success. He was replaced in 1800 by Governor King. King had a small success in breaking the officers' control of the rum trade, but by the time he left in 1807 few improvements had been made.

THE FIRST HOMEGROWN AUSTRALIAN MILITARY UNIT

Governor Hunter did have one significant achievement with the founding of the first truly homegrown Australian military units. In 1800 there were rumors of an Irish uprising amongst the convicts. The governor took immediate steps to strengthen the NSW Corps and raised two Volunteer Corps of free man. Each of these corps was to consist of fifty men and they were designated the Loyal and Associated Corps. One was to be stationed in Sydney under the command of Captain Thomas Rowley, while the other was commanded by Mr. James Thompson and was based at Parramatta. The membership of these corps was made up of men from well-to-do families who were determined to support the British government. Their arms were supplied by the governor and regular training session with the musket were held to ensure proficiency. They lived at home and were summoned by an alarm post fixed to Government House.

The troopers of the two units wore red coats with yellow facings, and the cross belts issued to all troopers. Undergarments, headgear and pants were probably civilian issue. The members of the organisation, later dubbed the Loyal Associations, attained a degree of proficiency and on one occasion mustered within twenty minutes when a suspect ship appeared off Sydney Heads. It proved not be a French man-of-war but an American whaling ship. The Parramatta Association proved to be particularly useful in the Battle of Vinegar Hill. They likely formed a second firing line behind the men of the NSW Corps. After the battle they proved their worth by scouring the countryside and bringing fugitive convicts to a bloody reckoning for their deeds.

With the arrival of the 73rd Regiment, the Associations were disbanded in 1810 by Governor Lachlan Macquarie.

Macquarie must have missed the auxiliary units. He soon founded the Invalid and Veteran Company from discharged marines and soldiers. He attached the unit to the 73rd and later regiments for light duties. The Veterans served until 1823 when they were disbanded.

BATTLE OF VINEGAR HILL

Even though the Rum Corps were soaked in corruption and sleaze, they could still put up a decent fight. Despite small scale punitive missions against the Aboriginals, there were no set piece battles in the first 30 years. This changed in 1804 when hundreds of ferocious Irish revolutionaries led a rebellion that threatened to destroy the new colony. The New South Wales Corps proved themselves in their baptism of fire.

In 1798 a rebellion had broken out in Ireland where the United Irishmen's Forces sought to free Ireland from English domination. This was a vicious affair and at least 30,000 people, English and Irish, died in tit for tat massacres. The uprising was finally squashed in the Battle of Vinegar Hill, County Wexford in 1798 and 400 hard core revolutionaries found themselves on convict transports bound for Sydney.

On 4 March 1804 a large number of Irish rebels rose in violent revolt at the government farm near Parramatta. They seized muskets and fashioned pikes from farm implements, threatening to march to Parramatta before moving on to Sydney town to proclaim a Republic of New Ireland. The leaders of the rebellion were former captains of the United Irishmen Forces, Phillip Cunningham and William Johnston, who lit beacons to attract convicts from the region to concentrate on Castle Hill before marching on Sydney. They called the newly liberated area 'New Ireland' and Cunningham was elected 'King of the Australian Empire.'

The rallying call was 'Liberty or death!'

At 11p.m. Major Johnstone of the New South Wales Corps was woken from his bed by the thunder of alarm cannons and told that hundreds of rabid Irishmen were threatening the colony. Sydney town was quite small at the time and 500 armed rebels posed a real threat. He mustered 29 soldiers and 50 militia of the Loyal Volunteers and set off to confront the Irishmen.

On Monday 5 March the redcoats caught up with the Irish rebels, who by this time numbered maybe 300 men. Many rebels had enjoyed their brief period of freedom by getting gloriously drunk. They had a good defensive position on Constitution Hill and Johnstone knew he'd have to use cunning to break their fighting spirit. Constitution Hill was later renamed Vinegar Hill in honour of the earlier battle.

Johnstone asked for a parley with the rebel leaders and, with a priest at his side, called for a peaceful resolution. In the middle of the meeting a small party that the major had sent to outflank the rebels appeared. Johnstone pulled out a concealed pistol, grabbed one of the leaders and swore to 'blow his soul to hell.' The other leader was seized and Johnstone gave the order for his line of 29 redcoats to advance.

Fired on from the front and flanks, the rebels were no match for the New South Wales Regiment's disciplined fire and soon broke and ran. Many fell and surviving ringleaders were hanged, while the others were placed in chain gangs and places of secondary punishment.

The convicts had no chance of standing against the disciplined fire of British redcoats, who would mete out the same treatment to Napoleon eleven years later.

FRONTIER VIOLENCE

The Corps did not only have to garrison Sydney; they were also responsible for the new settlements at Coal River, Norfolk Island and Hobart in Tasmania. Closer to home, they fought the Daruk people of the Hawkesbury River. This rich land was prized by the emancipist settlers as well as the indigenous inhabitants and a fierce guerrilla war soon broke out. By mid-1795 a quarter of the Corps – more than 100 men – were engaged around the rich river lands, hunting down Aboriginals and protecting settlers.

Attempts were made to terrorise the Aboriginals and a party under Captain William Patterson set out to destroy as many Daruk as they could. Failing to find any, the party erected gibbets in the bush as a crude warning. The Daruk, of course, had no idea what this crude symbolism meant.

THE RUM CORPS – REVOLT

William Bligh had been in the colony for six months before he became King's successor. He had ample time to observe the goings on of the Rum Corps and he was determined to break them.

Bligh already had a reputation for dealing crudely with subordinates and he spared nobody's feelings when cracking down on the rum trade. He seized stills, limited imports, favoured the poorer farmers and generally alienated most on his station. The last straw for the New South Wales Regiment came when in January 1808 he had an ex officer of the regiment, John Macarthur, thrown into the brig. This act coincided with a drunken free-for-all on 26 January (now of course Australia Day) when seemingly limitless supplies of grog was given to soldiers and civilians alike.

Major Johnstone had fought the battle of Vinegar Hill and he now had a new target in his sights – Governor Bligh. As commander of the Corps in Sydney he had Macarthur released, and a petition was drawn up requesting that he use his armed force to assume command of the colony. Five signatures were on this document, although after the coup many more were added. Using this most dubious of legal documents Johnstone emptied the Sydney barracks of its 300 soldiers, many of them roaring drunk, and marched on Government House.

The column marched with bayonets fixed, band playing and yellow regimental ensign flying. Different companies surrounded Bligh's official residence and one company entered the house and turned it upside down. The drunken soldiers arrested the Provost Marshal and several magistrates, as well as Bligh's secretary and chaplain. Bligh himself was reportedly found hiding under his bed, although this is a somewhat dubious claim. The coup leaders, Johnstone and Macarthur, effectively ran the colony until Lachlan Macquarie was sworn in as the new governor on 1 January 1810.

Bligh was placed under house arrest for a year before heading down to the newly established colony in Tasmania. He was determined not to leave until his command was officially terminated by government decree.

On 10 May Bligh sailed for England. Accompanying him were the members of the New South Wales Corps who had been relieved – it was no doubt an awkward arrangement. In the hearing that followed, Bligh was exonerated while Johnston was cashiered. Macarthur was prevented from returning to Australia for almost a decade.

CHAPTER 4

RULE OF THE REDCOATS

The New South Wales Corps was replaced by the 73rd Regiment of Foot. For the next 60 years a succession of British formations were the garrisons of the fledgling colony. Ostensibly the regiments were posted to protect the new colony from external aggression but in reality the troops were engaged in savage warfare with convict bolters, dispossessed Aboriginals and, eventually, disgruntled miners.

In fact, the new colonists did their bit to expand the British Empire and joined several overseas expeditions, including the New Zealand Wars against the Maori.

The equipment used by the regiments of foot remained largely unchanged through the years of occupation. Each man wore a red coat, with coloured collars and cuffs identifying the regiment. Varied patterns of lace were worn on the collar and at the front of the coat as an additional regimental insignia. Each musketeer was armed with a smooth bore musket or, later, with a rifled musket capable of firing a minie ball. The original Brown Bess was a flintlock, although later weapons utilised a percussion system. White trousers were worn during summer, while blue-grey pants were issued for winter wear. Each musketeer had a cartridge box on one chalked white cross belt, while a bayonet was suspended from another crossbelt. A haversack and canteen were slung from the right shoulder and a black back pack with the regimental number stenciled on the rear flap was used to carry equipment. Shakoes were tall cylindrical hats made of felt or leather with a brass plate carrying the regimental number on the front.

THE BRITISH REGIMENTAL SYSTEM

Twenty-four British regiments of foot were posted for service in the fledgling colony. They were part of a common rotation that usually saw the regiments shipped from England to Australia, then to the subcontinent, before heading back to the motherland. The posting to Australia averaged seven years. Most regiments were made up of 800 to 1,000 effectives. Unlike the New South Wales Corps, each line regiment was made up of center companies, a grenadier company and a light skirmisher company. The regiments were rarely shipped together and different detachments arrived on separate ships and often in turned up in different locations. This meant that detachments could be spread all over the continent. For example, detachments of the 57th West Middlesex served in New South Wales, Western Australia, Tasmania, the Northern Territory, Victoria and Queensland during their posting between 1825 and 1832. The colonial governments paid half the cost of maintaining the regiments.

No cavalry formations were dispatched to Australia, although artillery batteries were occasionally supplied, as were commissary and engineering assets.

The regiments were crucial for the continued expansion of the colonies. Their contribution allowed Great Britain to be able to claim that they were the only European Empire to possess an entire continent as part of their imperial domains. In March 1788 Norfolk Island was claimed and garrisoned by marines who were then replaced by a detachment of the NSW Corps. In 1803 a settlement was established in Hobart and Governor Lachlan Macquarie ordered the construction of a fortification barracks for the garrison. Soon detachments were sent to the fledgling settlements at Newcastle, Port Macquarie, Moreton Bay, Wollongong and Bathurst.

In 1826 a detachment of soldiers from the 39th Regiment and a party of convicts pre-empted the French by settling Albany in Western Australia. In 1829 Perth was established as the new colony of Western Australia and a detachment of 68 members of the 63rd West Suffolk Regiment were entrusted to protect the colony from foreign aggression. With the foundation of Western Australia every inch of the southern continent was deemed to be a British possession. In September 1836 Captain William Lonsdale of the 4th King's Own was sent to take control of Melbourne from the civilian settlers. This military force was massively boosted with the outbreak of the Crimean War in 1853. Determined to defend the Victorian goldfields from Russian aggression the garrison of Melbourne was expanded to 700.

As well as guarding convicts, garrisoning fortifications and defending from foreign incursions, many military personnel were engaged in exploring the vast 'empty' continent.

Major Thomas Livingstone Mitchell (b. 1792, d. 1855) was a decorated veteran of the 1st Battalion 95th Rifles, and fought in some of the fiercest sieges of Wellington's campaigns in Spain. He was also a gifted cartographer. In 1828 Mitchell was appointed as Surveyor General of New South Wales, and in the next two decades led expeditions that mapped much of the hinterland of Eastern Australia. His third expedition into Victoria during 1836 discovered such bountiful grazing lands that he called the area *Australia Felix*. Of course, the lush meadows dotted with stands of trees that reminded Mitchell so much of the pastures of England were a result of millennia of Aboriginal fire stick farming.

ONEROUS DUTY – CONVICT GUARDS

The main reason for replacing marines with infantry regiments was the marine commander's refusal to allow his men to guard convicts. The redcoats had no such reservations and much of the early infrastructure of the Australian colonies was built by convicts who were guarded by detachments of British foot. This arduous duty was well removed from the glories of battle and no doubt many an officer or soldier regretted being placed on dreary duty at what was considered to be the ends of the earth. The pernicious effect of Indian rum, bad company and poor conditions played havoc with morale. Added to this was the isolation that being 'on command' brought. Placing small detachments under the supervision of an inept subaltern to garrison vast tracts of virtual wilderness was a recipe for trouble.

Even worse was a posting to a place of secondary punishment. These locations were where the most recalcitrant and difficult convicts were sent. A hard hand and an absence of finer feelings was required to survive in these hell holes. Despite some regimental officers trying to alleviate the suffering of their charges, there is no doubt that some took out their frustration on the convicts they guarded.

Newcastle was founded in 1804 as a place of secondary punishment, and some of its first inmates were 37 rebels from the Battle of Vinegar Hill. Convicts were given one of two unenviable tasks; mining the rich coal seams that produced the colony's first exports or producing lime from burnt oyster shells at Fullerton Cove. Major James Morisset (b. 1780 d. 1852) was posted with his regiment, the 48th, to Sydney in 1817, and a year later was appointed commander of Newcastle. He was known as King Lash. The major delighted in tormenting the thousand or so convicts under his care while parading in full dress uniform. He believed in preventative measures and convicts were often lined up and one in three would be given 50 lashes for good measure. This was particularly painful on the lime burners who had to hump, on their ravaged back, hessian sacks full of broken oyster shells while wading through seawater. One possibly apocryphal story has Morisset ordering a prisoner to be lashed with 'the cat'. Unhappy with the effort of the flogger he had another convict flog the first flogger, and so on until six prisoners were all in a row laying in with the cat-o'-nine tails.

Despite his harsh treatment of the prisoners, Morisset earned nothing but praise from his superiors.

Perhaps the worst posting of all was Sarah Island in Macquarie Harbor. Not even the soldiers could escape the biting south-westerlies that swept up from Antarctica, making life on the exposed island a misery to all. Newcastle was considered too close to Sydney and many convict bolters managed to escape to cause more trouble. Macquarie Harbor on the south west coast of Tasmania was so removed from any other habitation that successful escape was almost impossible. Established in 1822, the 33 kilometre long inlet is surrounded by some of the densest and most inhospitable bushland in the world. Even now seasoned bushwalkers have to be cautious when they set out to explore so hostile an environment. The entrance to the harbor was aptly named – the Gates of Hell. Only shallow draft boats could penetrate the crashing seas and dangerous rocks at the mouth of the inlet and many ships, complete with their crews of soldiers and convicts, foundered at the lethal spot.

A party of 110, including 74 convicts and troops of the 48th Regiment, arrived in early 1822 and began building barracks. The commandant, named Lieutenant John Cuthbertson, made terrific progress. For ten months of the year winds lashed the settlement, blowing down buildings and setting ships adrift. It took as long as 27 days for ships to make the 300 kilometre voyage from Hobart, but could often take much longer. Supplies were always an issue and fresh water had to be carted from the mainland.

On 22 December 1823 Cuthbertson was drowned while trying to tether a ship that was blown off its moorings. He was replaced by Lieutenant Wright of the 3rd, who was forced to begin farming on the mainland to alleviate the scurvy that was tearing through convicts and soldiers alike. The 40th and 63rd Regiments of Foot also saw service on the island.

In the 11 years of the settlement 85 convicts died: 27 were drowned, eight killed by accident, three shot by their guards and twelve murdered by fellow inmates. There was usually no need to investigate the identity of the murderers. Many killed their fellows so they could escape the torment of Macquarie Island at the end of a hangman's noose.

Large numbers of convicts bolted into the bush, but almost all of them died of exposure or at the hands of the natives. Those who escaped with the infamous Alexander Pierce ended up in his stomach.

Transportation of convicts was stopped in New South Wales in 1852. The last convicts disembarked in Tasmania in 1853. By the decade's end the convict system was dismantled in many respects and few redcoats were still engaged in convict management – no doubt one of the least pleasant aspects of a posting to Australia.

BUSHRANGERS AND BOLTERS

The other threat that the regiments of foot had to deal with was the scourge of bush ranging. Two Aboriginal 'bush rangers' were the first to be captured and hanged in the colony of Victoria, when they were captured by Ensign Samuel Rawson and eight privates of the 28th Regiment in 1841.

These small police actions were nothing like what was required in Tasmania, where whole regiments were required to hunt down large gangs of bushrangers who almost toppled the colonial government.

In 1804 the garrison of Van Diemen's land was limited to approximately 50 personnel of the New South Wales Corps. By 1845 there were 2,000 soldiers stationed on the Apple Isle.

Tasmania became something of a dumping ground for convicts and many escaped into the bush to cause trouble. Governor Macquarie sought to bring these men back into society and granted an amnesty to all bushrangers allowing them free pardon if they surrendered by 1 December 1814. The problem was he issued the amnesty in May of that year, allowing miscreants a free hand to get up to all kinds of mischief for another eight months. Powerful criminal leaders formed large and well armed ragtag gangs. There were even reports of armed bands marching in formation through outlying settlements and demonstrating their might by drilling with volley fire.

In 1814 the 46th Regiment of Foot was called to eradicate the outbreak that was terrorising farmers and merchants throughout the settled districts. Initially the 46th was hopelessly outclassed by the bushrangers, who would disappear into myriad hidey-holes at the approach of the redcoats. The tables were turned when convict constables were attached to each detachment. Soon tactics very much like those used in Malaya and Vietnam more than a century later were employed. Small parties of soldiers patrolled the bush, setting up ambushes and looking for signs of activity. The monotony was broken by brief sharp actions.

In March 1817 three bushrangers, William Elliot, James Parker and John Chapman, were discovered by a patrol. A brief firefight ensued. The first two were shot dead, although Chapman took to his heels. The heads of the dead bushrangers were severed from their bodies and taken into Hobart for positive identification.

Perhaps the greatest opponent of the redcoats was Michael Howe. Shipped to Van Diemen's land in 1812 as an assigned convict (a convict who worked for bread and board in a settler's household) he soon fled. He became leader of a notorious gang that terrorised farmers, forcing many off their land. At one stage Howe's gang plundered the town of New Norfolk. Howe titled himself the 'Governor of the Ranges' and organised his gang along paramilitary lines. Members were drilled, did fatigues and were punished if they broke 'regulations'. In April of 1817 he was almost caught by the 46th. Although he escaped, his gang was rounded up and his hideouts burned.

Howe had an unlikely nemesis in the 48th Regiment. Young Private William Pugh suggested to his officer that he had a cunning plan to capture Howe. The plan involved sharing the reward money with a kangaroo shooter called Warburton. The hunter had a hut up in the hills and was known to be on good terms with Howe. On 21 October 1818 the kangaroo shooter lured the bushranger to his hut where the young private waited. The bushranger presented a bizarre sight and was clad only in kangaroo skins while sporting a bushy black beard. Howe sensed a trap and bolted but came unstuck when he slipped down a creek embankment. He turned to fight his pursuers but private Pugh knocked the fleeing bushranger down with the butt end of his firelock, jumped after him, and battered his brains out just as Howe was opening a clasp-knife to defend himself.

Howe's head was hacked off and taken into town for the bounty money while his bones were left to bleach in the Tasmanian forest.

Life for the redcoats in Van Diemen's land was notoriously difficult. Supplies were often hard to come by and marching through the thick bush took its toll on men, uniforms and equipment. During their posting to Tasmania, the 40th Regiment of Foot missed out on an issue of equipment and clothing. Forced to extemporise, some men made haversacks and knapsacks from kangaroo and wallaby hides. Recognising the suitability of these furs in the frigid Tasmanian weather, some soldiers dressed themselves entirely in furry coats and trousers, even having kangaroo cartridge skin boxes and possum skin shakoes! Things came to a head just outside of Launceston when two parties of soldiers shot at each other, each thinking that the other were bushrangers. Corporal John Deane was killed in this unique case of friendly fire.

The settlements of Bathurst, Sydney and Newcastle were plagued by bandits and bushrangers. They were so bad that Governor Sir Thomas Brisbane (b. 1773 d. 1860), the governor from 1821-1825, declared that only the military could restore order. Initially he dispatched a detachment of the 3rd Regiment of Foot (The Buffs) to the Bathurst region to hunt down the predatory gangs. The troopers were mounted on cart horses and met with instant success. Brisbane was so pleased with the result that he established the Corps of Mounted Soldiers, under Colonel William Stewart of the Buffs, with the express purpose of hunting down bushrangers.

Regiments volunteered men for this service from 1825. Beginning as a small unit, there were 100 mounted soldiers by 1830. They were increasingly effective as their bushcraft grew and convict bolters could expect to be captured one or two days after escape. There were 500 miscreants rounded up during the months of 1838 and1839. The mounted soldiers initially wore their laced red coats but this proved impractical for hard duty on the roads of the colony. They were soon fitted out with a broad brimmed hat (forerunner of the slouch hat perhaps), one cross belt to hold their carbine, a sword and white trimmed dark blue trousers and coat. Despite being seconded from the infantry, the Corps of Mounted soldiers became in reality a unit of light horse. The British government never sent a cavalry regiment to the new colony.

The troopers were deadly efficient and no doubt could have taught soldiers in Vietnam a thing or two about stalking a deadly foe. John Donahue was transported in 1824 and escaped from assigned service. For three years he roamed the territories outside of Sydney, robbing coaches, terrorising wealthy settlers and generally making a nuisance of himself. He earned the moniker 'Bold Jack', and after being captured and sentenced to death managed to escape before the sentence was carried out. The authorities were made something of a laughing stock and it was up to a small party of mounted soldiers under Sergeant Hodson of the 57th Regiment of Foot to bring him to justice.

As the sun set over the Cumberland Plain on 1 September 1830, a keen eyed trooper saw a suspicious group. The area was known as a haunt of the bold bushranger and his men. After tethering their horses, the soldiers crept up to within one hundred metres of the party. They noiselessly split into several groups to encircle the suspects. They opened up on the bushrangers and Donahue with his gang scrambled into some scrub and began firing. The bold bushranger hurled lead and imprecations at his pursuers. While peering around a large tree to take a shot he was hit by a ball fired from the carbine of Private of the 39th, John Mugglestone. Donahue fell to the ground dead.

The mounted troopers were also used to 'disperse' hostile Aboriginals. Major Nunn led an expedition of perhaps 20 soldiers against the Kamilaroi peoples of the Liverpool plains in 1838. The superior equipment and mobility of the troopers allowed them to win one sided 'victories' against the indigenous populations at locations such as Slaughter Creek. This was the last major expedition of a military force against the Aboriginals, and by the 1850s the back of black resistance was broken. Civilian police and trackers combined with settlers and stockmen would henceforth fight on the frontiers.

AUSTRALIA'S FIRST OVERSEAS MILITARY ADVENTURE: NEW ZEALAND

The first time Australian soldiers charged entrenched positions defended by a well armed and determined opponent was not at Anzac Cove but much closer to home – at Tauranga Bay, about 250 kilometres south east of Auckland, New Zealand. The Maori were a fierce people and their large tribes had been involved in wars for the thousand or so years since they had first settled in New Zealand. Unlike the Australian Aboriginals, who were unable to organise large forces to fight the colonial settlers, the Maori gave the British armed forces many a bloody nose.

Despite a treaty being signed between the indigenous population and the Empire in 1840 conflict soon broke out and in 1863 the British began a recruitment drive for volunteers from the Australian colonies. By 1864 almost 2,700 had volunteered for service and most found themselves in the 'Waikato Militia' divided into several regiments.

The enlistment drive in the Australian colonies had offered grants of land to the volunteers who were expected to settle after the war. They would provide a readymade militia who could be called out should the Maori begin another rebellion. Conflict in New Zealand had been almost continuous since the 1820s and the volunteers were given a modern and functional uniform without any of the normal parade ground trappings. A woollen 'Pork Pie' forage cap, a dark blue 'jumper' (tunic), matching shirt and thick blue trousers with a red stripe down the side kept the troops warm in the New Zealand chill. A black leather cartridge box belt completed the ensemble. Blankets and great coats were often rolled up and strapped across the chest. This uniform was perfect for moving through thick New Zealand foliage and keeping off the elements. Efficient rifle Enfields or French Minie rifles were issued to most recruits.

The glorious picture of a heroic battlefield soon paled into a much less pleasant reality. The cold and dismal New Zealand weather was not the only thing the militia had to struggle against. The Maori were fierce enemies who would torture and murder any prisoners. Tales of cannibalism were made worse when the recruits witnessed the fierce Haka and the grotesque tattoos carved onto mature warrior's faces. In the skirmishers that the Australians were involved in the Maori proved to be a doughty and dangerous warrior.

On 23 October 1863 seven Australians died in a skirmish with 150 warriors. The first Australian to die in overseas service was Lieutenant J.S Perceval of Bendigo, who found himself and his men surrounded by the Maoris at a small church, named Mauku church, on Titi Hill. It seems the lieutenant may have gotten carried away at the battle of

Titi Hill and had to be restrained from charging the Maori skirmishers single-handed. As the warriors closed he stood and shot two before being gunned down himself. Other Australian casualties were caused when the Maori dropped their muskets, drew their long handled war clubs and engaged in hand to hand combat.

The battered militia withdrew behind their stockade soon after.

The Maori knew the effectiveness of the modern firearms used by the British and countered this advantage by digging formidable forts known as *pā*.

A large *pā* contained successive lines of entrenchments and palisades built into dominating terrain features. Rear reserve positions were included and the fortifications resembled some of the sophisticated trenches used in World War I.

Storming a *pā* could be a bloody business. Many Maori had learnt to use firearms and, once the open ground had been crossed by assaulting soldiers, British units had to fight in deadly hand-to-hand combat with fierce warriors armed with greenstone clubs and spears. In June 1845, 220 men of the 58th and 99th Regiments stormed a *pā* and suffered a staggering loss. Of the 220-man storming party 40 were killed and 70 were wounded in the Maori cross fire.

Fortunately for the Australians in the Waikato Militia, they were chiefly involved in protecting the flanks of the major British drive in 1863. They also secured the rear areas and it was in this role that the Australians' bushcraft and marksmanship served them, and their British commander, well.

There was one set piece battle where the Australians were required to charge an entrenched Maori position. On 21 June 1864, approximately 600 men of the 1st Waikato Militia along with elements of the 43rd and 68th Regiments were ordered to drive a considerable body of warriors from a string of rifle pits dug into the heights dominating Tauranga. Many of the Maori were armed with rifles and they were intent on building a *pā*, which would dominate communications with Camp Te Papa.

The Europeans marched on the position and for two hours the sides kept up a lively fire at each other. Finally, after some reinforcements arrived, the three units charged the rifle pits in the face of the Maori fire (most of which went high). Sixty-eight natives were killed in the rifle pits and many more in the pursuit that followed. Captain Moore was the commander of the Waikato militia and his men excelled in the pursuit through difficult country until nightfall. In all 180 Maoris were killed. This significant loss of life led to the Maori's surrender soon after.

This was one of the last set piece battles of the war and soon after the militias were all but disbanded. Most of the Australians returned to the colonies of NSW and Victoria. The land they had been granted was poor and the weather even worse! Not to mention the unfriendly locals.

The New Zealand Wars saw Australia's first naval commitment. The HMVS *Victoria* was a sloop-of-war that was built in 1855 and was owned by, you guessed it, the state of Victoria. The fast ship had a complement of 90 men and her first official duty for the Crown was to carry 120 troops of the 40th Regiment of Foot from Hobart to New Zealand. They were then involved in running supplies to New Plymouth and hunting down blockade runners seeking to sell arms to the Maori. Some men from the crew were armed with cutlasses and pistols. United with members of other crews they were formed into a naval brigade and participated in the storming of several *pā*.

BLOOD AT BALLARAT

British regular regiments were involved in one set piece battle during their tenure as the garrison of Australia – the Battle of Ballarat, otherwise known as the Eureka Stockade. When disciplined regulars marching in line and column advanced to overcome a semi-trained group of poorly armed rebels, there was only one possible outcome: a massacre. Adding to the drama of the battle was the poor decision made by the miners to pick a fight with some of the best equipped and most battle hardened regiments in the British Empire.

In 1851 payable gold was found in Australia. During the next decade waves of migrants streamed into Australia to make their fortunes. Many set themselves up for life with the plentiful alluvial gold that was found in the first Gold Rush.

After one or two years this initial bounty dried out and miners had to toil in dreadful conditions far removed from civilisation's amenities for increasingly meagre returns. Simultaneously with the worsening conditions came a government impost – each miner was required to pay for a Gold Licence. The cost of these licences was no mean amount and ranged from 1 pound, ten shillings a month to two pounds for three months. These fees equated to many months average wages for a working man.

All prospectors had to pay for the privilege to mine whether they found gold or not. The money was used by state Gold Commissioners to police the goldfields, to issue licences, to guard gold convoys as well as the post and to maintain general order on the diggings.

There were the usual grumbles among the miners. The fees were too high, they were being taxed without voting rights, roads and services weren't being improved, and so on.

What really drove the diggers into open rebellion was the attitude of the police. These mounted troopers, or 'traps' as the diggers called them, were tasked with hunting down any diggers who did not have a licence. There is some dispute about the origin of these troopers and some maintain that they were ex-convicts in uniform. It is more likely that the bulk of the police were ex-soldiers. Their performance on the battlefield of Eureka would indicate the latter. Nevertheless, they brought the savage discipline that they had experienced to the gold fields. They seemed to revel in 'digger hunts', which would be carried out twice a week.

The traps spared the miners no humiliation. Many were tied up behind a trooper's horse and dragged in a resentful convoy with other diggers to the Commissioner's tent, where they had to fork out another five pounds to pay a fine. Some, who had paid their fee but were not holding their license, were chained to trees for days without being tried. Others were thrown into rude slab huts without water or even a bucket and confined through broiling hot days and freezing nights. Anybody who has been to Ballarat will know that temperatures there are extreme. Nights in particular are enough to 'freeze the bollocks off a bullock' in digger parlance. The traps resented the diggers, most whom could be called entrepreneurs, and they used any excuse to torment them.

Even the act of paying for a licence was humiliating. Men had to wait for hours in a wooden pen for their turn to fork out 30 shillings – time that would have been better spent digging for gold.

Throughout NSW and Victoria tensions bubbled along with miners meetings to express discontent and argue for less restrictions. The miners were a mixed group. Ex-convicts, European adventurers, hardened men from the Californian gold fields, ex soldiers and ex sailors. All these groups were combined with a leavening of politically literate radical Irishmen. These were hot spots of discontent and a detachment of troops from the 40th Regiment were sent to support the traps in Bendigo.

The situation came to a head in Victoria with the appointment of Governor Hotham. He had heard much of the continued disturbances and was determined to stamp out any more shenanigans. He made it clear he would use the military if necessary.

During August 1854 Hotham toured the Victorian goldfields. He was initially welcomed, but when Hotham found that less than 60% of the diggers held licences he determined to stamp out any evasion of payments. In September he ordered the traps to check licences twice a week rather than once a month. On 7 October disgruntled miners caused several disturbances at Ballarat and Hotham sent a group of soldiers and troopers to arrest the culprits. While they were able to carry out his order and arrested three suspects, there were not enough soldiers to stop violent riots and arson. Reinforcements were needed and further troops were summoned from Melbourne.

The arrests further inflamed the situation and, on 11 November, 10,000 miners gathered on Bakery Hill, Ballarat to found the Ballarat Reform League. The choice of Bakery Hill as a rallying point for this huge horde of miners was provocative – it was close to the government encampment.

On 23 November the three accused were found guilty. The following day 16,000 miners gathered on Bakery Hill to burn their licences. Firearms were issued and ammunition stores gathered. Many guns were fired into the air. It seemed that the Victorian Government was in danger of losing control of the richest district in the colony. Hotham responded by ordering further intensive licence checks.

Reinforcements from Melbourne marched into Ballarat, past what later became the Eureka Stockade. Thousands of miners turned out to attack several companies from the 40th and 12th Regiments of Foot, which may have numbered a couple of hundred men. Soldiers were jeered at and spat upon, carts were turned over and even a couple of shots were fired, allegedly killing a young drummer boy. Several soldiers were beaten.

The column got through to the government encampment, but the miners had made a crucial mistake. They had humiliated some of the Empire's toughest soldiers. There would be a reckoning. A reckoning in blood.

The 12th Regiment of Foot had yellow distinguishing marks and was also known as the Suffolk Regiment. Raised as the Duke of Norfolk's regiment in 1685 it was intended to help in breaking the back of the Monmouth Rebellion. The regiment went on to fight in crucial battles such as Dettingen and Fontenoy in the War of the Spanish Succession. They earned further laurels while fighting Tipu Sultan in India and during many battles in the Napoleonic wars.

The 40th Regiment of Foot, the 2nd Somersetshire, were originally raised in Canada in 1717. It fought in many frontier conflicts as well as serving in the American War of Independence from 1775, and was involved in almost every major battle that the Empire was engaged in. The regiment added to its lustrous reputation and fought under the Duke of Wellington in most of his battles in the Peninsula from 1808 to 1813. These battles included the hard fought victories at Rolica, Vimeiro, Bussaco, Talavera, Salamanca, Vitoria and the Battle of the Pyrenees. In all of these battles the 40th utilised Wellington's favourite tactic. An accurate volley fired at close range followed by a charge with cold steel. Few French units could withstand this tactic and it is to the miners credit that they resisted for as long as they did.

Perhaps the 40th's greatest battle honour was that of Waterloo. Kept in reserve for most of the day they were moved into the centre of Wellington's line, where they stood firm amongst shot and canister fired at close range by French horse artillery during Napoleon's final attack. The square held in this desperate moment despite losing a third of their number, who lay dead as if in formation.

The regiment was no stranger to Australia and served in New South Wales and Tasmania from 1823 to 1828. In Tasmania they played a key role in defending colonists, moving into the island's interior during the increasingly savage 'Black War' which saw the virtually complete genocide of the nine Tasmanian tribes. The Big River and Oyster Bay tribes were almost wiped out in several massacres carried out by members of the 40th, aided by local settlers.

Before returning to Australia in 1852, the regiment fought in savage battles in India and Afghanistan. The men who landed on Victoria's shores were hardened veterans indeed. Any man who fell into the hands of a sub-continental enemy could expect a hideously violent death. No quarter was given or asked for – something the diggers would soon experience.

After supressing the Eureka breakout, the regiment would take part in the Taranaki and Waikato campaigns during the New Zealand Wars in the 1860s.

The 1850s saw the zenith of the British Empire. This was in large part due to the efficiency of their red coated infantry regiments. The 12th and 40th would have an extra advantage over the diggers. In the early 1850s regulations had been passed ordering that every overseas regiment was to be issued with 200 rifled muskets. The Hobart *Colonial Times* newspaper reported that the 12th issued rifled muskets to 24 men in each company. While most men in a company were issued with a smooth bore Lovett musket accurate to perhaps 100 metres, the 24 soldiers equipped with a rifled Lovett could fire a minie ball accurately to at least 600 metres.

These sharpshooters were to be crucial in the coming battle.

The two regiments were not only equipped with the latest weaponry but were wearing the trim and functional uniform introduced for service in overseas domains. In comparison with unwieldy earlier uniforms, they wore a simple red fatigue jacket without laced lapels, tails or waistcoat, light white summer trousers, short boots and the compact 1844 Albert shako with visors both fore and aft to give protection from the sun. The 1850 regulations stipulated that only one cross belt was to be worn over the right shoulder to support the cartridge box while a white waist belt held the bayonet frog. NCOs still had two cross belts. As shown in William Lincoln's excellent pamphlet *Uniforms and Accoutrements of the British*

Army 1854 Eureka Stockade, the infantry were well equipped to fight on the Ballarat goldfields.

It seems that long tailed regimental coatee were still issued for parade and guard duties, but while in action the infantry wore the shorter fatigue jacket.

On 1 December things came to a head. A group of at least 1,000 armed and angry diggers marched from a meeting at Bakery Hill and, under the leadership of Irish firebrand Peter Lalor, marched to the 'Eureka lead' – site of a deep seam of gold. On the knoll-like hill adjacent to the Melbourne road were many mineshafts, along with tents and huts. An immense tree was cut down to be fashioned into a flag pole. Hauled up its side the Southern Cross flag made it first appearance. An estimated 1,000 diggers knelt in a circle around the Southern Cross Flag and, led by Lalor, swore a solemn oath: 'We swear by the Southern Cross to stand truly by each other and fight to defend our rights and liberties.'

The men then turned their hard and calloused hands to building the stockade. Carts were overturned, fallen trees were woven together to make primitive firing platforms and loosely packed logs were driven into the ground. The stockade, which enclosed about an acre of the goldfields, had at its center some tents and huts packed with ammunition.

The stockade was also used to intercept carriages on the Melbourne road; wealthy travellers were subject to violent attacks. Armed parties of miners roamed the goldfields seizing weapons and enlisting 'volunteers' for the coming fight. One group went so far as to arrest a Mining Commissioner. In effect they were setting themselves up as an alternative government.

Over the next two days men in the stockade were brigaded into units and drilled. Ex-soldiers helped to instruct the miners in rapid musket fire while others were made to practice close order drill with rudely fashioned pikes and halberds. Miners flocked to the colours, including the Californian Rangers. These considered themselves to be an elite unit of hardened miners, dripping with pistols and mounted on fine horses. This 'unit', along with some of best trained miners, departed down the Melbourne Road with the intention of ambushing a large group of redcoat reinforcements. They had heard that the remainder of the 12th and 40th, supported by two cannon and two Howitzers crewed by naval gunners, were marching for the goldfields. Reports came in of a large unit of Bendigo miners heading south to help their comrades.

The authorities seemed to be paralyzed in fear of the huge mass of rebels. Even during a torrential storm, the British on government hill were ordered to remain on guard ready to defend against an attack by Lalor's men.

All seemed well on the Eureka Stockade. So well that on Saturday 2 December the rowdy miners indulged in a drunken knees up. It was presumed that the British would not attack on the Sabbath so they blew off some steam, intending to sleep in on the Sunday morning. After much carry on, most of the miners returned to their huts and tents, many of which were outside the stockade. What's more, Lalor made a crucial mistake. Two score of his doughtiest fighters were English ex-servicemen. When they heard he had given the password for the evening as 'Vinegar Hill' they left in disgust.

By the morning of 3 December 1854 there were between 150 and 200 miners still behind the stockade. No doubt many were nursing sore heads.

Informers kept the authorities well informed of the goings on and when Captain J Thomas of the 40th heard of the reduced number of defenders, he decided to attack.

Mustering half of the 500 or so troops under his command he had them fall in early on the morning of the 3rd. The remainder were left to garrison the government camp lest his forces suffer a reverse.

Precise numbers are hard to determine but a reasonable estimate is that his regular forces included 65 men from the 12th Regiment, 87 infantry from the 40th and 30 mounted infantries from the same regiment. This later detachment testifies to the ability of the British Army to adapt to circumstances. Several gold coaches had been attacked and as a response to this threat soldiers from the 40th had been mounted on horses and acted as a well armed escort able to fight off any would be bushrangers. No doubt a proportion would have been armed with the new rifles and they could be seen as something of an elite unit. Making up the numbers of the attackers was a detachment of 70 mounted police and some foot police.

Thomas knew his stuff. The entire formation was neatly arrayed behind cover just as dawn began to creep over the horizon. To his left he placed his mounted infantry and some mounted troopers. A storming party of perhaps half of his regulars were arrayed in loose formation to his front supported by close order foot. Out to his right Thomas deployed some police troopers.

The whole formation marched in the pre-dawn darkness up the sides of a gully towards the stockade on the rise before them.

Thomas wrote in his official report to Hotham:

> We then advanced quietly towards entrenchment where the revolutionary flag was flying, at about one hundred and fifty yards we were received by a rather sharp and well directed fire from the rebels-without word or challenge on their part; then, and not until then, I ordered the bugle to sound 'commence firing.' For about ten minutes a heavy fire was kept up by the troops advancing, which was replied to by the rebels. During this time I brought up the infantry supports and the foot police. The entrenchment was then carried and I ordered the firing to cease. All persons found within the entrenchments were taken prisoners, and many of the fugitives were intercepted by the cavalry.

This report is useful on two fronts:

Firstly, it is an excellent indicator of the sophisticated tactics that a British infantry force was capable of. A line of skirmishers emerges from cover. They attract enemy fire which is dissipated on the attackers' loose formation. In short rushes the skirmishers advance on the enemy fortification. It is likely that the skirmishers approached in pairs. They would have been Thomas' trained marksmen and would have used the fire and movement tactics that are still used by the modern military. The rifled muskets accurate fire kept the miners heads below the parapet. Under the cover of this galling fire the main body of assault troops approached the stockade and, melding with the skirmishers, let off a devastating volley before launching an effective bayonet charge over the stockade. All the while the mounted infantry would have been supporting the attack by skirmishing on the main body's flank, effectively splitting the rebel fire and causing confusion. Dismounted police troopers did the same on the opposite flank.

So effective were Thomas' tactics that his men suffered minimal casualties while attacking an entrenched foe.

The source is useful on another point – it demonstrates how official reports can be total whitewashes! After ensuring that the diggers were portrayed as the aggressors, Thomas spares the reader the violent details of the attack.

It was a well-documented and bloody battle.

Once the first volley broke out men poured from their tents into the entrenchments. The retired servicemen among them knew what the resounding bugle call meant – they were about to be assaulted. Tumbling out of their tents they saw a solid line of flame as the redcoats approached. The diggers could only reply sporadically. In what seemed to be an instant the 40th were at the defences. The regimental adjutant, Captain Wise, was first over, calling out '40th, follow me!' As the captain leapt over the abatis he was wounded several times. The wounds would prove to be mortal but in the short term they served to further infuriate his men. The redcoats surged into the rebel defences. Lalor was hit by a musket ball which destroyed his shoulder. Other miners were bayoneted or shot. Some that sought refuge had their tents burnt down and were bayoneted as they emerged. Many diggers disappeared never to be seen again. It is likely that they were seized by vengeful redcoats and tossed down one of the mineshafts that covered the hill. Some miners may have thrown themselves into the shafts in despair. The 40th almost got out of hand in their fury and it is reported that a large group of diggers owed their lives to an officer who interceded to stop a bloody massacre at the last moment.

A diary entry of a witness to the aftermath of battle painted a somber picture. On the morning of Sunday 3 December, 19-year-old Charles Evans followed the route taken when the infantry attacked the compound. The first thing he noticed was a large body of soldiers leading three dray loads of dead and wounded through the gully where they had assembled for the attack. Proceeding up into the stockade he encountered a ghastly scene. Scattered around the camp lay 18 to 20 lifeless bodies that displayed clear signs of mutilation. Some had gunshot wounds that had torn off their faces while others appeared as if peppered by a fusillade of shots. What particularly shook the young man was a figure who lay at the entrance of his burnt tent. It would appear that his legs and groin were thoroughly charred while his torso and head were intact, despite suffering several bullet wounds. Another digger was still breathing and choking out his last despite the fact that his brains protruded from a hole in his skull. Charles counted the wounds on a German miner he used to know – there were 17, all of which could have been mortal.

Evans was not the only civilian to visit the site. Women and children scoured the terrain looking for their loved ones and many were screaming and crying upon finding dead husbands and fathers. Evans reported several eyewitness accounts claiming that the troopers had fired at innocent women and once they had broken into the stockade the mounted troopers had delighted in cutting down defenseless men as they emerged from their tents.

While the official death count of the rebels was about 20 men, it is likely that it was much higher. Up to 60 received wounds and many of these died. Many deaths no doubt went unreported. Innocent bystanders were captured and beaten, only being released days after the event.

One member of the 40th died during the assault. Private Michael Rooney received a ball in the head. Six of the attacking force died and some were wounded leading to a casualty rate of perhaps 5%. Maybe 30% of the defending rebels were casualties and 110% captured!

The short, sharp attack broke the rebellion. The column of 800 men from Melbourne arrived soon after but they were not needed. The California Rangers wisely disbanded themselves while the miners from Bendigo turned back on news of the assault.

Observers noted that, from the 3rd onwards, miners who used to abuse and scoff at soldiers and troopers learnt to hold their tongues.

Hotham may have won the battle but he lost the war. Public opinion turned against him, many of the miners demands were met and Lalor was rehabilitated.

Nevertheless, any who thought to ferment rebellion against the Crown would perhaps have looked at the performance of the 12th and the 40th Regiments of Foot and reconsidered their options!

The military could also be a positive force in the new society. One hundred and one men of the 12th were dispatched to Lambing Flat in May 1860 to protect Chinese diggers from rioting white miners. They maintained the peace until 1862.

BRITAIN PULLS THE PLUG

By the 1850s life for the British regiments of foot in the new colonies was pleasant. The decades before had seen hard fighting against defiant Aboriginals and bloodthirsty bushrangers. Civil authorities and armed frontiersmen had taken over most of those duties. What's more, after 1840 the flow of convicts was reduced to a trickle, and in the 1850s ceased altogether. The onerous duty of guarding these reprobates became less and less of a feature of garrison life. New, comfortable barracks were built and many soldiers gave themselves over to cricket, music and drinking. Indeed, it was considered better to be a private in Australia than a general in India! The Corps of Mounted Soldiers was disbanded in 1860 as they were not considered necessary.

The American War of Independence (1775-1783) was provoked by the perceived need that the American colonies should pay the English exchequer for their defence. The following rebellion changed world history and led to the colonisation of Australia as a convict dumping ground.

By the mid-19th Century history seemed to be repeating itself. But rather than levying unpopular taxes on the colonies of Australia, Great Britain simply pulled out her land forces. In March 1862 the House of Commons resolved that those colonies which had achieved stable self-government would have to pay for their own land defences. The Empire would still provide naval protection but by March 1870 the last British regiment of foot – the 18th Royal Irish – sailed from Australian shores. They were farewelled from Port Phillip by an adoring crowd of 20,000 well-wishers.

A new era began where the colonies, scattered around the 26,000 kilometers of Australian coastline, were to be responsible for their own self-defence.

CHAPTER 5

FIVE ARMIES TO FEDERATION

As early as the 1850s there were rumblings from the Empire's capital, Whitehall in London, that the colonies of Australia would soon have to pay for their own defensive needs. The situation crystalised during the New Zealand Wars of the 1860s when many British regiments of foot were sent to fight in those savage wars. This stripped the Australian mainland of most of its defence assets. The colonial governments themselves realised that they would have to look to their own protection in the future. When the last British regiment pulled out in 1870 the nascent Australian Army had a multiplicity of tasks. Capitals needed defending from the French, Russians and Germans. It was necessary to defend the Queen's peace within the colonies and, if necessary, the Empire might call on her colonial sons for service abroad. What's more, the social order needed to be maintained.

All of the states built their own units. The larger states of Victoria and New South Wales were able to field what would now be called an all-arms force of cavalry, infantry and artillery. The limited resources of the other states reduced the types of formations they could raise.

While it is impossible here to go into detail on every colonial regiment, this chapter will examine some of the most important. It must be noted that many of the regiments raised had a huge range of uniforms and insignia over a relatively short period of time and to note every intricacy of these would require a much longer book than this one.

While serving in these regiments many soldiers gained the necessary skills to carve out successful careers in both the Boer War and the First World War.

VOLUNTEERS TO MILITIA

During the 1850s hundreds of volunteer companies were raised throughout Australia. Royal permission was required for the establishment of such forces. It seems that the key attraction for many of the volunteers may have been the desire to dress up in fancy uniforms and parade around looking splendid. Men paid for their own uniforms and accoutrements so it was an activity open only to the better off within the community.

State governments usually supplied weaponry to the volunteers and, if a unit had the good fortune to possess a wealthy benefactor, particularly splendid uniforms could be provided. Each unit was free to choose its own uniform and the diversity could be mind-boggling. During the 1880s many states sought to consolidate their forces. Acts were passed which abolished the volunteer movement and introduced militia units; these were partially funded by the state and were more like our current reserve forces. The Militia Acts led to greater standardisation of uniforms, training and equipment.

With Federation most of the militia units were absorbed into the new federal army. Despite this many proud units fought tooth and nail to hang on to their splendid militia uniforms.

The story of the 1st Regiment Adelaide Rifles is a terrific example of how these units changed over time.

THE 1ST REGIMENT ADELAIDE RIFLES

The Brigade of Volunteer Militia was founded in 1840 to battle convicts and outlaws in the foothills around Adelaide in the new colony of South Australia. In 1841 the title 'Royal' was added but this was pointless. The small component of volunteers was too darn busy to spend time parade bashing. Within a few years the brigade disbanded itself.

The outbreak of the Crimean war saw the Governor call for 2,000 volunteers and units sprung up around the still sparsely populated state. There was a monetary reward and, for the one day a week they were requested to train, the volunteers received six shillings plus a 4 shilling allowance.

In 1860 there was a rationalisation of several units into the Adelaide Rifles. The number of units which ceased to exist is illustrative of the proliferation of small volunteer units throughout the colonies. The Port Adelaide Rifles, 1st Adelaide Rifles, Gawler Rifles, Glen Osmond Rifles, Edwardstown Rifles, Glenelg Rifles, Sturt and Brighton Rifles, Nairne Rifles, Munro Para East Rifles, Noarlunga Rifles Adelaide Marksmen and the Mitcham Rifles all vanished with the rationalisation, and their numbers were reduced to 1,000 men.

The Adelaide Regiment was a particularly splendid looking formation, with grey coatee and trousers combined with a grey kepi. The whole unit would not have looked out of place in a Civil War rebel battle line. Intricate black and red Hungarian loops decorated the cuffs and collars, and what could be better than a white shirt and black bow tie to finish off the ensemble?

In the mid-1860s the unit was renamed the Adelaide Regiment of Volunteer Rifles and within the year was renamed the South Australian (Prince Alfred's Own) Volunteer Infantry.

Soon after, the whole unit was disbanded, until being re-raised in 1877 to become the Adelaide Rifles. In 1891 it was called the 1st Regiment Adelaide Rifles. It retained this title until Federation.

THE VICTORIAN VOLUNTEER RIFLE CORPS

With the outbreak of the Crimean war in 1854, Governor Charles Hotham approved an Act to establish a volunteer corps not exceeding 2,000 men with officers approved by the governor. The units were unpaid, but such was the enthusiasm for enlistment that by 1860 the Act was amended to allow a force of 10,000 men. In 1870 the Victorian Volunteer Force became the primary defence of the colony, until they were disbanded in 1884 and replaced by the full-time professional Victorian Militia Force.

In 1854 the Victorian Volunteer Rifle Corps was raised. Numbers of enlistments skyrocketed and by 1862 companies, all with different uniforms and regulations, were established throughout Victoria. They were organised into three battalions with a combined strength of 2,400 men. The North Battalion had companies in Pentridge, North Melbourne, Fitzroy, Williamstown, West Melbourne, Collingwood, Carlton and East Collingwood. The South Battalion included volunteers from many southern suburbs including St Kilda, Hawthorn and Prahran. The Country Battalion included detachments from Geelong, Portland, Warrnambool, Ballarat and Geelong. The uniforms employed by the regiment were similar to the frock coat, pants and kepi worn by soldiers in the American Civil War, although the dominant colour was green. In 1883 the battalions were disbanded with the Militia Act, and in 1884 four new battalions were raised. These continued as Victoria's main defensive shield until 1901 when they became Commonwealth formations.

The Rifles were supported by the Royal Victorian Volunteer Artillery, which expanded to 11 batteries of 611 men. They were trained by staff officers and NCOs of the royal artillery and were noted for their proficiency in the field. In 1870 a permanent artillery battery was formed and defences were erected at Williamstown, Queenscliff and Portsea.

In the period leading up to 1870 many small cavalry units were raised in different districts throughout the colony. They were brought together as the Prince of Wales Victorian Volunteer Light Horse in 1863, and in 1870 the unit was outfitted in a dashing Prussian Blue Hussar uniform complete with silver lace and black fur busby. Their moment of glory was when they acted as a guard of honor to Prince George (later King George V) in 1881. In 1885 the unit was incorporated into the Victorian Mounted Rifles.

THE VICTORIAN MOUNTED RIFLES

The Victorian Mounted Rifles were the crack unit of their day. It was an entirely volunteer corps first raised on 2 December 1885 by Colonel Tom

Price. Only those who were proficient with both rifle and horse were accepted to appear on the regiment's rolls. By 1885 the regiment had a strength of almost a thousand men divided into nine depots (or company headquarters) throughout Victoria.

The Victorian government supplied to the troopers the state of the art .45 calibre Martini-Henry Rifle, a fifty round bandolier, uniform, accoutrements and horse gear, although the recruit had to supply his own horse and saddle.

The troops had a modern khaki tunic with subtle crimson facings, corded riding breeches and brown pull on leggings. Most importantly the Victorian Mounted Rifles were the first Australian unit to be issued with the distinctive slouch hat, which has become a symbol of the Australian armed forces ever since.

In 1891 the regiment was divided into two battalions with one at HQ, Ballarat, and the other in Melbourne. Volunteers from all companies fought in the Boer War and Lieutenant Leslie Cecil Maygar was the first Victorian to receive the Victoria Cross.

Maygar had tried to volunteer with the first detachments to leave for the new war but was refused due to ill health. He was finally accepted for the 5th Detachment and was promoted to Lieutenant in the 5th Detachment Victorian Mounted rifles. He soon proved to be terrifically brave when under fire from the crack marksmanship of the Boers. The *London Gazette* reported how Maygar earned the Victoria Cross:

> On 23 November 1901 at Geelhoutboom, Natal Maygar galloped out and ordered men of a detached post, which was being outflanked, to retire. The horse of one of the men was shot under him when the enemy were within 200 yards and he dismounted and lifted the man on to his own horse which bolted into boggy ground, making them both dismount. As the horse could not carry two, Maygar again put the man on its back and told him to gallop for cover at once, while he himself went on foot. All this took place under very heavy fire.

Lord Kitchener himself pinned the VC to Maygar's breast.

After Federation the Victorian Mounted Rifles became the 8th and 11th Light Horse Regiments.

Maygar went on to see distinguished service with the Light Horse and was one of the last men to be evacuated from Gallipoli, as Colonel of the 8th Light Horse. He was mortally wounded at the Battle of Beersheba on 31st October 1917.

TASMANIAN VOLUNTEER RIFLE REGIMENT

Unlike the colonies to the north, Tasmania had very few volunteer troops when the British pulled out in 1870. In 1877 the Tasmanian Volunteer Rifle Regiment was formed. It consisted of two companies in Hobart and two in Launceston. It was armed and equipped as British regiments at the time with an impressive white laced red coat, black spiked pith helmet and black trousers with a red seam. When parliament passed the Defence Act of 1886 the regiment become a partially funded militia. By 1899 the Tasmanian infantry were wearing a modern khaki uniform with red collar, shoulder straps, and cuffs. Black gaiters and a slouch hat turned up on the right completed the outfit. As a result, the formations were well equipped to send volunteers to the Boer War. The first contingent of 80 men raised from the Rifle Regiment left for the war 16 days after the commencement of hostilities in October 1899. In all 36 officers and 821 men volunteered for the Boer War. The second contingent was drawn from militia forces and volunteers and upon arrival were given the impressive title of the Tasmanian Imperial Bushmen. This elite formation of mounted infantry was renowned for their proficiency with horse and rifle.

Two members, Private John Hutton Bisdee and Lieutenant Guy George Egerton Wylly, won the Victoria Cross. Wylly was leading a small scouting party on 1 September 1900 made up of eight men, including Bisdee. They were ambushed by a large group of Boers. Wylly was wounded almost immediately but gave his horse to another trooper before holding off the Boers as the rest of his men retreated. Bisdee saved another wounded man by putting him on his horse and, despite a hail of Boer bullets, managed to mount up behind him and escape.

THE QUEENSLAND MOUNTED INFANTRY

Among the colonies Queensland, separated from New South Wales in 1859, seemed the least keen to set up defence militias. Although there were numerous attempts to raise large bodies of foot, cavalry and artillery, it was only in 1884 when the Defence Force Act was passed by Queensland's parliament that the locals begin to take defence seriously. This Act made all suitably aged men liable for military service and divided the colony into three districts. With the added stimulus of monetary support men flocked to the colours, with troops being raised throughout Queensland. Soon the companies were organised into regimental strength, and designated the Queensland Mounted Infantry, with a common uniform and training.

Like the Victorian Mounted Rifles, the uniforms of the regiments were suited for Australian conditions. The slouch hat was fitted with an emu feather or a cock's plume. Khaki uniforms with scarlet facings and an ultra-modern Martini-Henry breach loading rifle were issued. Each trooper had a 50 round bandolier.

In 1900 the regiments were reorganised into three battalions. Although slow to commit to their own defence, Queenslanders flocked to the Boer War. Almost 3,000 men and 3,200 horses rode against the guerrillas.

In 1903 with the reorganisation of the army, the three mounted battalions became the 13th, 14th, and 15th Australian Light Horse Regiments with many of the men providing sterling service in the Great War.

THE FIRST FORMED UNIT SENT OVERSEAS: THE SUDAN

In response to a British government request, NSW offered to send a self-contained contingent to the Sudan to help avenge the fall of Khartoum and the death of General Gordon, which had occurred on 26 January 1885.

On 3 March 1885, 750 volunteers from various militia units marched through the streets of Sydney. They were seen off by a rapturous crowd of 200,000 and embarked from Circular Quay. The contingent consisted of one artillery battery equipped with five 16 pounder guns; a battalion of infantry with 500 effectives; a military band and an ambulance corps (76 of the infantry were drawn from the 1st Regiment of Infantry, otherwise known as the Sydney Battalion). The men were splendidly outfitted with scarlet tunics, dark blue pants with a red stripe down the side and white tropical helmets. This was named the New South Wales

Sudan Contingent and was the first fighting force raised in Australia to fight overseas.

Upon arrival they were attached to the British Guards and issued with khaki drill. The Australians soon established a reputation for toughness and were able to cope with harsh conditions well. However, they did not see much action and the main enemies they had to face were heat, dust, thirst and the stench from the bodies of dead Arabs. Six men died during the expedition, all from illness or disease, while three men suffered wounds in battle. 50 infantrymen did volunteer for service with the nascent Camel Corps and saw more fighting.

The contingent returned in June 1886 to a rapturous welcome. They brought home with them a donkey. The unit's mascot saw out its days eating grass at Duntroon sheep station which later, of course, became the nation's officer training school.

NEW SOUTH WALES: THE DUKE OF EDINBURGH'S HIGHLAND VOLUNTEER RIFLE CORPS

There is no doubt that the most inappropriate clothing for a volunteer corps in NSW would be a red coat, a heavy woollen kilt, tartan leggings, a great six-tasselled sporran and a wire hat covered in feathers. That was the kit that was issued to the Duke of Edinburgh's Highland Volunteer Rifle Corps in 1870. The visit by His Royal Highness Prince Alfred Duke of Edinburgh in 1868 set off such a stir that the New South Wales government set up a Highland Regiment in his honour. As the first English royal to visit the colony it was thought appropriate to honour his tour with a dedicated unit. Two companies were raised and, basing their uniform on the tartans and colours of the famous 42nd Highland Regiment of Foot (The Black Watch), the unit caused quite a stir in Sydney society. To the shrill keening of the bagpipes, the Corps would thrill audiences with their proficient drill and martial air. Sham battles were held with other regiments on the open fields that were still to be found at Kensington, and they were able to crank out a decent volley on their Hay pattern muzzle loading percussion rifle.

A rare photo of Colonial troops in the Sudan in the 1880s.

Many Australians based overseas joined the British troops in their war against the Boers.

Members of the 8th Australian Light Horse Regiment moving out of a ravine close to the beach not long after landing at Anzac in May 1915. Photo by James Pinkerton Campbell.

Only 20 of Germany's A7V tanks were built and saw limited action on the Western Front in 1918. Only one survives, 'Mephisto' - captured by Australian diggers and now on display in Queensland.

Australians of the Imperial Camel Corps on the sandhills, lined up on their camels. An original Paget Plate negative by James Francis (Frank) Hurley.

A fatigue party from the Australian 7th Brigade pass the former German bunker known as 'Gibraltar' at the western end of Pozières, 28 August 1916, during the Battle of the Somme.

An emotional farewell as Australian soldiers depart for the war, 1940.

Private Ryner of Manly and Private Cullen of Summer Hill, members of the 9th Australian Division manning a Vickers Gun position overlooking German positions at Tel-el-Elsa, Egypt, July 1942.

On arrival at Crete in May, 1941, Australian troops make their way across the fields from the harbour which was subjected to heavy dive-bombing attacks.

A German photograph taken at 'Retimo' (Rethymon) airfield of British and Australian troops captured on the island of Crete, June 1941.

Triumphant Australian troops enter Beirut, Lebanon, and are mobbed by the locals, 8 July 1941.

Members of the WAAF parade through Spring Street, Melbourne, in 1941. The Women's Auxiliary Australian Air Force was formed in March 1941 and was both the first and largest of the Australian Women's services during the war, with more than 27,000 members.

Kalang aerodrome, Singapore, a few minutes after Japanese bombs hit, 3 February, 1942.

A famous image from documentarian Damien Parer's Oscar-winning film 'Kokoda Front Line' showing an Australian soldier helping his injured mate to cross a river during the New Guinea campaign, 1942.

Australian soldiers open fire on Japanese troops fleeing from their pillbox position nearby, during the Pacific campaign. The Diggers did not always receive armoured support.

With Victory in the Pacific in August 1945, Australian troops finally came home to a hero's welcome.

Despite the glamour of the unit it was disbanded in 1878. Perhaps that bizarre Highland kit was just too much for the Sydney heat.

THE NEW SOUTH WALES LANCERS

Not many pubs can say they have contributed to military history. The exception to the rule would be the Oxford Hotel, Sydney where in 1884 a meeting was held where the participants decided to raise a crack unit of light horse. By the next year a troop of 45 riders had been assembled with the title the Sydney Light Horse. The men were well-to-do volunteers who provided their own mounts, saddles and uniforms, although the horse furniture was supplied by the mounted police. Other troops were formed and the amalgamated units were termed the First New South Wales Regiment of Cavalry.

After experience in the Sudan where the 5th Royal Irish Lancers had put on such a show it was decided to rearm the mounted riflemen as lancers. In 1891 the regiment was given a splendid uniform of salmon khaki with scarlet lapels and trim. In imitation of the Victorian mounted units they adopted the slouch hat turned up on the left with black cockerel feathers in the scarlet puggaree.

Showmanship was never far from the New South Wales Lancers. They were well known for their mounted band, where all of the musicians rode splendid white chargers. Thirty-three officers and men attended Queen Victoria's Diamond Jubilee celebration in London during 1897. Their fine colonial bearing and horsemanship caused a stir among the appreciative crowd.

The Lancers were also known for their professionalism. A cadre of instruction was set up in 1888 to ensure that all members were drilled to the highest professional standards. This professionalism bore fruit when a training squadron was dispatched to England in 1899 to bone up on the latest tactical innovations. On the way home, the Boer War broke out and the squadron disembarked at Cape Town to become the first Australian volunteers to fight in that bloody and vicious conflict. Over the next few years, many other members volunteered and many died to Boer bullets.

After Federation the regiment was renamed the 1st Australian Light Horse. In 1912 they were redesignated the 7th Australian Light Horse Lancers.

THE SLOUCH HAT

Whether fighting in the Egyptian desert or the wilds of Vietnam, the Australian digger is immediately recognisable by his iconic slouch hat.

The first Australian slouch hat was issued to the Victorian Mounted Rifles in 1885. The distinctive high crowned khaki hat with a broad brim initially had the brim turned up on the right to facilitate firing the unit's Martini-Henry rifles. The Rifles' slouch hat had a distinctive pleated puggaree (hat band).

Colonel Tom Price of the Mounted Rifles first saw the slouch hat in Burma, where the native constabulary used a similar head dress when on duty.

The brim was held up on the right by a cord which was attached to a gilt lion's head boss fastened to the left side of the crown. The hat also had a two pieced buckled chin strap. This slouch hat saw service in the Boer War when many troopers of the Victorian Mounted Rifles volunteered for service.

The slouch hat soon spread into the other colonies when in 1890 local military commanders all agreed that their armed forces should adopt the distinctive headgear. The New South Wales Mounted Infantry wore the hat but, in an early sign of Melbourne-Sydney rivalry, decided to turn up the left side of the brim. Tasmania followed the Victorian lead while the other Australian colonies all followed the NSW fashion. Different units used different badges and puggarees.

The Defence Act of 1903, which united all Australian units under a central command, standardised the slouch hat, giving it a lower crown and a left side turn up. Units still used different insignia and the Queensland Mounted Infantry was the first unit to place emu feathers in the crown of their hat. This was then adopted by the Light Horse in the Gallipoli and desert campaigns of World War I.

It was in the Great War that the slouch hat reached its definitive form. The varied puggarees were replaced with a plain khaki hat band and the 'Rising Sun' badge was displayed on the left turned up brim.

BOER WAR – THE FIRST GUERRILLA CAMPAIGN

The Boer War could possibly be termed the first modern war. Parade ground formations gave way to skirmish warfare where small, well armed groups of guerrillas fought the increasingly mobile columns of the enemy. Railways, blockhouses and vast wire obstacles became for the first time the sinews of war, while whole populations of women and children were locked up in the first concentration camps to break the economic back of the Boers' resistance. On this vast theatre of war Australians proved themselves to be a match for even the most skilled Boer opponents.

But when the first contingents marched through Sydney to the cheering of 200,000 well-wishers, little did the enthusiastic soldiers know that for the next three years they would be thrown into a hornet's nest. Tens of thousands of well armed Boers, convinced that they had God on their side, would fight to the end in an effort to defend their homelands from the English aggressors.

The Boers (farmers) were a mix of Dutch, German and French settlers who had migrated to the southern tip of Africa since the 17th Century. Many had fled religious persecution and they were determined to avoid rigid governmental control. By 1899 many Boers had migrated north from Cape Colony to the Transvaal and the Orange Free State to escape British controls. Several minor wars were fought and the British came off second best. The two new Boer states strengthened links with the German Empire and, when gold was discovered in the Transvaal, Britain decided to act and sought to annexe the two territories.

War was declared on 11 October 1899.

The Boers were well prepared. Each man between sixteen and sixty was expected to fight the Imperial forces. Most were equipped with a modern Mauser, with which they were proficient marksmen, and all were mounted on horses. While they did not have uniforms the Boer civilian clothing was perfectly suited for blending into the environment. Swarms of irregular mounted rifles were supported by state-of-the-art breech loading horse artillery purchased from the German war machine.

The British thought the war would be a walk in the park. They were disabused of this notion during Black Week (10-17 December 1899). Three battles were lost with almost 3,000 British casualties. Using tactics better suited to the Napoleonic battlefield, columns of British infantry were cut down by sharp shooting Boers.

At least the British were able to learn from their mistakes. The Australian colonial troops who arrived in the theatre of war had originally been, due to a British request, foot soldiers, but they were soon reunited with their mounts to become mounted infantry, a role at which they excelled.

The Boers were a worthy foe. Troops could be moving through kopjes (broken terrain covered hills) or the veldt (grassy plains) with no idea that there was an ambush waiting. Hidden behind insignificant rocks or plants the Boer would wait until the last minute before opening up in a deadly fusillade. They had an intimate understanding of their land and always kept escape routes clear once many casualties had been inflicted on their enemies. The most common weapons were Martini-Henry rifles or Mausers. Both were effective to 2,000 metres in the hands of an experienced marksman. Australians learnt to recognise the type of weapon being used against them. The Martini-Henry fired dum-dums which made a sound like a blowfly rushing by their ears, while the Mauser bullets hissed as they passed. Each Boer was an experienced horseman and equipped themselves with cartridges and supplies of biltong enough to last eight days. Boer biscuits, consisting of hard baked biscuit filled with dried fruit such as raisins, could last for months along with the biltong. Aiding the 'commando' were horse artillery batteries of modern German breech loaders, whose crews had been trained by German officers.

Despite all this, the Australians soon developed a reputation for efficiency on the battlefield rivalled only by the Boer himself. Expert with horse and rifle, they were able to track their elusive enemy. When engaged in a fire fight the Australians would coolly fix the enemy to their front while working around the flanks. Once an enfilade was set up the Australians would get stuck in with cold steel – most Boers would surrender before this.

One of the Australians' first major successes came on New Year's Day 1900. The Queensland Mounted Infantry stalked a Boer position at Sunnyside and ended up capturing the entire commando of 40 men. The town of Kimberley was captured on 13 February 1900 and a squadron of New South Wales Lancers were among the leading parties into the town after encountering stiff resistance.

The colonial bushcraft proved to be most useful. Australian troops could navigate at night as easily as if it were day, while the English would often get hopelessly lost in a similar predicament. One Boer historian lamented that there was no way to defend against the Australians. In the dead of night, they would scout the Boer positions, kill the sentries, release the horses and generally terrorise the veteran fighters. He thought them very formidable and commented that they were far more dangerous than any British troops that were opposed to the Boer.

The pitiless environment was the other major danger faced by the Australians. Men and horses alike suffered from the terrible conditions. Columns could be traced by the rows of dead horses they left behind. As the British columns penetrated deep into the Transvaal and the Orange Free State, short rations led to sickness. The daily ration of four biscuits (hard tack), a tin of bully beef and a small quantity of tea or coffee was never enough. The need to drink from contaminated water sources led to dysentery. A lack of clean clothes and poor sanitation also saw the rise of typhus. Letters home complained of lack of latrines, having to wear the same clothes month after month and no soap for weeks on end. Men were not issued with tents. Two blankets were not enough to keep out the freezing cold of nights on the veldt.

Perhaps the worst aspect of the war was its increasing violence against men, women and children.

The Transvaal capital of Pretoria fell on 31 May 1900. This ushered in a new period of ruthless guerrilla war. Determined to track down the last of the Boer fighters, the British and colonial fighters resorted to economic warfare. Isolated homesteads were burnt on the slightest suspicion that fighters were taking refuge in them. Although no menfolk were to be found the houses would be turned over. Almost invariably Mauser ammunition or other weapons would be found. Families were herded into a new institution: concentration camps. All crops, livestock and farms were indiscriminately burnt and block houses with wire barriers were built to criss-cross the countryside and prevent movement of the Boer commandoes. At least 26,000 died in the camps while the war degenerated into a merciless exchange of tit for tat killings. Prisoners on both sides could expect little mercy from their captors. The Boers concentrated on hit and run raids. As the Boers targeted rail networks, to protect the precious locomotives from demolition, Boer prisoners were strapped to flatbed rail trucks by their captors and pushed in front of the trains.

It was during this time in August and September that Harry 'Breaker' Morant's unit executed some Boer prisoners. There was an order from the British high command that declared any Boer found in a British uniform was to be shot. It seems that Morant followed accepted veldt practice but made one crucial mistake – he was implicated in the shooting of a German missionary. In order to avoid an international diplomatic incident, the British high command made an example of the bushman and put him in front of a firing squad. After this incident the new Commonwealth Parliament passed an act that only Australian military courts could pass judgement on matters of military discipline.

By this time the Boers, the British and the Australians were all heartily sick of the war. The African territories were ruined and 35,000 Boers had died, the majority of them being children. There were 1,400 Australian casualties, with at least 578 dead from Boer bullets or disease. The war ended as a British victory but it was by no means seen as a glorious triumph.

AUSTRALIA'S FIRST NAVAL DEPLOYMENT: CHINESE BOXER REBELLION

The Righteous Harmonious Fists (the Boxers) wanted all foreigners out of China.

In 1900 the British government sent an urgent request for naval assistance to fight the Chinese Boxer Rebellion. New South Wales immediately agreed and three British warships in the state's service were released to sail to Hong Kong on July 1900. The South Australian government did not want to be left out of the action and offered to send the Heavy Cruiser *Protector*.

The *Protector* was a state-of-the-art piece of kit built in Newcastle upon Tyne in response to the Russian Gunboat scare of 1882. It was classified as a Light Cruiser, with a displacement of 920 tons, and could travel at an impressive 14 knots. She had a massive 8 inch (203mm)

Armstrong rifled breech loading cannon mounted on the bow that could hurl a 180 pound shell (82 kg) almost 7 kilometres. The *Protector* had five more 152mm guns, four quick firing 3 pdrs and five 10 barrel Gatling guns. What's more she was equipped with 200 Martini-Henry rifles, 100 revolvers and 30 boarding pikes. The *Protector*'s crew was only 95 men!

The Admiralty accepted the offer and HMCS *Protector* set off for Hong Kong on 6 August. On 23 September the cruiser arrived at the mouth of the Yangtze river. After serving as a bit of a workhorse and not getting into too much of the action, the *Protector* retuned to Australia just in time for the Federation celebrations. In this time the *Protector* had travelled 16,000 nautical miles, but it's only fight was with an out-of-control junk which rammed the starboard hull by accident.

FEDERATION

1 January 1901 saw the death knell of the colourful militias and volunteer forces that existed through the colonies. On this date defence became a Commonwealth matter. The Staff, Militia and Volunteer's forces, numbering 29,000, were to be joined together into one force under the stewardship of Major General Sir Edward Hutton. After much staff work, on 1 July 1903 General Order No.169 and the Defence Act of 1903-04 gave the Governor-General powers to appoint officers and re-arrange military districts. Many regiments were given new Commonwealth titles. They were the fortunate ones as many others were disbanded or amalgamated.

The 1903 dress regulations introduced the new standardised khaki and officially recognised the slouch hat as the standard head gear of the new nation's army. A system of badges and insignia were introduced so that all regiments, corps and arms of service were instantly recognisable to all other members of the armed services.

CHAPTER 6

WORLD WAR I
– FIGHTING THE TURK

'When the Empire is at war, so is Australia at war.' So said Prime Minister Joseph Cook in response to Britain declaring war on Germany in August 1914.

Cook was of course pledging allegiance to the British Empire, which had entered an alliance with France and Russia with the aim of preserving their colonial possessions against the threat of German expansionism.

Australian recruiting centres were swamped with eager recruits determined to join up and fight the Hun. But it was the nature of global politics that saw these first enthusiastic Australians and their comrades from New Zealand (the ANZACs) steaming towards the Middle East rather than to the Western Front. Instead of fighting the Kaiser they found themselves in Egypt ready to fight the 'sick man of Europe' – the Ottoman Turks.

The Ottoman empire had been shrinking for at least 100 years. However, their military was reinvigorated by German tactical advice and training. As a result, expectations that the Turks would rapidly crumble were dashed and Australian forces received a bloody nose while perched on the steep slopes of the Gallipoli peninsula.

In the months that followed, most of the Anzacs refitted and were shipped to the Western Front, where they finally had a chance of getting to grips with the Hun. Mounted units, including the Light Horse, stayed behind; first as defenders of the Suez Canal and then to carry Australian horsemanship deep into the heart of Turkish Palestine. Their free riding daredevil attitudes led to significant Allied victories at Beersheba and then Damascus.

GALLIPOLI

On 1 November 1914 the first Australian troops sailed to war. In 36 transports out from Albany, Western Australia, 20,000 soldiers of the 1st Division and the 1st Light Horse Brigade thought they were heading for Europe. These troops were to combine with New Zealand Brigades and be known forever after as ANZAC: Australian and New Zealand Army Corps. They would be commanded by General Birdwood.

The troops found themselves camped in the shadows of the Pyramids of Giza just out of Cairo. Here they stayed for 14 weeks, training, drinking, playing football or cricket, and whoring. It was during this time that the Anzacs first got something of a reputation for disobeying orders and larrikinism, especially if they came across the class-based English Officer Corps.

The Australians were initially posted to Egypt to act as a bulwark defending the Suez Canal from the Turks. Lord Churchill of the British Admiralty came up with a more aggressive plan. He organised an expedition to outflank the Germans by going through the 'soft underbelly' of Europe.

By 1915 the British Army was bogged down in a belt of trenches that ran from Switzerland to the Channel. Advances in machine guns and artillery had made any attacks over open ground akin to suicide. With no end to the stalemate in sight the Allies sought to outflank the central powers by knocking Turkey out of the war, allowing direct access to the Russians through the

Black Sea. The plan was to go through the Dardanelles straight into the sea of Marmara. The English Navy was intended to front up to Constantinople and shell the Turks into submission.

There was one problem. The Dardanelles was a narrow strait between north western Anatolia and the Gallipoli peninsula. Modern artillery batteries and extensive minefields made it absolutely impenetrable to Allied surface shipping.

On 18 March the Royal Navy with French allies had sent a huge fleet consisting of 18 battleships and numerous cruisers in an attempt to break through the defences. Minefields and accurate fire from the shore batteries reduced the attack to a blazing fiasco. Many ships were severely damaged and the French battleship *Bouvet* capsized with most of the crew of 600 still on board.

The only way the Allies were going to achieve their plan of steaming to Constantinople was to seize the high ground of the Gallipoli peninsula so that accurate fire from Allied battleships could be directed onto the Turkish defences in the Dardanelles.

As a part of this plan it was decided that a submarine would steam through the narrows and enter the Dardanelles. It was hoped that this would prevent reinforcements being sent to oppose the landings.

Australia had two submarines at the start of the war, HMAS *AE1* and *AE2*. *AE1* had been lost in mysterious circumstances to the north of German Papua. Only *AE2* remained and, after a perilous trip from Australia to the Mediterranean, it was chosen to conduct the daring mission.

HMAS AE2 – THE ONLY SHIP TO PASS THE DARDENELLES

French and British surface ships could not pass the 50 kilometre long narrows at the Dardanelles. Several submarines that made the attempt foundered. It was imperative that a submarine get into the Sea of Marmara, to interdict reinforcements being shipped to the Gallipoli peninsula to help repel the coming landings.

One Allied craft did manage: HMAS *AE2*, an E-class submarine purchased by the RAN from the British Navy, managed to penetrate the deadly Turkish defences.

The skipper of *AE2* Lieutenant Commander Stoker knew that his trusty sub could travel submerged for 80 kilometres on battery power. The strong currents into the Mediterranean from the Sea of Marmara meant that it was the equivalent of 100 kilometres to pass through the Dardanelles. Stoker realised that he would have to edge his ship past some of the fortifications on the surface to preserve his batteries.

At 2.30a.m. on 25 April 1915, the moon set over the entrance to the deadly waters. Stoker gave the order to travel at a steady 8 knots on the surface. Searchlights constantly swept the water and patrol boats could be heard chugging in the distance. In the calm clear night, it was remarkable that *AE2* was able to travel unmolested for almost two hours.

Suddenly, at 4.30a.m., cannon belched flame from the northern shores and shells whistled above the small submarine. The order to dive was given and *AE2* began its passage through the deadly minefields. The mines were tethered to the sea bed with chains and for the next half hour the crew heard these mooring wires scraping along the sides of the submarine. Iron nerves were required – if a chain caught on any part of the hull a mine would be dragged down to detonate against the submarine, sending all of its crew to a watery grave.

On occasion the boat rose to periscope depth to get its bearings, and at 6.00a.m. the end of the straits was in sight. Alert Turkish gunners sent shells at the sub and several warships steamed in her direction. Several torpedoes were fired at the Turks before Stoker gave the order to dive.

The boat made its way into the Marmara straights and for the next four days played havoc in the Turkish shipping lanes. While no ships were sunk by the Australians the threat that the submarine posed meant no capital ships could remain in the area. Nevertheless, the Turks maintained active patrols and on one occasion the submarine was grounded on a shoal. Only by pure luck did the boat manage to dislodge itself and return to the depths, all the while under Turkish shellfire.

On 30 April *AE2*'s luck ran out. Some lucky shots from a patrol boat punctured the hull in three places. Stoker scuttled the sub but not before all hands had abandoned ship.

This was the only known RAN vessel lost to enemy action during the war. All of the crew except for four who died in captivity were repatriated at war's end.

THE LANDINGS

Several years ago a sad discovery was made in the hills above Anzac Cove. In the approaches to the peaks of Chunuk Bair – one of the high points of the Gallipoli peninsula – a group of skeletons was discovered. The bleached bones had endured almost a hundred years of freezing winters and broiling summers. Hidden in the underbrush for years the skeletons still bore remnants of clothing and equipment which identified them as Australians, part of the AIF. The skeletons were still strung out in a skirmish line and lay where they had been killed on the early morning of 25 April 1915.

These unknown Australians reached the objective of the entire Gallipoli landing but did not take the objective. If sufficient forces had attained the objective on the confused morning of the landings, the Allies would have been able to dominate the entire peninsula. They would have been able to direct the massive naval assets lying offshore onto Turkish defensive positions in the straits and on shore, rendering any defence untenable. Churchill's strategy would most likely have been a stunning success.

If these heights were not seized the Turkish defenders would be able to bring up reserves and use the heights to dominate the attacking Allies. Trenches would be dug, machine gun pits created, bunkers dug into the friable soil and artillery positions built. The exact same circumstances of deadlocked trench warfare would prevail on this far flung outpost as existed in Europe. The stalemate would continue.

This is of course exactly what happened. The initial landing fell short of their objectives and for the next nine months the Australians desperately fought to break thought the Turkish stranglehold. They did not succeed and the Battle of Gallipoli became a heroic failure. The 'soft underbelly' of Europe turned out to be an armoured carapace.

Why did the attack fail?

After stewing in Egypt for many months, the Anzacs were keen to get stuck in. As in many battles, a seemingly insignificant point on a map was to assume significance beyond all measure. The Gallipoli peninsula on which the allied landing was to take place was a rugged and inhospitable piece of land with steep slopes cut by innumerable gullies.

Tipped off by the March naval attacks, the Ottomans had four weeks to dig trenches, lay barbed wire entanglements filled with mines and place machine guns with clear fields of fire. Roadways across the peninsula were built to allow rapid deployment of reserves, and reserves were concentrated where they could easily move against any potential landing point. Ready to fight, 84,000 well trained Ottoman soldiers of the 5th Army awaited the Allied onslaught.

What's more, the Allied landings were faced with two brilliant commanders. When the Ottoman and the German Empires formed an alliance in the middle of 1914, large amounts of modern equipment, including several cruisers, were sent by Germany to her new ally. Included in the aid were up to 70 advisors from the German Heer (army) who were to train the Turks in modern offensive and defensive tactics. General Otto von Liman (b. 1885 d. 1929) served in staff and divisional commands before becoming head of the German military mission to the Ottomans in 1913. Before war broke out the Turkish Army was reorganised into strong divisions and officer training was based on merit.

Liman made one other key contribution – he appointed the dynamic commander Mustafa Kemal to the command of the 19th Division. This aggressive commander proved the difference on the morning that the Anzacs landed.

General Sir Ian Hamilton was appointed to command the landings. His force was composed of 78,000 men and included the Anzac corps under Lieutenant General Sir William Birdwood. Two divisions were under his command: the 1st Australian Division and the New Zealand and Australian Division.

The British plan called for the major effort to be made on the southern tip of the Gallipoli peninsula around Cape Helles. At the same time the

Anzacs were ordered to land 20 kilometres to the north at a promontory named Gaba Tepe. They were tasked with driving inland to interfere with any reinforcements heading towards the British at Cape Helles. Little did the Australians know it at the time but the beaches around Gaba Tepe were held by well entrenched Turkish forces. Artillery and machine guns on the promontory would have enfiladed the landing sites, turning the whole affair into a massacre. Barbed wire entanglements were actually below the waterline and the flat beaches would have turned the entire area into a killing zone. Von Sanders had predicted that the area around Gaba Tepe and the beaches near Cape Helles were the most likely sites for the expected landings and had taken extensive counter measures.

Perhaps fortunately for the leading Australians of the 3rd Brigade, an unexpected current forced their landing boats northwards into a small sheltered bay that became known as Anzac Cove.

As the first wave of 1,500 men rowed ashore at dawn on 25 April they saw above them towering hills and steep cliffs. They had expected to find open beaches but the broken terrain ahead posed a real challenge even for the athletic Australians. Nevertheless, they began an unopposed advance until a yellow flare was fired from the heights above. Two companies of Turkish infantry were lying in wait and soon accurate rifle fire began to tumble the arriving Australians out of their boats. Turkish shells began to arc over the 100 metre heights onto the crowded beaches, causing more casualties. The Australians had no choice – they had to advance. Shrugging off their packs, a wave of Australians swept up the steep slopes, bayoneting Turks and clearing the beachhead. By 5.30 the 3rd Brigade had cleared the beach and at 7.30 the other two brigades (1st and 2nd) of 1st Division began to land. All the while the Australians pushed into up the hills towards the two points dominating the landscape, the 260 metre high Chunuk Bair and Sari Bair.

In one of the maddest orders given in the entire war, the Australians had been forbidden to have any bullets 'up the spout' and were ordered to fight with the bayonet until dawn. As they pursued the fleeing Turks they could at least began shooting them once the sun came up. Their orders were to keep going at all costs and soon intrepid Anzacs were rewarded with a clear view of the Dardanelles. These scattered groups, still encountering stubborn pockets of Turkish resistance, had actually attained their objective.

It was at this crucial moment that von Sander's decision to place Lieutenant Colonel Mustafa Kemal in charge of his reserves bore fruit and changed the course of the battle. The Australians were in disarray. They did not have maps of the area in which they had landed, and command and communications were snarled on the crowded beach at Anzac Cove as thousands of men came ashore. What's more, efficiently handled artillery from the Turkish positions inland and from Gaba Tepe were smashing into the landing fleet. Without spotters ashore the Allies could not call in effective supporting fire from the massed cruisers and battleships lying offshore.

If the Australians had been given a breathing space their troops would have been able to dig in and, by using Chunuk Bair as an observation point, they could have dominated the battlefield.

Kemal grasped the threat immediately and a battalion was dispatched to counterattack the Australians. He soon realised this was not enough and went to find out for himself exactly what was happening. Kemal's autobiography gives a vivid account of his actions that morning. A landing at Anzac Cove had not been expected, so there was no road or even track to the battlefield. Setting off cross country through scrubby vegetation and cleft hills the Colonel, at the head of several regiments and an artillery battery, walked up the slope of Chunuk Bair. He describes how he and his aide intercepted a platoon of fleeing Turkish riflemen and asked why they were running. They pointed towards the beaches and Kemal saw the first Australians approaching his position. He ordered the platoon to turn about and face the Australians. When his soldiers protested that they had no bullets the Colonel ordered them to fix bayonets and face the enemy. They did so and the Australians went to ground. Soon after, the first elements of the Turkish 57th Regiment arrived and under the direct commands of their division commander began to build a defensive line. Soon the 28th came up on the Turkish left and Kemal ordered his artillery battery to unlimber and start firing at the approaching Australians.

The Turks launched counterattacks against the scattered Australian advance and by 11.30a.m. the Australians were in retreat. This was repeated all around the perimeter, and positions which the Australians had seized, including the Nek and Baby 700, were soon back in Ottoman hands. Much blood would be spilt in the following months as the Anzacs sought to reclaim these vital terrain pieces.

By the end of the day the Anzacs had 18,000 men compressed into a battlefield about 3 kilometres wide and slightly more than 1 kilometre deep. Turkish fire from all sides smashed into their positions. Evacuation was considered but several factors, including the news that *AE2* had penetrated the Dardanelles, gave the commanders hope, and Hamilton gave the order for the Australians to dig in. The last of Kemal's counterattacks was held and the Australians were to spend the next nine months perched on the steep slopes of Anzac Cove.

It was during this phase that the Australians earned the name 'digger'. The only safe place was below ground, and the diggers took to the task of entrenching with a will.

The landings at Cape Helles were bloody affairs. The well prepared Turks held the Allies back from taking most of their objectives. Once the British had been stopped, von Sanders decided to wipe out the Anzacs' precarious beachhead.

On 19 May, 42,000 Turkish infantry stormed the frail beachhead with orders to sweep the invaders back into the sea. Fortunately for the outnumbered Australian diggers, they received the 1st Light Horse Brigade as reinforcements which brought their strength up to 17,000 men. In addition, the Australians were tipped off by air recon which noted large troop movements to their front.

The Anzacs were on full alert. At 3a.m. on 19 May massed waves of almost suicidal Turks charged at the well entrenched troops. For hour after hour the Turks attacked. Even with the light of dawn Turkish officers ordered their men to hurl themselves against the Australian machine guns and Lee Enfield rifles. By the time von Sanders halted the attack, 10,000 of his men had fallen. There were 160 Australians dead and 468 wounded.

The Turks had more than earned the Australians' respect. They too had shown that they could die bravely. This mutual regard was reinforced when a truce was arranged enabling the Turks to retrieve 3,000 dead lying in no-man's-land. Both sides helped clear the battlefield of the swollen and hideous corpses. The heat had swollen them up to twice their usual size and giant rats had to be shooed away from the fly blown remains. 'Johnny Turk' and the Anzacs cooperated and swapped tobacco and cigarettes. To remove the bodies, picks and entrenching tools had to be hooked around their belts to drag them into mass graves. The truce was honoured by both sides until:

'The bugle sounded and I had to run up a stiff hill and just before I jumped in (to a trench) I gave a wave back, and the Turks waved back too….A Few minutes after that, two red flares were fired…The war was on again.'

Recollections of James Donaldson, quoted in T Matthews,
Crosses: Australian Soldiers In The First War 1914-19

TRENCH LIFE

After the carnage of the first month the front settled down to a uniquely unpleasant form of trench warfare.

Since the Turks had managed to retain the high ground the Australians were forced to dig in to survive. Even rear areas, out of direct line of sight of Turkish observers, were subject to continued artillery harassing fire.

Fortunately, the ground around Anzac Cove was easy to dig. The earth consisted of small pebbles and shale, mixed in with a loose soil that was soft enough to dig away by hand. Despite the ease with which it could be dug it was curiously resilient to rain and wind, and even now many trench systems remain on the peninsula.

Major trench lines were knitted together over the next few weeks and dugouts appeared everywhere – on the cliffs facing the cove, in all rear areas and in the sides of trenches. Tarps and blankets were strung on rudimentary frames to give a modicum of shelter.

Such a concentration of men led to new hazards – flies feasted on sweaty bodies, piles of faeces and dead bodies strung out in no-man's-land. The act of eating was almost impossible. Troops would try and hide under greatcoats or pull their heads inside their shirts to try and stop flies descending on their biscuit and bully beef or jam. This rarely succeeded and flies would beat about in the digger's mouth while they tried to chew their tucker. Lice and fleas tortured all ranks. Any water had to be brought in by boat making basic hygiene almost impossible.

Toilets were open pits and flies would congregate in the filthy heated cess polls before spreading dysentery, diarrhoea and gastroenteritis. Men lost weight and at one stage at least 20% of the Anzacs were not considered fit for duty. Only the worst cases were evacuated to offshore hospital ships. Most suffered in silence and even kept their place in the line.

GALLIPOLI ANGEL OF DEATH – BILLY SING, SNIPER

Once battle lines were drawn into trench warfare a new type of fighter emerged – the sniper. Marksman had been used in previous wars but the new war needed a new type of killer. Snipers would sneak out into no-man's-land or take up a camouflaged position in the trenches and wait patiently until some luckless opponent exposed himself long enough to earn a bullet through the head.

William 'Billy' Edward Sing stood out as Australia's most successful sniper at Gallipoli. Considering that many of the Anzacs had been reared with a gun in their hand Sing's reputation is all the more remarkable.

Sing almost looked like a Turk himself. He was short and swarthy and sported a black moustache and goatee. As a young'un he was a member of the Queensland Proserpine Rifle Club. He joined the 5th Light Horse and with the rest of his regiment was shipped to Gallipoli without his mount. Here he teamed up with some spotters and took out hundreds of Turks.

There was no military designation of sniper in 1915; the team were titled as scouts. Between May and September Billy was credited with 150 Turkish dead. While Billy waited with loaded rifle his scout would use a powerful camouflaged field glass to look for targets. Once one was located Sing would carefully draw a bead and fire. The rules for claiming a kill were quite specific. Two men had to see the target go down and if there was any doubt a hit had been made it could not be claimed. It seems Sing erred on the side of caution and his tally may have been much more. His most successful day registered 9 kills.

There is no doubt Sing was ruthless – no matter how old or young the target, once they were within Sing's sites they were as good as dead.

He used a short magazine Lee Enfield which was the standard issue rifle for all Australian forces from 1907 until after the Korean War. At maximum range this rifle could take out an opponent at up to 3 kilometres but usual drills allowed for each man to get off 15 aimed rounds a minute. Marksmen using special 'Aperture' sights were trained to place five bullets within a two centimetre bullseye from 100 metres, perfect for the close confines of the Gallipoli trenches.

By the end of November 1915 Sing's score was well over 200. He became quite a famous character and there were newspaper reports detailing his success. A sniper works on stealth and this notoriety was counterproductive – two Turkish marksman were dispatched to the 5th Light Horse's front with one aim – get Sing.

They almost succeeded, wounding Sing and pulling him out of contention for a period of time – and making the ace sniper much more cautious.

He went on to continue his work on the Western Front and during his career earned both the Distinguished Conduct Medal and the Belgian Croix De Guerre. But like many of his comrades the decorated soldier took much more unwanted baggage home. Shrapnel wounds, damaged lungs and possibly shot nerves meant he could not make a go of civilian life and he died alone in a boarding house in 1943.

LONE PINE AND THE NEK

As the Allies and Turks poured reinforcements into the peninsula, desperate measures were taken to break the deadlock. Scattered outposts had turned into lengthy trench systems with a succession of trench lines, communications trenches and bunkers. The initial Allied deployment had swollen from five divisions to 16.

In August 1915 Hamilton determined to seize Chunuk Bair and turn the campaign from a stalemate into a victory. At the same time, new British formations were to land at Suvla Bay to the north of Anzac Cove in a desperate effort to outflank the Turkish lines.

The Australians were tasked with two major attacks: one at Lone Pine and the other at the Nek. While the Australian assault at Lone Pine was a costly success, the Battle of the Nek was a tragic failure.

The Lone Pine assault went in at 5.30p.m. on 6 August 1915. Standing on the Lone Pine Memorial today one is amazed at the small size of the battlefield. On either side of the – now well manicured – grass lay the opposing trench systems. It was the Australians' job to storm across no-man's-land and seize the Turkish trenches. Tunnels had been dug on the approaches to the enemy positions and, when the heavy preparatory barrage finished, the Australians leapt at the Turks from a mere 80 metres away. Upon reaching the enemy trenches the Australian troops were surprised to find that the Turks had roofed their trenches with solid pine logs. A confused hand-to-hand melee developed where desperate diggers would wrest off the logs while others tossed handmade grenades in to the Turks below, or leapt in to attack with the bayonet. Many Australians took the open communication trenches to the rear and then charged back into the front trenches to finish off the foe. Some Turks were seemingly stunned into inaction by the ferocious bombardment, but most fought bravely to the death.

By 6.00p.m. Lone Pine was in Australian hands. Divisional sized counterattacks were launched in the following days. Storming parties of Turks swept up to their lost positions, hurling a shower of bombs at the Australians. Many of these were picked up and hurled back by the diggers. Turkish reserves were sucked into the fray and only when their butcher's bill exceeded 7,000 casualties did the attacks cease. The Australians suffered too. From 6 to 10 August, when the fighting stopped, 80 officers and 2,197 men had fallen.

Lone Pine is recognised as one of the greatest examples of Australian military heroism. Seven Victoria crosses were earned on that tiny expanse of scrubby dirt.

Lone Pine succeeded thanks to well planned cooperation between artillery and infantry. The attack on the Nek failed because this was lacking. The 3rd

Light Horse Brigade was tasked with attacking from Russell's Top to the Turkish trenches on the Nek. A tiny section of land separated the lines, maybe as much as three or four tennis courts wide. But most of it was flat and the Turkish trenches were well supplied with Maxim heavy machine guns. The attack was planned to act as a decoy from other assaults, such as the New Zealand assault on that crucial high ground at Chunuk Bair and the British attack at Suvla Bay. Ironically both positions had been held for a small amount of time after the initial landings.

The troops of the 8th Victorian and the 10th West Australian Light Horse Regiments were to jump off at 4.30a.m. on 7 August. The attacks were to be made in four waves of 150 men. Preceding the attack was a ferocious bombardment where all available land guns as well as naval artillery were to soften up the Turkish trenches. For some reason most of the shells fell behind the Turkish positions and the barrage ceased seven minutes before the attack.

By this stage of the war a common tactic was to land a barrage on top of the enemy lines. It was then halted, luring the opposition out of their trenches to take up position in order to repel the assault. But then one more barrage would crash down, catching the defenders in the open. At first the Australians thought this was what was intended when the barrage ceased early.

It was not. It was a colossal stuff up. At 4.30a.m. whistles sounded and the first wave went over the top. The well prepared Turks mowed down many Australians before they were half way out of their trenches. Most of the Light Horse had fallen before crossing 12 metres of the 70 metre objective. The two waves of the 8th Regiment were mown down. The commander of the 10th, seeing that the attacks were futile, asked permission to stand down. His request was denied and the West Australians charged bravely into the maelstrom of death, resulting in 234 Australian deaths; 138 were wounded. Few Turkish casualties were inflicted and it is doubtful that any of the Light Horsemen reached their objective. If they did they were soon dispatched by bayonet or bullet by the Turkish defenders.

To add insult to injury, no reserves were drawn to this battle. The New Zealand assault went in at 11a.m. and was a costly failure. The assault on Suvla Bay met with little opposition, but thanks to incompetent British leadership the success was not exploited and the salient was soon sealed off with Turkish reserves.

Hamilton was not ready to give up and further assaults were launched. On 8 August the New Zealanders seized most of Chunuk Bair but a fanatical counterattack, once again led by Mustafa Kemal, hurled them off the dominating feature. The August offensive was a costly failure and Hamilton's command had lost 12,000 men. The Turks had won their finest victory of the war.

Soon after these offensives the exhausted 1st Australian Division was relieved by the newly arrived 2nd Division. The Australian New Zealand Division was relieved by the British 54th.

The end was in sight. The cost of maintaining such a large army across dangerous beachheads was proving too much. The Turks were close to their supply depots and continued to amass reserves of ammunition and men. The Australian press, led by Keith Murdoch, were drawing attention to the squalid living conditions suffered by the diggers as winter approached.

It was decided to withdraw from the peninsula.

Difficult as the decision was, the withdrawal went off without a hitch. In early December the first evacuations were made, continuing until by 19 December only 1,500 men were left holding the Anzac perimeter. They were all taken off by December 20th.

7,600 Australians were killed at Gallipoli and 19,000 were wounded.

This tragedy marked in a sense Australia's coming of age as a nation – the Aussie digger would become a recognisable figure of bravery and heroism throughout the world.

EGYPT AND PALESTINE – TRIUMPH OF THE LIGHT HORSE

After the successful evacuation at Gallipoli the Australian troops were returned to Egypt. Here they licked their wounds and received thousands of new recruits. Soon there were enough men to create two new divisions. Cadres from the older formations were mixed with the new troops to provide a leavening of experience. Once again the Australians trained intensively in the shadows of the pyramids.

In March the first Anzac corps left for Europe, followed in May by the second.

The bulk of the mounted troops stayed behind to defend the Suez Canal on the edge of the Sinai Desert from Turkish incursions.

The British theatre commander was General Archibald Murray. His greatest military asset was the ANZAC Mounted Division commanded by Major General Harry Chauvel.

The division was initially composed of the 1st, 2nd, and 3rd Australian Light Horse Brigades as well as the New Zealand Mounted Rifle Brigade. Most of the men had seen action in Gallipoli and were excited by the prospect of mounted warfare in the new theatre.

The campaign for the domination of Egypt and Palestine began in August 1916. Fouteen thousand Turks advanced on the Suez Canal. Chauvel was tasked with stopping this attack and, with his heavily outnumbered horsemen, conducted a dogged fighting withdrawal. His troopers harassed the Turks and by the time they were closing in on the crucial town of Romani, Chauvel felt he had their measure. As the tired and thirsty enemy forces made ready for their final attack against the 1st and 2nd Brigades he unleashed the fresh 3rd Light Horse Brigade onto their flank. Four hundred and twenty-five Turks surrendered and the rest were bundled back to their starting positions with 50% casualties.

After this resounding victory for Australian arms the decision was made to clear Turkish troops out of Palestine. By February 1917 the Sinai Peninsula was clear and Murray set his sights on seizing the gateway to Palestine: Gaza.

Sadly, the operation on 26 March 1917 was badly handled by the British general. Although the mounted brigades swept around Gaza to isolate it from reinforcements, Murray failed to press the infantry assaults on the beleaguered garrison and he ordered a precipitate withdrawal. Another bloody assault on 19 April failed with 6,000 casualties. By this time the Turkish high command had realised the threat to their position. Reinforcements had poured into the front and a solid 45 kilometre line of defences stretched from the coast at Gaza to Beersheba.

Murray was replaced by General Edmund 'the Bull' Allenby. He was a distinguished cavalry leader who led from the front and was known for his aggression. The first thing Allenby did was to reorganise his command. Recognising Chauvel's talent he placed the Australian general in charge of the newly organised Desert Mounted Corps. Three divisions were placed under his care and Chauvel became the first Australian to command a corps in battle. Allenby also had seven infantry divisions divided into two corps.

The Gaza-Beersheba line was a tough nut to crack. Allenby decided to assault Gaza with one infantry corps while directing the other at the centre and right of the Turkish defences. But the key to his plan was to take Beersheba, a challenging task that Chauvel and his Australian Light Horse relished.

On 31 October Allenby threw his infantry corps at the Turkish defences.

Hard fighting was experienced all along the lines. The Turkish defences were well supplied with ammunition and batteries of German 77mm cannon and 150mm howitzers helped to keep the Allied forces at bay. There were even battalion sized formations of German machine gunners adding a bit of extra stiffness to the Turk defences. As dusk approached it seemed that Allenby's attack might end in a costly failure – he called on Chauvel to break the deadlock.

Beersheba was the crucial position; if it fell the entire Turkish line would unravel. A more immediate concern for Chauvel was his need for water. His mounted troops needed 400,000 gallons of water and that could only be found in the wells behind the ancient city's walls.

Two British mounted divisions made a frontal attack on Beersheba and created some headway. Nevertheless, there were still thousands of Turks armed with machine guns and howitzers barring Chauvel's desert Mounted Corps from the vital wells.

The Australian commander had a fine sense of timing and he decided that the time was right to launch a do-or-die attack on the defences. He ordered the 4th Victorian Light Horse and the 12th New South Wales Light Horse to saddle up some 7 kilometres from the defences. He ordered that they form up in three lines from 400 to 500 metres apart with 5 metres between each horsemen. Lacking lances or sabres he ordered the horsemen to charge with bayonets drawn. At 4.30p.m., with shadows lengthening on the ground, the horsemen set off at a trot towards the Turkish lines. Spontaneously, it seems, the cream of the Australian military broke into a gallop.

For some reason the defenders couldn't draw a bead on the attacking horsemen. Whether it was late in the day and they thought the battle won, or the setting sun threw out their calculations, or it may have been the speed with which the unexpected attack came at their lines, neither artillery or machine guns or even rifles could stop the charge.

Maybe 5% of the charging troops fell but the rest ploughed through the Turkish trenches and on to Beersheba. Some dismounted and set upon the defenders in the trenches with bayonets and carbines.

After a brief but furious fight the Turks surrendered or fled – the door barring the allied advance into the heart of the Ottoman empire had been kicked open by hard charging Light Horsemen.

THE END IN THE EAST

With the fall of Beersheba, the Turkish lines were shattered. Despite the tenacious fighting withdrawal of his enemies, Allenby's spearhead, including the 10th Light Horse, took Jerusalem on 10 December 1917. By February the ANZAC Mounted Division had captured Jericho.

The German Spring Offensive in March 1918 saw much off Allenby's strength being sent to the Western Front. He was forced to conduct an 'active defence' for much of the year until reinforcements arrived in September. He decided to finish off the dispirited Turkish forces to his front and on 19 September multiple attacks were launched all along the line. Aided by the 1st Squadron Australian Flying Corps the columns burst through the enemy front lines. Chauvel's mounted troops were deftly handled and whenever the enemy sought to establish a new defensive position they would find themselves outflanked or cut off by wildly charging sharpshooter cavalry. As the defences crumbled the Australians found themselves responsible for thousands of filthy, ill equipped and even starving enemy prisoners.

On 1 October the 10th Regiment of the 3rd Light Horse Brigade mounted a charge into Turkish Palestine's capital Damascus. As the troopers clattered into the town, which they thought would be stoutly held, they were greeted by thousands of jubilant Arabs who had taken control of the city hours before.

Chauvel and his crack troops then proceeded to take Lebanon and Syria. They were near Homs when news came of the Turkish surrender on 30 October.

The freewheeling Australian Light Horse Regiments, under the inspired leadership of Lieutenant General Chauvel, had proved the difference in the penultimate battle between the British and the Ottoman Turkish Empire.

CHAPTER 7

WORLD WAR I - FIGHTING THE HUN

The diggers arrived on the Western Front in 1916. The scale of the battle dwarfed anything seen in the east. Rather than being confined in a battlefield limited to several square kilometres of difficult terrain, the Australians were thrown into a cauldron of total warfare where millions of men fought for survival and victory over a deep trench system extending from the neutral Swiss border to the English Channel.

In 1916 and 1917 the lesson was learnt that each man was a tiny cog in the huge machine of war, expendable and insignificant. Nevertheless, the Anzacs built a reputation for courage. In 1918 they proved to be an elite force within the British Empire's forces and were instrumental in halting the last great German offensive of the war. Under the command of Sir John Monash the Australian Corps were used in devastating offensives that led to the 'Black day for the German Army.'

After helping to turn the tide in the Allies' favour, the Australians returned home. Once again the Australians had made a bloody sacrifice for the British Empire. Of the 295,000 Australians who served in and above the trenches between March 1916 and November 1918, 46,000 died and 132,000 were wounded.

1916 AND 1917 – CARNAGE IN THE TRENCHES

The stirring stories of Gallipoli had led to a rush of enlistments back home. When the 1st and 2nd Australian Divisions returned to Egypt they found thousands of reinforcements. It was decided to create a new AIF corps. Each of the initial divisions was split down the middle to create the 4th and 5th divisions AIF. At the same time the 3rd Division was being raised in England under the splendid leadership of General John Monash.

In February 1916 the Germans struck at Verdun. It was vital that troops be shipped to Europe to help the Western Allies at this time of crisis. On 26 February the 1st ANZAC Corps, under General Birdwood, was ordered to the Western Front. The 1st and 2nd AIF combined with the New Zealand Division was to make up the first wave of Anzacs. The 2nd Corps, comprising the 3rd and 4th divisions, was still fitting out support services and wasn't dispatched until May.

Finally, after overcoming the initial disappointment of being sent to a secondary theatre, the Anzacs were heading to the heart of the war. The infantry was issued with new kit to suit the conditions. Thick greatcoats, hand grenades, ammo pouches and British steel helmets were exciting novelties. Each division's artillery regiments were beefed up with 12 batteries of modern 18 pounder guns and three batteries of heavy 4.5 inch howitzers. Added to the heavy Vickers machine guns at battalion level were light Lewis guns for use at squad level.

The 1st and 2nd division were placed in the line in what was called the nursery. This quiet sector near Armentieres was used by the British to 'blood' new formations. The occasional artillery stonk was intermixed with patrols as the corps became familiar with the new conditions.

The 5th Division was not so lucky.

They weren't 'blooded' in Field Marshal Haig's Somme offensive. They were decimated.

On 19 July 1916 the new division was ordered to attack a salient near the town of Fromelles. The attack was badly botched. A seven hour bombardment, beginning in the morning, was too light to inflict any real damage on the German defences, but tipped them off to the coming attack. Nevertheless, the prolonged barrage gave heart to the Australians, who charged forward enthusiastically. Small sections of German trench were captured by the 8th and 14th Brigade, but the 61st British Division – which was given the role of protecting the Australian formation's flanks – made almost no headway. Surviving German machine guns tore into the flanks of the Australians, and a counterattack by the 7th Bavarian Division hurled the Aussies out of their hard won gains and captured 400 prisoners. Whole battalions had been eviscerated in the 'butcher shop' of Fromelles and the ferocity of the German response unnerved the division, which had been out of action for months.

With hundreds of wounded men screaming out for succour in no-man's-land, the battle was over less than 24 hours after it started; 5,533 men of the 4th were casualties. The 61st Division suffered losses of only 1,547. The attack had been intended as a decoy from the main Somme offensive but not one German reserve unit was drawn into the futile fight.

Part of the problem at Fromelles was the new kit the Australians had to carry. Each man was issued a spade, twelve bombs, 250 rounds of ammunition, two gas masks, haversack, greatcoat, rations and their rifle.

Men were thrown over the top into massed machine gun and artillery fire from the Germans.

In order to continue the offensive, the 1st Division was ordered in to assault the town of Pozieres on 23 July. This vital defensive position on the Somme battlefield had resisted four major attacks by British infantry one week earlier. The experienced division swept through the German positions and evicted hundreds of Germans with grenades and bayonets. As soon as they had occupied the positions, the diggers made ready and decimated a battalion size counterattack; hundreds of Germans went down to Australian machine gun fire.

The 1st Division had made the first concrete advance of Haig's bloody Somme offensive. The Germans weren't happy. Reserve artillery divisions were brought up to pound the Australians. The 2nd Division was sent in to relieve the drawn and haggard 1st. German shellfire fell like hail; whole companies of men were cut down like scythed wheat. Many men cracked and committed suicide. Some dug shallow, shell scrape trenches only to find themselves buried by mud thrown up by heavy calibre shells. Others were thrown pin wheeling through the air only to find themselves whole and sound in a shell hole. For the first time Australians experienced the horrific experience of 'vapouring': a comrade would suffer a direct hit and become so much sticky, bloody vapour, covering his comrades in a disgusting clammy goo.

The Australians had their wish – they were fighting the Hun for their mother country. The only problem was they were fighting for the Butcher Haig, whose ill planned attacks led to almost 30,000 Australian casualties in the six weeks of battle on the Somme. Pozieres alone had led to 24,100 casualties suffered; 6,741 were dead. A shallow stretch of trenches two kilometres long was all the AIF had to show for their efforts.

As the chill winds of autumn swept across Flanders, the pace of battle slowed. The Australians were faced with a new foe; the coldest winter in two generations made life in the shallow mud bound trenches almost impossible. Twenty thousand more Australians were evacuated to the rear suffering dysentery, trench foot and frost bite.

1917 saw similar assaults to those that had been fought the previous year. Names such as Messines, Ypres, Glencorse Wood, Menin Road, Polygon Wood and Passchendaele are now just places on a map. In 1917 tremendous deeds of heroism occurred in these locations as thousands upon thousands of Australians fought, bled and died in futile attempts to break through the formidable Hindenburg Line. It seems difficult to imagine but their losses exceeded those of the previous year. Thirty-eight thousand men fell to the German defences before Ypres alone.

There were some positive developments which would later bear fruit. General John Monash began to develop his theories of combined arms attacks and the British tank arm was evolving into a battle winning formation.

Widespread mutinies in the French Army in April 1917 caused almost as much concern as the Russian Army's collapse later in the year.

As 1918 approached it seemed the war must come to a conclusion. Fortunately for the British, they had the Australians, who would once again make the difference in their hour of need.

1918 – YEAR OF DECISION

With Russia out of the war it became obvious to the Allied command that the Germans would seek a killing blow in the West. While crack divisions were transferred from Russia and the Ukraine, the Australian, British and French formations brushed up on their defensive tactics and dug in to await the onslaught.

There was a recognition of the Australians' crucial role in the fighting when the five divisions of the AIF were consolidated into the Australian Corps. This formation, under General Birdwood, was the largest independent Australian force in our existence.

As well as moving large formations to the Western Front, the German high command finally formalised a new style of warfare that had been developing in front line units for several years. Their mighty offensive would be led by a new type of trench fighter: the Stormtrooper.

These troops were specialist trench busters and used what would now be termed shock and awe tactics – combining speed with massive fire power.

Instead of being weighed down by a heavy backpack stuffed with rations and personal items, the new type of assault troops had a blanket or greatcoat wrapped around their torso and a simple mess bag. Modern gaiters and boots replaced the antiquated jackboots, allowing them to run at greater speed. Within a squad each man could choose his favourite weapons. Some reprised the role of 18th Century grenadiers and carried sacks filled with long handled grenades that resembled 'potato mashers'. Despite the amusing nickname, the *1915 Stielhandgranate* was a lethal weapon that had either impact fuses or time delays depending on the need.

Grenades were hurled in volleys to shatter strongpoints before other troops, armed with cut down Maxim machine guns, magazine pistols or even sub-machine guns, went in to finish the job. Thousands of British Lewis machine guns were added to this array, along with captured mobile Russian artillery pieces. Section based tactics where each platoon was divided into several groups led by NCOs became the norm. Each section was based around a light machine gun, which would suppress enemy positions while troopers armed with grenades would close in to destroy the positions and seize enemy trenches.

Gone were the linear attacks of previous campaigns. These stormtroopers essentially used modern day infantry tactics. Small units would be given objectives and it was the responsibility of the NCO or officer in charge to work out how best to achieve the objective. 'Gun groups' or 'rifle groups' would utilise fire and movement to approach enemy positions. These positions would be supressed with assault artillery, mortars and machine gun fire before being assaulted with close in weapons such as grenades or pistols and, by 1918, the Bergmann MP 18 submachine gun. On a localised section level rifleman would snipe at the enemy, keeping their heads down while the bombing parties worked their way forwards.

New artillery techniques were used in support of the Stormtroops. The Germans amassed thousands of guns and gave them preregistered targets. Different types of gas shells were mixed in with high explosive shells. The gas, which tended to settle in trenches, forced the defenders out to the surface, while the high explosives decimated the men once they had emerged into the open. Other batteries produced a curtain of fire that prevented reinforcements reaching the enemy trenches. Meanwhile fighter formations, such as Jagdgeschwader No 1 (roughly translated as interceptor group number 1) under Manfred von Richthofen, wrested air superiority from the Allied Flying Corps allowing German bombers and reconnaissance planes to operate over the unprotected enemy trenches. New liaison methods allowed the German artillery to pick new points of resistance and pour fire onto them.

Flanks and weak points were sought. Troops were trained to bypass enemy strongpoints and take them from the rear or roll the remaining positions up from the flank. If these weak points could not be found a point of maximum impact would be chosen where all of the battalion assets would overwhelm the enemy with massed firepower, allowing the assault troops to break through. Once a breakthrough had been achieved these elite soldiers were trained to penetrate into the enemy's rear, disrupting communications, causing confusion and cutting off remaining enemy formations from supply.

At 4.30a.m. on 21st March, the Ludendorff Offensive began. Supported by 6,000 guns, massed infantry divisions, each spearheaded by a battalion or regiment of Stormtroopers, descended on the British 5th Army defending Amiens. Huge holes were punched in the British lines and the shocked and shattered formations were withdrawn to behind the Somme. It had taken nine months for Haig to capture the blood soaked battlefields, and the Germans had retaken the entire front in a matter of weeks.

Australian flyers of the Australian Flying Corps saw swarms of Germans overrunning battlefields such as Pozieres, where so much Anzac blood had been spilt the previous year.

The German advance towards Amiens looked as if it was about to tear a hole between the French and British armies and allow the Germans to roll up either adversary and win the war. On 22 March the Australian Corps was ordered to Amiens to prevent this catastrophe and trucks and trains filled with diggers moved to the front. Previously despondent French citizens, who had been loading their possessions on to carts to escape the Hun, gave a cheer and began to unload their belongings when they saw the Australians.

On 26 March the Australian 3rd and 4th divisions reached the front. Between 27 and 30 March they fought savage battles with the Germans to deny them access to the vital transport hub at Amiens. Hamel was seized, but the Australians managed to stabilise the line at Villers Brettoneux. At Dernancourt the Germans broke through the Australian lines and encircled an entire battalion of diggers. These plucky colonials managed to fight their way out and were involved in a spirited counterattack that threw the Germans back. By 5 April Ludendorff's Spring Offensive on the Somme had been halted. Extended German supply lines and heroic defensive actions by the Australians had helped to save the Allied front.

As the lines solidified along the Somme, the Australians scored one more notable victory, shooting down the Red Baron.

WHO BROUGHT DOWN THE RED BARON?

The Australians on the Western Front had a reputation for blazing away with Vickers machine guns, Lee Enfield rifles, Owen machine guns and even their revolvers at any plane that crossed their positions in the mud of Flanders. Experienced British and Canadian pilots advised new members of their squadrons to steer clear of any Australian positions unless they wanted to experience a hail of friendly fire. The greatest pilot of his age, Manfred von Richthofen, the Red Baron, made the fatal mistake of pursuing a novice pilot over the Aussie trenches and paid with his life.

On 21 April 1918, in the skies over the Somme, the greatest fighter ace of World War I was brought down by an Australian machine gunner. A Canadian pilot claimed the kill, but three Australian machine gunners poured fire in the direction of the Red Baron and his distinctive red triplane after the Canadian had left the fight. It is likely that one of those gunners brought down the greatest fighter pilot of World War I. With the passage of time it is impossible to say exactly who brought down the famous pilot with one bullet through his chest, but it is possible to narrow the field.

Manfred Albrecht Freiherr von Richthofen was born on 2 May 1892 in what is now part of Poland. Born near Breslau in Silesia, he was a member of the Prussian nobility. As a youth he grew up to have blond hair and piercing blue eyes. The young man exceled in gymnastics and used to love hunting deer and wild boar in the forests of his homeland.

By the outbreak of World War I he had enlisted in a glamorous Uhlan (lancer) regiment, but once the war became static he rallied against the diminished importance of cavalry units, who were reduced in many cases to mere couriers. As soon as possible Richthofen transferred to the new German air force (Luftstreikrafte) where he became an observer and machine gunner in a two seater reconnaissance plane. In this role he was able to display his iron nerve, and he soon entered flying school.

Richthofen did not prove to be a 'natural' and on his first solo flight misjudged the landing and crash landed. Nevertheless, he persevered and soon won his wings. While the young pilot was never an elegant flier he possessed a killer instinct and became the greatest German ace of World War I.

Manfred's comrades in the air force all mention his self-control. Of average height and quite stocky, the Baron's piercing blue eyes weighed up all the pilots attached to his unit. Any who did not have the right attacking attitude were soon moved on. The captain was always measured and concise with his speech and avoided familiarity or profane language.

Once in the air he became almost supernatural in his understanding of air combat. He could pick out an enemy formation before any of his comrades and would launch a calculated attack as soon as possible. By the time many of his comrades were still working out their targets, Richthofen would already have sent an enemy plane flaming towards the ground. His great talent was closing up as close as possible to an opponent and dispatching them with unerringly accurate shooting. Once the planes had returned to their base he would still be able to offer advice to all of his pilots, describing their role in the combat, despite the confused nature of an air melee. His advice was always good – one thing he stressed was the need for pilots not to pursue enemy pilots far behind their lines. Advice that he followed...until 21 April 1917.

Contrary to post-war rumours, the Red Baron did not thrive by picking off damaged planes or slow reconnaissance jobs. Most of the planes he downed were up-to-date interceptors flown by experienced airmen. In fact, if he cooperated with a fellow pilot to bring down an enemy plane Manfred invariably credited the kill to his comrade.

By January of 1917 Richthofen had 16 kills and he was placed in charge of Squadron (Jasta) 11 and was awarded the Blue Max. By April 1918 he was in charge of the famous 'Flying Circus' composed of many of the elite flyers of the Luftstreikrafte. Four squadrons were combined to form Jagdgeschwader No 1. His squadrons, which could put up 40 to 50 elite flyers at a time, had been instrumental in seizing air superiority and allowing the great German Offensive of March 1917 to almost break the allied lines. By April they were stationed near the Somme River and regularly engaged above Australian positions around Hamel and Villers Brettoneux. On 20 April Richthofen made another milestone and shot down his eightieth victim North East of Villers Brettoneux.

The following morning the Red Baron prepared for a final sortie above allied lines before he was to go on leave on the 22nd. He became known as the Red Baron thanks to his beloved bright red Fokker DR 1 Triplane, which gave him and his fliers superlative manoeuvrability combined with heavy firepower, a lethal combination in the skies over the Western Front in World War I. Every part of the plane was painted bright red except for the large Maltese crosses on the fuselage, wings and tyres.

At first, as 21 April dawned wet and muggy, it seemed that there would be no flying that day. However the clouds cleared and reports came in of Allied flyers penetrating across no-man's-land. The Germans were preparing for one last push against the Australian positions and Richthofen's unit was given the orders to shield German infantry assembly areas from prying British and Australian eyes. At 10.30 the German planes took off and set out towards the area between Hamel and Villers Brettoneux to intercept any Allied squadrons.

Soon there were about 25 German fighters flying in formation just behind the German front line – waiting to pounce on any prey.

That prey was spotted soon enough. Fifteen Sopwith Camels belonging to 209 Squadron, commanded by the Canadian Roy Brown, were tasked with protecting some slow moving Australian recon planes from 3rd Squadron Australian Flying Corps. Brown had been fighting for several years and had 12 victories to his credit. He was suffering from what we would now call combat fatigue. He was emaciated with dull eyes and was severely fatigued due to lack of sleep. Nevertheless, he was still a professional fighter and he gave orders to a rookie pilot, 'Wop' May, to stay out of any combat and observe what happened during his first combat mission.

The two forces clashed above the Somme River. Brown signalled May to stay behind as the rest of the squadron joined the melee. Soon the drab planes of the RAAF were pitching and weaving among the brightly coloured triplanes and biplanes of Richthofen's Flying Circus. As the planes ripped past, pilots would seek to get a bead on each other, and bright tracer trails filled the air. The German and Australian infantry on both sides of the line stopped whatever they were doing and watched the action from below.

During dogfights in World War I the planes might begin fighting at 10,000 feet, but as the planes dodged and weaved the combat gradually lost elevation. At one stage May, who was still at the original height, saw what seemed to be a sitting duck below him. He chose to disobey orders and dove onto his target. In his excitement he missed the German plane and found himself in the chaotic melee as the best German pilots tried to shoot him down. May did the only logical thing and dove towards the Somme River, intending to head home.

Richthofen saw the Camel and dove to pursue. Soon he was on May's tail, closing in on him and seeking to get a clear shot. The experienced German airman might have recognised the other pilot as a rookie. May proved no easy mark and threw his plane about in unpredictable turns, dives and climbs that made it impossible for even the superb marksman behind him to draw a bead. It was at this stage that Brown saw May's predicament and turned to follow the German. Even as Richthofen was shooting at May, Brown was shooting at the German – with no effect.

Richthofen wouldn't abandon his prey and soon he was pursuing the Camel along the route of the River Somme and across the lines into Anzac territory. In a matter of moments every armed Australian was loosing off shots at the speeding triplane.

Why did Richthofen ignore his own precepts on this fateful day in April? After this sortie he was going on leave – maybe the thoughts of hunting animals rather than men caused him to relax. Or there could have been other, darker reasons. In mid-1917, while on leave, he had admitted to his mother that he thought there was little chance that Germany could win the war. During the Ludendorff Offensive which had just been halted, the Germans had seen the wealth of supplies and kit that the Allies were blessed with. When that last major attack had petered out it was obvious to many, even the very young and very old soldiers who were now manning the front line, that it was only a matter of time before the war ended.

Perhaps the Red Baron was just sick of killing people. It is possible that, with his eightieth victory, the greatest German pilot had simply had enough.

Perhaps he was frustrated that a rookie like May had evaded his well aimed fire.

Whatever the reason, on that April morning the Red Baron did not finish May off but followed him behind the Allied lines into a hail of gunfire – well aimed fire from a succession of Australian positions. It seems that sometime in this brief window of time Brown sheared off from the pursuit. Australians reported two planes but not the third. One lieutenant saw Brown's plane attack with a heavy burst of fire before it disappeared in a northerly direction.

The Australian 4th and 5th Divisions were entrenched before and along the imposing Morlancourt ridge facing the Germans. In front of this ridge ran the River Somme. Richthofen pursued his quarry just above the river and was actually below the ridge line for a fair proportion of his journey. Australians looked up out of their dugouts and many took pot-shots at the Baron while, from the top of the ridge, rear echelon squaddies did the same.

One Vickers machine gun belonging to the 24th Machine Gun company was manned by Sergeant Popkin, and he managed to draw a bead on the red triplane as it flew near his position on the ridgeline. Popkin was renowned as a good shooter and he estimated that he got 80 bullets off as the bright red triplane traversed his front from left to right. No hits were observed.

At one end of the ridge was the 53rd Battery of the 14th Australian Field Artillery Brigade. This was one of the batteries supporting the 5th Australian Division and was composed of six eighteen pounder field pieces with two post mounted Lewis machine guns for anti-aircraft defence. The Battery was emplaced in pits and one Lewis was positioned at the rear left of the centre gun while one was on the left flank. The cannon were shrouded in camouflage netting and it is likely that Richthofen was not aware of the threat below until he was fired upon.

Commanding the 53rd Battery was Major Leslie Ellis Beavis. His command post phone rang with news that some flyers were heading his way and he checked that his Lewis guns were manned. One gunner was Robert Buie, who had been on lookout since dawn and was waiting with a fully loaded Lewis and several drums of ammo at his feet. Buie was a crack shot and a man of few words. The other Lewis was crewed by Gunner William John Evans. Evans was manning the left hand gun while Buie was at the rear position.

After evading Popkin's burst, Richthofen banked steeply up and over the ridge in pursuit of May – right on top of the two Lewis machine guns. Beavis saw that he was a perfect target and as he banked towards their position the Australians could see the German pilot clearly, almost into the cockpit. Both gunners were ready and waiting and, as soon as the Camel had passed, they poured fire directly onto the pilot. One observer even saw the look of surprise on Richthofen's face when Gunner Evans opened up – so caught up in the chase was Richthofen that he hadn't realised the danger he was in. As soon as the Lewis gunners fired, Richthofen was out of action – May's desperate evasion techniques were not enough to get the Fokker off his tail. He did cease the pursuit immediately after the two Lewis guns had emptied their magazines.

Many observers had no doubt that as soon as the two Lewis' had done their work, the Fokker did a rapid climb, as if Richthofen had been slammed against his throttle stick with the impact of the bullet, before levelling out and descending gradually to a forced landing. The mortally wounded Richthofen threw his goggles out of the cockpit. It was during this descent that Popkin got another burst at the plane, which had done a 180 degree turn at the edge of the ridge.

The triplane crashed and the first Australian on the scene found a bruised and bloody Red Baron dead in the cockpit. It is likely he had guided the plane to a crash landing in his last moments of life.

The autopsy revealed that a single .303 bullet had penetrated Richthofen's chest and lungs, nicked his heart and exited on the opposite side. Buie, Evans and Popkin's weapons all fired the same kind of bullet, as did all of the Australians armed with Lee-Enfield rifles. All had an opportunity to fire into the right of the plane. While no definitive answer can be found as to who fired the fatal bullet, my money is on Evans. As soon as nearby soldiers heard the rattle of his light machine gun discharging its magazine, the Red Baron stopped his pursuit of May, levelled out and flew to his death.

May suddenly realised that the Fokker triplane was no longer pursuing him. His remarkable evasive actions had allowed him to survive an attack from the deadliest hunter on the Western Front. Brown appeared soon after and guided the disorientated rookie back to their base.

JOHN HAY – THE RED BARON'S 17TH VICTIM

John Hay was in the wrong place at the wrong time. Born in Sydney on 22 January 1889, on the outbreak of war he left Sydney University and volunteered for service in the Royal Flying Corps (RFC). He soon proved to be a capable pilot and a charismatic leader of men. Flying the difficult to control FE 8 as a member of No 40 Squadron, he made three confirmed kills in 1916, just north of the Somme.

Also in the region was Jasta 11. This squadron had not nailed an Allied plane in four months, so early in 1917 Richthofen was sent there as a new commander. On 23 January he led out his new squadron with a point to prove. In his red painted triplane the German ace, who had 16 kills to his credit, singled out Hay and pumped 150 bullets into the FE 8 at a range of 50 metres. Hay's fuel tank ruptured and his plane became a blazing fireball. At 500 metres the Australian leapt from his plane and fell to his death in no-man's-land.

Many mourned the fine young man and a bell with his name inscribed upon it still calls students to class at Sydney University.

THE FRONT STABILISES

Ludendorff had been halted on the Somme but he still had some shots in his locker. On the 19th he attacked towards the Channel Ports. If they fell, the British Army would be effectively cut off from supply and reinforcements. At Bethune and Armentieres, the Allied defences were overrun and the Germans were bearing down on Hazebrouck – a vital cog in the Allied supply network. The 1st Australian Division was sent to defend the town on 12 April and, when the Germans attacked on the 17th, they threw them back with heavy losses.

One more attack was made by the Germans on Villers Brettoneux. Although it was initially successful, the Australians made a night-time bayonet attack that swept the Germans out of their positions and stabilised the front. This attack was considered by many to be the finest action of the war.

It was around this bloody battlefield that the diggers recovered one of the finest souvenirs of that bloody conflict – Mephisto.

A UNIQUE QUEENSLANDER – MEPHISTO

Since 1919 a unique and strange beast has been in residence at the Queensland Museum. It is an A7V built by Daimler Benz in World War I. Twenty of these vehicles were built by the Germans, and Mephisto (Unit 506) is the only one to survive. It was hauled out of the front line by a battalion of Queenslanders, despite German efforts to destroy it.

The A7V was built in response to the tanks introduced by the British and was an absolute leviathan. Boasting a 57mm gun mounted in the front sponson, six machine guns built into the side of the hull gave extra support. It was relatively heavily armoured for the time (maximum 30mm steel plate) and had a crew of up to 17 men! Despite this, the seven meter long vehicle could attain speeds of almost 10km an hour in good conditions. Conversely, the overhang at the front and rear of the vehicle meant it was easily bogged in rough terrain and this factor sealed Mephisto's fate.

Mephisto was assigned to a Kampfwagenabteilungen (fighting vehicle battalion). The insignia of this battalion was the skull and crossbones, which can still be seen on the front of the vehicle.

The tanks took part in the German Spring Offensive in March 1918 and cooperated with Stormtruppen detachments to help break through the Allied lines. Unit 506 fought around the St Quentin sector and was instrumental in destroying several strongpoints.

On 24 April, Mephisto and 13 other tanks were involved in an assault on Villers-Bretonneux. While the assault was a success, the A7V drove into a shell hole and the Germans found it impossible to extricate the bulky vehicle. The tank was used as a pillbox for the next several months until the Germans, when they were forced to retreat, tried to demolish it with high explosive charges.

Australian troops of the 26th AIF Battalion saw the stricken beast to their front and the battalion commander, Major J.A. Robinson, who was obviously something of a big game hunter, decided to add a new trophy to his unit's home town of Brisbane. On 22 July a raid was launched to seize Mephisto, with the aid of two gun carriers and with air and artillery support. The Queenslanders successfully extracted the vehicle and brought it behind Allied lines.

Battered and bruised Mephisto is still an imposing beast. The Australians decorated the vehicle with signatures and their unit insignias.

Once shipped to Brisbane, Mephisto spent 60 years exposed to the elements on a terrace outside the Queensland Museum. Here its condition deteriorated somewhat, but this was a fortunate fate compared to its brothers, which were all scrapped after the war. Recently, extensive restoration work has been undertaken to bring Mephisto back to its former glory.

THE END APPROACHES

With the strategic failure of the Ludendorff Offensives the Germans had lost their last opportunity to win the war. American soldiers were pouring into the Allied rear areas while the blockade of German ports was making life for the Germans behind the lines intolerable. There was, however, still much hard fighting to be done, and the Australians would once again be crucial to Allied plans.

The mishandling of the British 5th Army during the March offensives resulted in its commander being sacked. He was replaced by the Australian corps commander General Birdwood.

Birdwood was replaced as Australian commander by General John Monash. Monash had several things working against him when this appointment was being decided. First and foremost, he was originally a member of the militia rather than the professional army before the war. Also, he was descended from Polish Jews, something of a liability in class-conscious Edwardian society. Thankfully for the troops under his command, Monash's positive attributes outweighed these base prejudices. Monash was a trained engineer and this, combined with his knowledge of historical battlefields, gave him a unique perspective. Monash's plans were meticulously prepared, he always made sure his men were well looked after and that casualties were kept to a minimum. What's more, Monash proved to be solid. Even in the darkest days at Gallipoli the then brigade commander had kept his cool and followed orders without complaint.

Once in charge of the Australians Monash proved to be more than competent – he demonstrated an outstanding and innovative approach to warfare that would echo throughout the century. Monash was one of the chief pioneers of what became known as 'combined arms' warfare. Armour, artillery, infantry and air power were combined to brilliant effect to smash through the German lines.

His assault at Hamel on 4 July is considered to be the first modern combined arms battle. The troops of the Australian corps attached to the British 4th Army drilled with the tanks attached to the attack and experimented with tank-infantry cooperation, working out how best to attain set objectives. Secrecy was paramount, with few written orders and radio silence being the norm. Allied aircraft were deployed before the attack to ensure that troops were able to move into position without enemy reconnaissance planes alerting the defenders. The row from the low flying planes served to drown out the noise of tanks approaching.

The attack went according to plan. A massive artillery barrage from hidden gun positions destroyed preregistered defensive targets. Ammunition was dropped to the forward troops as they advanced, waves of low firing aircraft strafed enemy positions and smoke and dust concealed the troops as they stormed into the enemy trenches. A creeping barrage moved forward in front of the troops. The successful assault was carried out in 93 minutes. Monash had estimated it would take 90 minutes.

General Rawlinson, who was the commander of the British 4th Army to which the Australians were attached, saw that the innovations were widely adopted by the rest of the British Army, and similar successful battles such as the battle of Amiens used the same tactic but on a wider scale. The other innovation pushed by Monash was to attack weak points and flanks rather than relying on frontal attacks. Amazingly, even as late as 1918 this concept was novel to many in the Allied high command.

Other offensives soon followed. They followed the blueprint laid down by Monash and were spectacularly successful. On 8 August the Australians corps (reinforced by a Canadian division) spearheaded the assault during what was known as the Battle of Amiens. At 4.20a.m. the 2nd and 3rd Australian Divisions advanced south of the Somme, and had broken through the German front by 7.30a.m. The 3rd and 4th Divisions passed through their comrades and maintained the attack. Thousands of Germans were taken prisoner while their front line was pushed back between 13 and 15 kilometres. General Ludendorff declared 8 August to be the 'Black Day of the German Army.' He and many of his colleagues on the General Staff finally realised that the war could not be won.

Soon afterwards Monash's achievements were recognised and he was knighted by King George V.

The hammer blows continued to rain down upon the Germans. On 31 August Monash launched three brigades at the heights of Mont St Quentin. The shocked German defenders soon caved in under the Australian combined arms attack and four of their divisions suffered tremendous casualties. One of the few remaining elite divisions still held in the German arsenal, a German Guards Division, launched a counterattack but the Australians managed to fight them off.

These and other catastrophes were too much for the Germans and they pulled their remaining forces back to the Hindenburg line by September.

The Allied supreme commander Field Marshal Foch ordered his subordinates to throw everything they had at the German defences. By this time the Australians were nearing exhaustion. In six months of heavy fighting many formations were at quarter strength and some battalions had less than 300 effectives.

Most brigades were pulled out of the line to be rested and only two more major actions were fought, at Bellicourt in late September and Montbrehain in October. As usual the diggers gained their objectives, but with terrible losses.

By mid-October the Australian Corps had been withdrawn for a well earned rest. They were not involved in the pursuit battles that saw the final destruction of the German positions and the armistice on 11 November 1918.

Australia had paid a heavy price: 330,000 men were sent overseas from a population of only 4.9 million. In the course of the conflict, 59,342 perished and 152,171 were wounded. Just over 4,000 were made prisoner of war.

Thus, almost 65% of Australians who volunteered for service were casualties.

But many who were deemed fit upon discharge suffered terrible psychological problems and found it difficult to readjust to civilian life. It would take a long time for the emotional and physical scars to heal from Australia's involvement in the Great War.

AUSTRALIAN FLYING CORPS' GREATEST AIR ACE: THE KILLER CLERK

The 2nd, 3rd and 4th Squadrons of the Australian Flying Corps arrived in France in late 1917. They were just in time to play a crucial part in the battles that stopped the Ludendorff offensives in March and April, and fought continuously until the armistice in November 1918. In that time the squadrons were credited with downing 435 enemy machines. Captain Harry Cobby (b. 1894 d. 1955) was credited with at least 29 of these victories.

On 9 September 1917 the 3rd Squadron arrived to take on reconnaissance duties with their RE8 scout planes. Number 2 and 4 squadrons flew over soon after. They were equipped with state-of-the-art fighter planes, which included the Sopwith Camel.

The Australian pilots were thrown into battle with as little as 12 hours flying time under their wings, but soon developed into crack formations. The fighter squadrons held their own against the best German formations, including Richthofen's Flying Circus during March of 1918. The 3rd Squadron gave immeasurable support to the Australian attack on Hamel with effective bombing and strafing of the German trenches and support positions.

Captain Harry Cobby epitomised the Australian fighter's dash and bravery. Cobby spent the first years of the war working as a clerk in the Commonwealth Bank. Despite repeated efforts to leave his work, the bank was keen to hang on to their star employee and were reluctant to release him for war service. Cobby finally got his way, joined the Flying Corps and began training at Point Cook, to the west of Melbourne.

Cobby arrived in France with the 4th Squadron and, with only 12 hours flying experience, was sent on his first combat mission. Cobby was absolutely terrified before his first mission and later wrote that if he could have performed any act to avoid going into action he would have done it. But once engaged in combat he proved to be a natural in the deadly game of aerial combat. He soon notched up an impressive tally of kills. These included 29 enemy planes and 13 observation balloons. These targets were well defended with anti-aircraft guns and enemy fighters which made them difficult to knock out. On 20 March he led a small patrol that managed to down several of Richthofen's Circus, including a red triplane.

The massed German offensives gave the Australian pilots unprecedented opportunities to shoot up convoys of marching troops and supplies. One of their greatest achievements was the virtual destruction of German depots and airdromes around Lille. On 16 August the three squadrons, with Cobby leading 19 machines from the 4th Squadron, strafed and bombed the enemy, destroying at least 37 German planes on the ground.

In October, the 4th Squadron received the Sopwith Snipe. This was a superior machine and in five days 30 enemy planes were downed, a squadron record in France.

By the war's end Cobby was in command of 80 machines. As the Australians fighters were demobilised in 1919 they had one more mission – supporting the AIF as it marched in a triumphant parade through the streets of London on Anzac Day. The 60 machines of the Australian Flying Corps were meant to perform a simple fly-by, but instead began low level strafing of the Strand. Cobby and some of his fellows found that they couldn't climb due to overhead wires until they came upon Trafalgar Square, where they managed to zoom upwards. While Cobby and his mates flew at ground level others performed loops, dives and rolls above Australia House. Fortunately, no one was injured – although many a chimney pot got a good rattling.

While Cobby was the most successful pilot in the Australian Air Corps, Flight Commander Robert Alexander Little (b. 1895 d. 1918) gained the most confirmed kills, with a tally of 47 planes, while serving with the RAF.

CHAPTER 8

WORLD WAR II – DESERT TRIUMPH

Never had England needed her loyal imperial domains to come to her assistance as she did in 1940. The Germans under Adolf Hitler had humiliated Prime Minister Chamberlain with the annexation of Czechoslovakia followed by the conquest of Poland. The British were then humbled militarily when their armed forces were bundled out of Norway and France.

Fortunately for Winston Churchill's British government, the 9th Division was on hand to prevent the British being ejected from Egypt with their magnificent defence of Tobruk in 1941.

The Australians fared less well in other battles. Thanks to poor decision making, thousands of Australians were captured or killed in the ill-fated Greek and Cretan campaigns. These blunders and the growing Japanese threat caused the Australian Prime Minister John Curtin to go against the wishes of Winston Churchill and transfer the AIF back to defend the Australian homeland.

While the AIF fought the enemy on land, the RAAF (Royal Australian Air Force) and the RAN (Royal Australian Navy) made a huge contribution to the eventual defeat of the Axis forces.

WAR IN NORTH AFRICA – DESERT DEBUT

The Australians' first major commitment in World War II proved that they were still an elite fighting force who could defeat the best, and the worst, that the enemy could throw at them. In late 1940 and early 1941 the Australian 6th and 7th Divisions were crucial in destroying the cream of the Italian forces – the 10th Army.

On 10 June 10 1940 Italy declared war on France and Britain. The Italian dictator Benito Mussolini (b. 1883 d. 1945) had long held dreams of building a new empire in the Mediterranean that would rival that of the Ancient Romans. Seeing the defeat of the Allies in France he thought he could pick up some extra territory with minimal effort. Italian forces were given a bloody nose on the Franco-Italian border but they made significant gains in North Africa against the British. On 13 September 1940 Field Marshall Graziani launched his huge 10th Army from Italian Libya into British Egypt. This army looked impressive on paper and possessed the equivalent of four army corps with 150,000 men, 1,600 guns, more than 500 armoured vehicles and almost 350 planes. Facing this formidable force was the Western Desert Force under General O'Connor, which consisted of slightly over 30,000 men.

Four well equipped Italian divisions with armour and artillery support penetrated 100 kilometres into Egypt, pushing the meagre British forces before them. They then dug into a chain of well defended fortifications near Sidi Barrani bringing up masses of supplies.

The British theatre commander, General Archibald Wavell, ordered that a plan be made to assault the dug-in Italians with the intention of giving them a bloody nose. His aims were initially limited but the fantastic success of his subordinate General Sir Richard 'Dicky' O'Connor's assault led to the first major Allied victory of World War II. This was in no small part due to the efforts of the 6th Australian Division, which was able to crack the toughest Italian fortifications. O'Conner's Western Desert Force was built around this well equipped formation.

Operation Compass, as the offensive was known, began on 9 December 1940, and soon the Italian fortified camps around Sidi Barrani were overwhelmed. Thirty-eight thousand Italians found themselves behind barbed wire while the Western Desert Force continued its attack into Italian Libya. It was here that the Allies came across their toughest nuts to crack – the border town of Bardia and the vital port of Tobruk.

In many ways Libya was the crown jewel of the Italian empire and no expense had been spared fortifying these vital towns. While the motorised elements of the Western Desert Force bypassed these formidable fortifications it was necessary to clear the Italians out of them lest they threaten British supply lines. The 6th Australian Division was ordered to seize Bardia and Tobruk.

The 6th Division had recently adopted the new triangular organisation of British infantry divisions. Three brigades, the 16th, 17th and 19th, each had three battalions. Each battalion had four rifle companies made of four platoons as well as a Battalion HQ with signals, antiaircraft, mortars, pioneers and anti-tank assets. This new organisation echoed the German Wehrmacht's key philosophy that every formation be an integrated, all arms battle group.

BARDIA

The Battle of Bardia was the first major stoush for the Australian Army in World War II, and it was planned and organised entirely by General Iven Mackay's 6th Division staff. They had a daunting task ahead of them. Sixteen thousand Allied soldiers were to be launched against 45,000 dug in Italians. Major General Iven Mackay was just the man for the job. He had been fighting with the Australian Army since the Gallipoli landings. As commander of the 1st Infantry Brigade in front of the Hindenburg Line he had become an expert at using combined attacks to breach defensive lines. Mackay saw the defences of Bardia as a much smaller cousin to the formidable defences of World War I.

Bardia was only 30 kilometres from the Egyptian border and was seen by the Italian Fascists as a defensive position that was absolutely vital for shoring up their North African empire. For years combat engineers had been working on a vast arc of defensive posts that extended for 29 kilometres around the small port. The first line of defence was an anti-tank ditch with a profusion of barbed wire entanglements intended to funnel attackers into deadly crossfire zones. There was a double row of concrete strongpoints beyond this line, each armed with 47mm anti-tank guns and several heavy machine guns. They were located close to each other so that each strong point could support their neighbours and pour deadly fire into the flanks of any attackers. Smaller anti-tank ditches surrounded many of these posts and the defenders could vanish underground into concrete bunkers to escape enemy artillery or air attacks.

Thousands of mines were laid between the bunkers and six major mine fields rendered large avenues of approach almost invulnerable to enemy attack. The Italian defences were dripping with heavy weapons. Almost a hundred 47mm anti-tank guns were supported by more than 300 artillery pieces ranging from 65mm to 149mm calibres. These were backed up by approximately 130 armoured vehicles, although most of these were the almost useless L3/35 tankettes. At the head of the Italian forces was the experienced General Bergonzoli who was confident that the 45,000 men of his XXIII corps could hold off any attacker and disrupt any further Allied advances.

He was wrong.

Mackay's 6th Division had two major trumps up their sleeve: the 23 Matilda tanks of the 7th Royal Tank Regiment, and the Australian infantry's desire to get 'stuck in'.

On the morning of 3 January 1941 a sustained barrage heralded the Australian assault. Mackay and his staff had used extensive recces to find the most suitable avenues for attack. He was not likely to sacrifice his men butting their heads against the strongest points in the Italian line. It was decided to attack the westernmost part of the line as it was there that the terrain was best for the Matildas.

The 16th Brigade, supported by Matildas, burst into the Italian lines. The 47mm anti-tank guns proved to be useless against the 80mm armour of the British infantry tanks and shells literally 'bounced off' the slow moving armour. But it was Australian élan that decided the issue. Well dug in Italians – each post had between 50 and 200 soldiers – had to be winkled out from their bunkers and trenches. The Australians didn't hesitate to get stuck in with the bayonet and used effective close assault tactics to carve corridors into the Italian defences. Many Italians fought with suicidal bravery as the diggers emerged from the dawn shadows, but once their positions were outflanked the attackers were able to pour fire into the Italian rear, rending their positions untenable. After sustained combat the Italians began to surrender. Many diggers, bursting into the warren-like defences, were astounded to find stockpiles of tinned tomato sauce, pasta, fine wine and cigarettes. The canniest diggers soon realised that the motherlode of booty could be found in the officer's dugouts, where fine cognacs and cigars were there for the taking.

The 17th Brigade entered the fray and moved southwards, while the 16th Brigade moved towards Bardia itself. On 4 January the port town fell, and after much hard fighting the last of the Italian resistance was broken. Many strongpoints held out until the last and by the end of the fighting most of the 7th's Matildas had been knocked out or immobilised.

By 5 January all resistance had ceased. One hundred and thirty Australians had died; 326 were wounded. Around 5,000 Italians were killed or wounded while the rest of XXIII corps – 40,000 of them – went into the bag, along with all of the garrison's guns and tanks.

The 6th Division was unblooded before Bardia but London's *Daily Express* called them 'the cream of the Empire troops and the finest and toughest fighting men in the world.'

Another prize awaited the Australians – Tobruk.

CAPTURE OF TOBRUK

While O'Connor's forces bypassed Tobruk, the town's role as a deep sea port made it vital that it be seized. The town had a deep water harbor that was well protected from the elements. The Italians had built jetties and cranes as well as a transport and storage infrastructure, ensuring that it was the most important town of Cyrencia. Even more crucial to an invading army were Tobruk's springs. It was the only source of fresh water for 1,300 kilometers of coastline.

Like Bardia, Tobruk had several concentric rings of fortifications linked with extensive minefields and barbed wire entanglements. The defences had been built in the thirties and utilised underground command bunkers, large supply depots and even observation towers. Hundreds of artillery pieces were ranged onto defensive positions and could be called on to pound any attacking formations. The Italian Commander General Manella had heard of the Bardia debacle, and behind his 50km of perimeter fortifications established another line of defences. Dug in tanks with infantry support were destined to give the attacking Australians a nasty surprise.

Once again 6th Infantry under General Mackay was given the task of reducing the fortifications. Mussolini's propaganda campaign had described the Australians as Britain's savage 'barbarians' who were to be turned upon the Italians. This was counterproductive, as once the 'barbarians' were released many Italians chose to surrender rather than face the Australian fury.

The 16th Brigade was given the task of breaking through the Italian defences. Before dawn on 21 January 1941 the regimental sappers crept into the defensive installations and began 'de-lousing' the perimeter's mines while cutting holes in the wire barricades. The sappers had blackened their faces and stealthily went about their business without disturbing the garrison troops. Behind the 16th waited the 19th Infantry Brigade and the repaired Matilda's of the 7th Royal Tank Regiment waiting to exploit the breakthrough. The last of the 6th Division's brigades, the 17th stood poised to launch diversionary attacks on either side of the breakthrough. Correspondents attached to the division commented on the professional and relaxed demeanour of the Aussies as they stood ready for battle; Chester Wilmot noted that they would have been more 'worked up before a football grand final.' Wellington bombers droned above the Italian positions and strafed ships in the harbor to help cover the noise of the Australian assembly.

At 5.40a.m artillery barrage began to fall upon the Italian positions, continuing for half an hour. Behind the barrage the last obstacles were cleared and the anti-tank ditches filled in. As the barrage cleared, the Australians emerged with fixed bayonets and stormed the defences. Italian resistance was patchy. Some Italians emerged almost immediately with white handkerchiefs, yelling for mercy. After an hour the 16th, supported by 18 Matildas, had punched a one and a half kilometer wide hole in the Italian defences and were heading for Tobruk harbour, while the 19th Brigade rolled up the northern perimeter.

Suddenly the attack stalled. Infantry marching into the centre of the position were hit by a massed artillery stonk at the same time as they walked into the final line of defence. Dug in tanks cut down Australian troopers with cannon and machine gun fire. Some Australians were killed as they stormed the entrenched tanks seeking to lob grenades through the commander's cupola. The Italians even launched a counterattack with a battalion of infantry advancing behind seven tanks. This was driven off and, after several hours of hard fighting, the Australians broke through the right flank of the Italian defensive line.

While some of the garrison were keen to surrender, many fought to the bitter end and had to be driven from their positions with bayonet and hand grenades. General Manella, in charge of the Italian corps, was captured but refused to order the surrender of his troops. It wasn't until late on 22 January that the last pockets of resistance were crushed.

The spoils of Tobruk were even greater than those of Bardia. Huge wheels of cheese, red wine, silk shirts and unlimited drinking water were seized by the attackers. The Italian flag in the old fortress was taken down and hoisted up on the flagpole was a digger's slouch hat. The Australians had arrived and they would not be ejected.

20,000 prisoners, hundreds of guns and 87 tanks were included in the booty. Almost 3,000 Italians were killed or wounded in their dogged defence, while the Australians lost 355 men.

Most importantly, by 22 January the harbour was taking in much needed supplies for the Allied drive.

This westward push continued remorselessly. While armoured columns motored through the interior, Australians marched along the coast destroying parties of Italians left behind in the headlong retreat. The climax of Operation Compass came on 7 February, when the last Italian troops in Cyrencia were cut off by flying columns of British armour at Beda Fomm, and forced to surrender.

Another 25,000 Italians went into the bag. Operation Compass proved to be a stunning success and 150,000 Italians had been killed, captured and wounded. There seemed to be nothing stopping General O'Connor's Western Desert Force from pursuing all the way to Tripoli and finally clearing the Axis power all the way out of Libya.

But as the last shots were fired in Beda Fomm two crucial decisions were made. Winston Churchill, the British Prime Minister, ordered that no further advances were to be made and the best troops from the Western Desert Force were to be dispatched to Greece to fight any planned Axis attacks.

At the same time Hitler, worried about the Libyan defeats, offered Mussolini a German armoured division on the proviso that the Italians didn't pull back to Tripoli. On 11 February General Erwin Rommel arrived in Rome, and three days later the first elements of the famed German Africa Corps (Deutsches Afrika Corps) were disembarked in Tripoli. The 3rd Panzer Reconnaissance Battalion and the 39th Anti-Tank Battalion were the first troops of what would become the 5th Light Africa Division (later renamed the 21st Panzer Division). They were immediately dispatched to bolster the Italian defences at Sirte.

Rommel turned the tables on the Allied forces. The 6th Australian Division was on its way to Greece and had been replaced with the 9th Division, under Major General Morsehead. This division was still shaking out and was missing much of its establishment. Second rate British formations were holding the line. On 24 March 1940 Rommel led the 5th Light Division and some Italian formations back towards Cyrencia.

The British command had no idea that the Germans could strike so quickly. The once derided Italian formations suddenly had teeth under Rommel's command and, with the Luftwaffe dominating the sky, the whole front was pushed back in what became known as the 'Benghazi Handicap'. By 12 April the Germans had reclaimed all of the lost Italian territory and were over the border into Egypt.

SEIGE OF TOBRUK

Four days earlier a decision was made that saved Egypt for the British.

The 9th Infantry Division, with the scratchings of some other units, were to withdraw into the Tobruk perimeter and hold it while the rest of the British forces withdrew to the east to protect the Egyptian frontier from Rommel's rampaging Africa Corps. Wavell presumed that the Australians might have to hold Tobruk for a couple of months before being relieved. It proved to be a wildly optimistic prediction.

Before flying back to Cairo, Wavell said to Morsehead 'There is nothing between you and Cairo.'

The 9th Division had, at its heart, three stout infantry brigades: the 20th, 24th and the 26th. Also attached, from the 7th Division, was the 18th Infantry Brigade. Supporting the troops were a battalion of Engineers, several British field artillery regiments, the 2nd/3rd Anti-Tank Regiment and the 8th Anti-Aircraft Regiment.

With the departure of Wavell on 8 April, the 9th Infantry Division took up positions around the perimeter. Following Wavell's requirement for a flexible defence, the18th Infantry Brigade was to form a second line of resistance with whatever armour had been salvaged from the recent debacle. There were available about 4 Matildas, 23 unreliable cruisers, some light tanks and several armoured cars. There were also some anti-tank guns mounted on portees that would prove useful in stopping any penetrations.

The double line of concrete posts and their covering anti-tank ditches were all still in good order. The gaps between the posts had proved to be too wide when the 6th had attacked, and it was often necessary to dig new positions between the larger concrete emplacements. Each brigade had a battery of anti-tank guns from the 3rd Anti-Tank Regiment attached. This regiment was equipped with a variety of weapons, including 2 pdrs, captured Italian 47s and Bofors 37mm, and Boys anti-tank rifles. There were approximately 35,000 mouths to feed in April but with the evacuation of non-combat troops this had shrunk to about 22,000 by May.

Each brigade had two battalions up in the 'Red Line', as it was called, and a second 'Blue Line' was constructed to hold the reserve battalions. Gradually the area between the two lines of posts was mined and wired so that the entire perimeter became one huge belt of defences. The larger posts had been built to accommodate 50 defenders, as the Italians had done. However, only 12 or 15 diggers could be spared for each post. The damage from the earlier battles was repaired. Lines of communication were laid down with the rear echelons. Batteries were sighted and ammunition was stockpiled. The Australians were about to meet their greatest challenge of the war. It was they who were tasked with stopping General Erwin Rommel – the Desert Fox.

The 9th Division was ready.

THE DESERT FOX

Mussolini was proving to be more of a hindrance than a help to his German dictator ally. Not only had he made a complete mess of his botched attack on Greece, it was now necessary to bail him out in the disastrous North African campaign. Thanks to Mussolini, Hitler would soon be fighting a war on three fronts!

Hitler chose General Erwin Rommel to sort out the mess in North Africa.

Rommel was no ordinary general. He had cut his teeth leading an elite regiment of alpine soldiers on the Italian front in World War I. Rommel was a natural soldier with an uncanny eye for terrain combined with an almost supernatural ability to find his enemy's weaknesses and exploit them. While other commanders in the rugged Italian Alps saw only obstacles, Rommel pioneered small unit assaults that penetrated into the rear of the Italian positions, then neutralised them with flank attacks and by cutting off their supplies. He was a natural Blitzkrieg commander.

For a period of time in the 1930s Rommel was in charge of Hitler's elite personal guard. As a reward for exceptional service, Hitler gave Rommel command of one of the new panzer divisions created for the invasion of France in 1940. The 7th Panzer Division was soon named the Ghost Division. Although the majority of his armour was made up of impressed Czechoslovakian T 38s, he was able to strike fear into his opponents by appearing at their rear mysteriously, like a ghost.

Rommel's experience made him a combined arms specialist. When facing opposition on the Meuse the General brought his 88mm Flak weapons into play. Over direct sights the high velocity weapons engaged French bunkers and destroyed them with precision shots through their firing slits. He was not afraid of leading from the front and boarded flimsy inflatable assault boats to lead his infantry as they stormed across the river to take out the remaining defences.

Rommel was no stranger to the British or the Matilda tank. As the French and British armies crumbled in the face of the German Blitzkrieg in France, the Allied high command decided on one last ditch defensive action to halt the panzers. Around Arras the cream of the French and British armour, including several regiments of the heavily armed Matildas, launched a counterattack into the flanks of the German columns – straight into Rommel's 7th Panzer. Rather than panicking, the divisional commander brought every gun he could muster to fight off the British. Howitzers, anti-aircraft guns, AT guns, rifles and machine guns – they were all mustered to concentrate fire onto the advancing armour. Rommel personally rallied broken units, placing them in the firing line, and he directed fire onto individual targets. It was too much for the British and the French (led by General De Gaulle), who scurried to their rear.

The counterattack was broken and France fell to the Germans.

This was the commander with whom the Australians in Tobruk would soon be doing battle.

TOBRUK BESEIGED

With the collapse of the Allied front, Rommel knew that once he took Tobruk the Suez Canal and Egypt would be his. He did not foresee any problems.

On 11 April elements of the Italian Brescia and Ariete Divisions arrived outside Tobruk. They were soon followed by the 5th Light Division with its V Panzer Regiment. Over the next few days several half-hearted attacks were launched as the Australian defences were probed for any weak spots.

None were found and Rommel turned the full weight of a Blitzkrieg attack on the Australians. None had ever resisted such an attack and it was presumed their front would be shattered.

On 14 April the 9th Division was hit with a combined arms attack the like of which the Australians had never experienced. Concentrating his resources in a Schwerpunkt (point of maximum impact) Rommel threw the entire 5th Light Division against the Tobruk perimeter. Preceded by Stuka attacks and artillery bombardments, the 5th Panzer Regiment came on in two massive armoured wedges forty to fifty tanks strong. They were supported by several regiments of German infantry, many of whom were riding on the tanks. In the rear were towed artillery and anti-tank assets.

The German tanks passed over the Australian emplacements and penetrated to the rear of their positions. German machine gunners dropped off the rear of the tanks and set up positions within the defensive belt. Following the tanks were waves of infantry.

In most previous German attacks in World War II, once the panzers had penetrated the German lines their opponents had panicked and allowed the supporting forces to enlarge the breakthrough. Unique to this battle was the order Morsehead had given to his men: they were to ignore the tanks and let them pass over the entrenched positions. Once the armoured wave had passed, the diggers were to emerge from their dugouts and take on the following infantry and other supports. As the German infantry approached the defences they were met with a hail of gunfire as the Australians opened up with Bren guns, Vickers machine guns and well aimed Lee Enfield Rifles.

Hundreds of Axis troops fell and any who penetrated the positions were swiftly ejected with bayonet charges.

Meanwhile, the two waves of German tanks made a beeline for the crucial El Adem crossroads, but they soon got a nasty surprise. Facing them were regiments of 25 pdr field guns firing over open sights. This gave the panzers pause. Usually supporting infantry and artillery formations would move forward to neutralise this threat, but they were all still being held up on the perimeter. Things got worse for the German tankmen when the 10th battery of the Australian 2/3 Anti-Tank Regiment drew up in their portees (guns mounted on the rear of trucks to give mobility) and poured fire into their flank. When the assorted tanks of the 1st Royal Tank Regiment launched an attack on the beleaguered German armour, it was the last straw and they beat a hasty retreat.

Rommel had lost hundreds of infantry: killed and captured. Seventeen tanks were totally destroyed and left smoking behind the Australian lines. Australian morale soared.

It soared even higher on 16 April, when the Italians of Ariete Division attacked. Rommel commented bitterly that after a half-hearted attack the Italians had 'retreated towards the enemy' and given themselves up.

But these were the first rounds and the German general planned a knockout blow. This time he would infiltrate infantry into the Australian positions before bringing his tanks up in support.

On 30 April the fully formed Afrika Corps (The 15th Panzer Division had recently landed) launched an attack on the south west corner of Tobruk's defences. It began with fierce artillery attacks and, under cover of this fire, German infantry infiltrated between the Australian posts while engineers deloused the minefields. Once a lodgement had been made the infantry used flares to guide German tanks onto the enemy positions. Four or five panzers would concentrate fire on the Australian bunkers and with their infantry comrades gradually reduce each post.

This was no battle from a distance against a remote enemy. It was close hand-to-hand combat where men were pitched against machine guns, armour, artillery and enemy bayonets. Stukas screamed down, pounding Australian positions and the gun lines behind the rear areas. Anti-tank shells cracked overhead as the few remaining British tanks came up in support. Men screamed as tanks drove over foxholes and turned on their tracks, reducing the occupants to mincemeat. Even though Australians in the red line found themselves cut off they held out to the last. If the Germans wanted to take a position they would have to kill every man in it. One post, R4, held out for 20 hours and seriously delayed the German schedule. Despite the fanatical resistance of the Australians, Rommel almost had the breakthrough he wanted. A four kilometre wide and 3 kilometre deep salient had been thrust into the Allied lines.

Most importantly for Rommel, he had managed to seize the old Italian fort on top of Ras el Medauur. It appears today as an insignificant bump on the horizon but in 1941 it dominated the Australian defences. Even the Ancient Romans realised the importance of this seemingly insignificant piece of higher ground; it appears that the Italian fort was built on the foundations of a Roman fortification. For the next five months the German possession of this point allowed them to dominate the surrounding battlefield.

The Australian defence remained undaunted. On 3 May a new enemy intervened – a dust storm whipped over the landscape, blinding men on both sides and making movement nearly impossible. It helped the Australians – they used the respite to dig a switch line that cauterised the German penetration. Fresh troops and guns manned these positions and, on 4 May, savage counterattacks were launched to reclaim the lost posts. These did not succeed in recapturing the posts, but at least broke up German formations mustering for further attacks.

The pitched battles continued but no further advances were made. Despite the possession of Ras el Medauur, the Axis forces were exhausted.

Rommel had thrown his best, fresh troops into the assault but, for the first time in the war, a panzer corps had been stymied.

Rommel was in no doubt as to why his troops failed to take Tobruk.

He wrote:

'The Australians fought with remarkable tenacity. Even their wounded went on defending themselves with small arms fire, and stayed in the fight to their last breath. They were immensely big and powerful men, who without question represented an elite formation of the British Empire, a fact that was also evident in battle.'

John Foley [1967] 'Tobruk Survives' in: History of the Second World War

The two sides retired to lick their wounds. The salient was a two-edged sword. It gave the Germans a potential jumping off point for further offensives, but it also meant some of the best German troops were required to occupy the salient, thus preventing them from being used in any attack on Egypt.

The 9th Division had done what it had been asked to do. Rommel could not take Egypt with this thorn in his side. The Allies had been given a vital breathing space.

HOLDING ON

Perching in foxholes in the featureless desert led to many hardships for the front line troops. Daily temperatures in the hundreds led to many soldiers becoming disorientated and they could often be found wandering in circles. Everything was eaten out of cans; the lack of fresh food or bread led to the diggers losing weight. The brigade commanders rotated battalions from the red line to the blue line regularly, but trips to Tobruk harbour for a refreshing swim were few and far between. Water was scarce and brackish. This took a particular toll on soldiers surrounding the salient, who had to lie motionless throughout the day in shallow foxholes where any movement would draw a stonk of artillery shells or a deadly sniper bullet.

One thing made life bearable for the troops on both sides. Movement was impossible during the day, but at dusk an unofficial two-hour truce was observed, allowing soldiers to get out of their shallow fox holes and move about. Ammunition and supplies were replenished, legs were stretched and soldiers could have a smoke and a chat in the cooling night air. After two hours the Germans signalled the end of the armistice with a burst of tracer fired into the night air. Everybody scrambled into their foxholes and it was business as usual.

Similar consideration to the enemy was displayed in the heat of battle. If a Red Cross flag was raised by a medic all fire would cease in that sector until stretcher bearers managed to evacuate the wounded soldier. Even in heavy exchanges of fire, ambulances had been known to approach safely.

An almost unique experience for the Australians was caused by the Luftwaffe domination of the air. The Nazi planes flew from two airfields just out of artillery range. The defenders were able to hear the planes start up, taxi and take off. On the still desert nights, many reported hearing the German aircrews singing as they went about their work.

The depredations of the Luftwaffe were making it harder for Tobruk to hold out. In June the water rations were down to half a litre per day and it became increasingly difficult to bring supplies into the harbour. The last Hurricane fighters had been withdrawn on 25 April and only flack, from ships like the ack-ack ship *Parramatta* of the RAN, were able to offer resistance to the Luftwaffe.

Supplies had to be smuggled in by night. All sizes of vessels were used, including a captured Italian fishing schooner captained by Australian Lieutenant Alfred Palmer. He frequently ran the gauntlet to get into Tobruk harbour with vital supplies, using a shaded green light to guide him. His successful run came to an end when the Germans placed a decoy green light to the east. The lieutenant only realised their trick when his ship, the *Maria Giovanni*, ran aground to be captured.

Tobruk was a great defensive victory but it came at no small cost to 9th Division: 744 Australians were killed, 1,974 were wounded and 476 were declared missing.

THE JOCK COLUMNS

The Australians cooped up in Tobruk were not the only thorns in Rommel's side. The 12th Battery of the Australian 2/3rd Anti-tank Regiment, had been moving up from the frontier when Tobruk was cut off by the Germans. Forced to retreat to Halfaya Pass with the rest of the British Army the Battery, with its 12 guns, formed a vital stop gap before other British troops came up to hold the position.

In the months that followed, the Battery's three troops were placed within small battle groups known as Jock columns. These columns could be small groups consisting of a battery of 25 pounders, a couple of companies of infantry and a troop of the 12th Battery with their four portee mounted 47mm anti-tank guns. Some columns were regiment sized and included squadrons of armour in support of a battalion of infantry. The role of the Jock columns was to strike deep behind the Axis lines and ambush bivouacking troops, destroy supply dumps and cut off communications.

The gunners of the 12th Battery, which had been recently equipped with 2 pdrs to replace the captured Bredas, soon gained a fearsome reputation and were credited with destroying large amounts of Axis materials. From April to September it destroyed six tanks, three armoured cars, an anti-tank gun, an 88mm gun, countless soft skin vehicles, and captured 126 enemy prisoners.

Under the legendary commander Major Jack Argent 'Silver John', the Battery only suffered one wounded soldier and became known as the Lucky Twelfth.

TOBRUK'S BUSH ARTILLERY

During Operation Compass the victorious Allied troops were astounded at the amount of luxuries found in the abandoned Italian frontier positions. It seems that Mussolini had provided his soldiers with limitless amounts of tinned tomatoes and dried pasta. The officers' quarters produced a spectacular bounty of fine wines, chianti, cognac and even cigars.

When the Australians marched into Tobruk there was a bounty of another kind. Neatly arranged inside or scattered among the desert were hundreds of abandoned artillery pieces. The Italians had not spiked the guns by placing double shells in the breeches and destroying the barrels, but had merely removed the sights from the artillery pieces and thrown them into Tobruk harbour. The pieces may have been missing sights but the Italians had left almost limitless supplies of shells.

And so was born the Bush Artillery.

In Tobruk the one luxury that the diggers had was time. What better thing to do when you've got time on your hands than to blow stuff up?

Cooks, clerks, drivers, medics – all the 'LOC (line of communications) wallahs' as well as infantry – chose their pieces, hauled them into position and started firing off the huge stores of ammo into the enemy's encircling positions.

This fire wasn't very accurate given that the sights had been removed. What's more, since the crews were not trained artillery men few knew the art of range finding. One observer noted that the manual found with one of the guns indicated the need for a FOP (Forward Observation Post). The 'gunners' dug a FOP within shouting range of the gun. That fact that the FOP had worse visibility than the slightly more elevated gun line didn't seem to worry the diggers at all. Another problem was the tendency of the shells to detonate within the barrel. It was necessary between each shot to haul the gun into position, aim it in the general direction of the foe, ram a shell home and run like blazes to the rear to take shelter behind a rock wall. Only when all of the diggers were safely in position would the extremely long lanyard be pulled to fire the shell.

Although it wasn't aimed fire, the fact that the Germans never knew where the next shot would fall surely played merry havoc with their nerves. One shell at least must have done some damage. A bush gunner told of an incident where they fired off a 75mm shell. Ten minutes later the Germans mounted a counterbattery barrage that lasted for almost an hour and must have used up at least 300 shells.

The most common type of captured weapon was the Italian 75mm. Possessing a handy range, it could do some damage. There were hundreds of 47mm anti-tank guns which were useless against most armour but which could fulfil a role as a useful infantry support weapon. The most popular gun was the 105mm howitzer, which was a reliable and stable gun platform.

The queen of all the captured guns was the 149mm howitzer. The personnel of the 3rd Anti-Tank Regiment adopted one of these outsized World War I relics. They used to delight in loading it up and lobbing a shell towards the Hun. There was only one problem: the age of the gun meant that after every discharge the entire gun seemed to shake itself down to its constituent parts. The gunners had to reassemble the piece between each shot, meaning it had an average rate of fire of one shell every two hours! Nevertheless, the Obice da 149/12 modello 14 did sterling service. They were originally made by Skoda in Czechoslovakia and were captured in World War I from the Austro-Hungarian Army.

Not all of the captured weaponry was second rate. Somehow eight German 50mm PAK 38s found themselves in the hands of the Australian forces – a modern weapon indeed.

GREECE AND CRETE

With the success of the Battle of Beda Fomm, General Wavell had seemingly proved that he was a talented commander who could make the right decisions. This reputation was sullied when he advised Winston Churchill that an expeditionary force of almost 60,000 men could successfully resist Nazi advances in Greece. He was wrong. The Australian 6th Division paid a heavy price for this misjudgement.

Hitler had been forced to come to the aid of his Italian ally after Mussolini's bungled attempt to take Greece. On 13 December 1940 the German leader had issued orders for the assault on the Balkans, and by early April 1941 no less than 15 divisions, including the crack Leibernstandarte Adolf Hitler Division, were poised to seize Yugoslavia and Greece.

By 6 April most of the Allied forces had arrived in Greece and the Australian 6th Division was placed in a new Anzac corps commanded by General Blamey. Whatever Blamey's shortcomings, he was able to appreciate the true nature of the situation: declaring it 'hopeless.'

On 11 April elements of the Adolf Hitler Division, with Stuka and armoured support, clashed with the Australian 19th Brigade. This was not Tobruk, and with an extended line to hold, of over 14 kilometres, the two forward battalions were soon forced into a fighting retreat.

The motorised German formations spread fear and confusion in the allied lines and whole companies of Australians went into the bag. Some battalions were reduced to less than half strength.

Nevertheless, the 16th Brigade to the Allied right managed to hold off the rampaging Germans for several crucial days, allowing the bulk of the Allied army to withdraw behind the new defensive Thermopylae Line. Brigadier Vassey's 19th Brigade came up in support, and it was in the midst of continuous attacks by masses of German armour and aircraft that he came up with his famous order: 'Here we bloody well are and here we bloody well stay.'

By 26 April most of the expeditionary force had been taken off the mainland and evacuated.

The 6th Division had paid a heavy price: 320 dead, 494 wounded and 2,030 taken prisoner. The butchers bill was going to get even higher in the defence of Crete.

Of the 6th, 6,500 soldiers joined about 25,000 British and New Zealanders for the defence of this strategic island. On 20 May the elite German airborne corps assaulted the main airfields. Maleme airfield fell. Soon Retimo airfield was attacked by 1,500 parachutists, who were opposed by the Australian 2/1st and 2/11th Battalions. Although the Australians fought off the Germans for eight days, by 30 May they found themselves encircled. Unknown to the diggers, Wavell had decided to abandon the island on the 27th. The order had not got through to the Australians, most of whom surrendered. Major Sandover, who commanded the 2/11th, gave his men permission to scatter, and 52 of his men managed to escape Crete.

While Australians helped give the German airborne a bloody nose in many other encounters on the island, the 6th was almost destroyed; 274 were killed, 507 wounded and 3,102 were taken prisoner. Additionally, much of the divisional anti-aircraft and artillery assets were lost.

British geo-political folly had taken a dreadful toll on the Australian soldiers.

SYRIA

May 1941 saw British forces in the Mediterranean at a low ebb. Powerful formations of German armour and Italian infantry were poised on the Egyptian border to drive to the Suez Canal and Cairo. Twenty-five thousand soldiers were encircled in Tobruk and there was no guarantee that they would hold out. Some of the best Allied armour and infantry units had been bundled out of Greece and Crete. A seemingly incessant stream of Axis bombers was pounding Malta.

To make matters worse, a new threat emerged in the Middle East. The French territories of Syria and Lebanon had been ordered by the Vichy French government under General Petain to allow German planes to operate over their airspace. Thirty-five thousand hardened French soldiers, including detachments of the French Foreign Legion, were dug in ready to repel any British aggression.

While the Vichy French forces had not been ordered to attack Anglo Egypt, there was no guarantee about the future. There was no love lost between the two powers, especially after the British Prime Minister had ordered the sinking of the French Mediterranean Fleet in July 1940.

On 31 May Churchill advised Menzies that Syria was to be attacked and requested Australian assistance. Due to recent losses no full division could be assigned to the campaign. Two brigades of the 7th Division (the third was in Tobruk), two battalions of the 6th Division and the RAAFs 3rd Squadron were committed to the fight.

Along with the Australian 7th Division under Major General John Laverack were units from India, England and even Free French Units. These troops had been raised by Colonel Charles De Gaulle, who had set up a government in exile after the conquest of France in 1940. Cutthroat Senegalese and Free French Foreign Legionnaires made up some of this force.

The Vichy forces outnumbered the Allies and possessed numerous thickly armoured tanks. It was thought they might put up only a token resistance but it was not to be.

At 2a.m. on 8 June 1941 a three pronged advance was staged from the British territories. The Australians of the 21st Brigade were tasked with taking the coast road towards Beirut while the 25th Brigade fought along the inland route towards Damascus.

The reception from the Vichy forces was defiant. They defended every terrain feature despite being pounded by air and sea bombardments. One of the fiercest battles was before Damascus, from 20 to 21 June. Seeking to encircle the town, Australian forces had to resist fierce attacks by French armour and infantry. A company of diggers was cut off and surrendered, before being released some hours later.

Approximately 60 kilometres separated Damascus and Beirut, but it took two weeks for the inland column to advance on their final objective. The French put up a stiff resistance and poured rifle, machine gun and mortar fire onto the attackers. During this time Private J.H Gordon of the 2/31st Battalion, 25th Brigade, crept up to within a few yards of a troublesome machine gun nest before charging and bayoneting the crew of four. He received the Victoria Cross for this heroic action.

The key defensive position on the coast road was a steep ravine through which the Damour river flowed. On 6 July Australians of the 21st Brigade seized the position. The two concentric pincers of the 7th Division was poised to enter Beirut on 12 July and, as a result, the Vichy French surrendered.

Once again, the Australians had been instrumental in helping the British government out of a sticky situation. But the cost had not been light: 1,600 of the attacking 7th Division were casualties.

HMAS *SYDNEY*: A TALE OF THREE CAPTAINS

The HMAS *Sydney* was the pride of the Australian Navy. She was built in Britain and commissioned into the RAN in 1939. The Leander-class light cruiser was a fast moving ship, well armed and well armoured with eight 6 inch guns in four turrets. She had four single 4 inch anti-aircraft guns, twelve .05 inch AA machine guns and eight torpedoes tubes in two quadruple mountings.

When *Sydney* arrived in Alexandria on 26 May 1940 her greatest assets might have been Captain John Collins and his crew, who had been trained to an absolute peak of efficiency. The *Sydney* was a welcome asset to the British Admiral Cunningham, who was tasked with keeping sea lanes free to allow supplies to reach the British forces engaged with the Italian Army in Libya.

Collins had joined the RAN in 1913 and in his successful career had excelled in naval gunnery. He brought this expertise to bear when training *Sydney*'s crew and this was soon to pay dividends.

On 19 July 1940 *Sydney* was off the north coast of Crete with orders to either support a flotilla of four RN destroyers engaged in an anti-submarine sweep, or to look for enemy targets near the Gulf of Athens. Collins used his initiative and decided to shadow the destroyers' movements around the west coast of Crete.

It is fortunate that he did so. At 7.17 a flotilla of Italian light cruisers spotted the destroyers and set off in pursuit. The *Giovanni Della Bande Nere* and the *Bartolomeo Colleoni* were state-of-the-art pursuit cruisers. Heavily armed with eight 6 inch guns they were more than a match for the four destroyers. Built for speed, the Italians soon began to close in on the RN ships. Armed only with 4.7 inch guns the destroyers headed northeast and sent an urgent sighting report to *Sydney*.

Unaware that Collins was only 65 kilometres to the north, things were looking grim for the destroyers. Shells from the Italians landed around the flotilla. None hit, but it was only a matter of time.

Collins used a sea mist to conceal his approach, so while his control tops were able to fix the position of the Italian cruisers, they could not see him. The concealed *Sydney* was adjacent to the fleeing destroyers but he had not radioed his position to them as he wanted nothing to spoil the surprise he had for the pursing Italians.

The first either of the protagonists knew of Collins were muzzle flashes seen in the mist at 8.29 as the first bracketing salvo landed around the *Bande Nere*. The Italians returned fire but were unable to hit the still concealed *Sydney*. Soon 8 inch shells were crashing into the leading cruiser and suddenly the *Sydney* emerged. Flying at full speed, pennons flapping in the wind and all her gun turrets facing starboard, she made 'the most welcome sight in the world' to the British sailors (Pelvin, 1998).

Unsure of what he was facing, the Italian commander decided to turn and head for the open sea. His cruisers laid down smoke, forcing the *Sydney* to switch targets between the two Italians. Collins pursued, but with only his forward turrets bearing on his foe, no hits were scored. At 9.15 he made an inspired decision. Trusting that his well drilled gunners could do the job, he turned the *Sydney* 30 degrees to starboard and brought all turrets to bear. A salvo crashed out and the decisive shot of the encounter hit home. One shell smashed into the *Bartolomeo Colleoni*'s boiler room, cutting off all power to her steering, controls and ammunition hoists. The Italian was dead in the water. Her crew began to abandon ship.

During this firefight one Italian shell hit *Sydney*'s forward funnel. One crewman was injured with a splinter wound.

Sydney pursued the remaining Italian but here superior speed allowed her to escape. The Battle of Cape Spada, as it became known, had ended in a significant Allied victory.

It was just as well; Collin's guns were down to only a few shells a piece.

The actions of Collins and the *Sydney* had major repercussions. The Aegean was effectively cleared of major Axis assets until the invasion of Greece in 1941.

As the *Sydney* steamed into Alexandria she was met by a tremendous roar of acclamation from every sailor present.

Admiral Cunningham wrote:

'The credit for this successful and gallant action belongs mainly to Captain J.A. Collins, CB, Royal Australian Navy, who by his quick appreciation of the situation, offensive spirit and resolute handling of HMAS *Sydney*, achieved a victory over a superior force which had important strategical effects.'

Richard Pelvin, Wartime No 2 April 1998, The Sinking of the Bartolomeo Colleoni.

After her Mediterranean triumph the *Sydney* returned to Australia to receive a hero's welcome in February 1941. The cruiser also received a new captain. The popular and experienced John Collins was sent to a posting at Singapore and replaced by Captain Joseph Burnett. Captain

Burnett received much praise from his superiors and had served in the navy since 1913. In 1939 he was on the Naval Staff where he proved efficient and hard working. When he was appointed to the command of *Sydney* there was only one thing he lacked: combat experience.

It was HMAS *Sydney's* misfortune to come up against a commander with a great deal more experience and cunning – Fregattenkapitan Theodor Detmers. When the German Kreigsmarine was preparing for the Second World War its leaders knew they would not be able to match the Allies for conventional naval strength. A policy of setting raiders out onto the high sea was adopted. Fast battle cruisers would patrol the world's oceans, pouncing on unescorted transports. Another tactic was to send out armed merchantmen to ambush and prey on shipping. By providing a multiplicity of threats it was presumed the Allied navies would have to spend inordinate resources chasing down these elusive predators.

Only the most promising captains were chosen for these commands and Detmers was to prove his skill and iron nerve. In 1921 he had joined the navy and spent much of his time on torpedo boats and destroyers. In 1940 he had commanded a destroyer during the invasion of Norway and soon after he was given the command of *Kormoran*.

This ship was a testament to German ingenuity. Outwardly the vessel appeared as a civilian merchantman. It flew Dutch colours and identified itself as the *Straat Malakka*. But behind hatches and panels, and on counterweighted platforms, this innocent-looking ship was armed with a deadly array of ordinance. There were six 15cm guns, six torpedo tubes and 300 sea mines used to play havoc in Allied shipping lanes. At the captain's word hatch covers would drop, panels over the quarterdeck and forecastle would be raised and the six deadly weapons, crewed and loaded, would be ready to fire. Since January 1941 the auxiliary cruiser had sent at least ten merchant ships to the bottom of the ocean.

It was this wolf in sheep's clothing that was sighted by *Sydney* on 19 November 1941. At 4.00p.m., off the West Australian coast, the Australian cruiser sighted the *Kormoran*, which immediately turned to the setting sun. The *Sydney* pursued and sent signals to the vessel to halt and identify itself. By 5.30p.m. Burnett's ship had, for some inexplicable reason, drawn almost alongside the German raider. Detmers knew that his only chance to escape was to get close to the Allied cruiser and pour shells and torpedoes into its side in a surprise attack. While Burnett could have kept his distance and sent an armed boat or even his scout plane to ascertain the true nature of the suspicious craft, instead he played right into Detmer's hand.

Only a small stretch of sea separated the two vessels when Burnett made his last, fatal, error. All Allied and neutral craft had particular secret signals to prove their bona fides. Burnett ordered the signal 'Show your secret sign.'

Detmers had no such sign; at 5.50p.m. he showed his true colours.

In the blink of an eye the peaceful scene was transformed into a full scale battle. As the Dutch colours were struck and a German flag was hoisted, *Kormoran*'s guns were revealed and they immediately began pumping shells into the *Sydney*. The RAN ship's bridge was almost destroyed and in a matter of minutes the two fore turrets and the rearmost turret with their six 5.9 inch guns were put out of action. Only Turret X was able to return fire and that caused some damage to the raider's funnel and engine room. At least Burnett had placed all of his crew in action stations, but tragically the initial RAN shots went high. To make matters worse for the Australians several torpedoes slammed into *Sydney*'s hull, making her begin to settle by the bows.

With this damage the *Sydney* sought to break off the battle, although as she moved away from her foe, four torpedoes were launched at the *Kormoran*. None of these scored a hit.

By 6.25p.m. the last shell was fired by *Kormoran*. She had hit the *Sydney* hundreds of times but was herself crippled. Detmers ordered the ship be abandoned, and as the crew boarded their lifeboats they could see flashes of light on the horizon as *Sydney* moved away.

In one of the great tragedies of the war, the RAN's pride sank with all 635 hands on board. It is still a mystery why not one sailor survived, but it could be in part due to the fact that no rescue operation was launched until five days after the battle. Rescue was only begun when the first boats containing the crew of the German raider were saved. From the *Kormoran*, 317 of the approximately 400 man crew were rescued.

Only in 2008 were the wrecks of the two ships found. *Sydney* still had 5 of her 8 lifeboats present on board, indicating that the order to abandon ship was never given. Why is that? Nobody is sure but it is possible that the crew managed to get fires under control and restore a semblance of stability before some kind of disaster struck, sending her down almost instantaneously. Some small pieces of debris and perhaps one dead sailor were all that were recovered in 1941.

Captain Burnett should have read up on his history. In World War I the original HMAS *Sydney* destroyed a similar German raider called the *Emden*. He stayed out of range from the German's cannon, forcing her to run aground as a burning hulk.

END IN THE DESERT – THE BATTLE OF EL ALAMEIN

If a man can be measured by his achievements, so can an army. The Australians had held out against fierce odds in Tobruk for more than six months. They were relieved by South African and English forces. By June 1942 the garrison had been built up to 33,000 men and included a South African infantry division and a British guards brigade.

During Rommel's offensive in June 1942, Tobruk was again encircled. This time Rommel captured the entire garrison within three days and forced the harbour's surrender on 21 June 1942!

Without the strategic thorn in his side, Rommel was able to push on through the border of Egypt and only came to a stop before the seemingly insignificant railroad town of El Alamein.

It seemed that Rommel was within spitting distance of a major strategic victory. Time after time he had broken through British defensive lines. It seemed that nothing stood between him and Alexandria and the Suez Canal. In Berlin fantastical plans were considered which would see Rommel link up with the Germans fighting on the Eastern Front and seizing the vital oil fields that kept the Allied war machine flowing.

It was not to be. After the Battle of the Coral Sea (8 May 1942) and the Battle of Midway (7 June 1942) General Macarthur had assured the Australian government that they no longer had to fear an invasion by the Japanese. The Australian government had been pressing for the return of the 9th Division to Australian shores, but with General Blamey's recommendation they instead released it for the action against Rommel.

From 25 June the divisional columns proceeded from their positions beyond Alexandria towards the front. The three brigades with attached AT and artillery assets thundered to the west along the coast road. To the Australians it seemed that the entire British Army was retreating in the other direction, but on closer inspection it proved to be the rear area squaddies bugging out from the front. The Desert Air Force, well supplied from the fields at Alexandria, kept the Luftwaffe from attacking the massed columns. These included the 3rd RAAF with their Kittyhawks, recently moved from the Syrian battlefield.

How Rommel must have cursed! Just as he launched an offensive around the flank of the British defences in early July, his intelligence reported that his old nemesis – General Moreshead's 9th Division – was moving into position.

Occupying crucial defensive positions on the Ruweisat Ridge, the Australian brigades set to knocking the Axis forces about. Battle hardened and refreshed after many months recuperating behind the line, the division had lost none of its fighting spirit.

On the night of 7-8 July the Australians launched a raid deep into the Axis position, destroying a battery of guns and inflicting many causalities.

A more ambitious attacked was launched on 10 July, when the 26th Brigade's three battalions seized a high point along the coast and destroyed Rommel's radio interception unit while taking more than 1,000 prisoners.

The high ground, known as Point 33, dominated the surrounding terrain. Rommel was desperate to get it back.

The next week saw the brigade fighting off numerous attacks. As the German panzers from the 90th Light and the 15th Panzer came up the coast, they were hurled at the Australian defences. Whole regiments of Italian foot were trucked in to the attack, well supported by massed Stuka formations. Groups of 20, 30 and 40 tanks tried to break through. The three Australian infantry battalions were well supported by 10 and 11 batteries of the 2nd/3rd Anti-Tank Regiment, just as they had been in Tobruk. The gunners were no longer forced to rely on captured Italian 47mm guns and most batteries had eight of the modern 6 pdrs supported by eight 2 pdrs or American 37mm anti-tank guns.

Having being the first AT regiment to stop the Blitzkrieg, the gunners knew how to get the best out of their equipment. The 6 pdrs used dominating terrain features to pick off tanks at long range. The weaker 2 pdrs were dug in on reverse slopes and heavily camouflaged. Their crew required iron nerves. Bombardier Muffet, supporting the 2/48th Battalion, had a hand in blunting a panzer attack with his 2 pdr anti-tank gun. As a platoon of Panzer IIIs approached his position, he waited until the last moment before opening fire. He managed to knock out three tanks before the fourth put a high explosive shell into his position, wounding or killing the entire crew.

In another notable incident four Mark IVs were knocked out and 'brewed up'.

The Germans were masters at recovering knocked out tanks and putting them back into action. If they were 'brewed up' the vehicles became just so much scrap metal. By 16 July the Afrika corps broke off their attacks. Surrounding the Australian salient were at least 40 totally destroyed Axis tanks. They would not see combat again. Axis forces lost 3,708, captured as prisoners, during this time.

The Alamein position was crucial as it was one of the few locations on the North African coast that did not have an open flank. The southern flank was guarded by the impassable Qattara Depression while to the north was the Mediterranean Sea. Rommel could not use his superior tactical mobility. What's more his supply lines were stretched, while the British had a short trip from the warehouses and ports of Alexandria.

Soon after these battles Winston Churchill visited the Desert Theatre. He took time to visit General Morsehead. Here he acknowledged that the 9th had 'stemmed the tide.'

Churchill made another contribution to the theatre – he appointed Lieutenant General Bernard Montgomery to command the 8th Army. Montgomery had 'made his bones' in the hectic withdrawal to Dunkirk in 1940. As the commander of 3rd Division he had held his brigades well in hand and erected a defensive line that halted the careening panzers, allowing the bulk of the British Army to escape.

Over the next three months both armies massed troops for a final desert showdown.

The forces on either side dwarfed earlier encounters. On the last day of August Rommel launched his last offensive to seize Egypt. It foundered on the defences erected by Montgomery on Alam el Halfa Ridge.

The Germans retired to lick their wounds and prepare for the inevitable counterstroke.

Montgomery was determined to throw the Axis forces out of North Africa. The Australians were to play a crucial role in his offensive.

The scale of the battlefield was like no other seen in the desert before. The 50 kilometre long front lines were packed with massed artillery and anti-tank guns defended on each front, and more than 300,000 men prepared to do battle.

1,000 Allied tanks confronted 500 German and Italian panzers.

The role of the Australians at the north of the battlefield, in the terrain they had seized in July, was to wear away the German and Italian defences. Their proximity to the coast road meant they were a constant threat and Montgomery hoped that the 9th would attract the bulk of the German reserves, allowing for a breakout against diminished Axis reserves. His forecast proved successful and as the battle wore on both the 21st and the 15th Panzer were used to contain the Australians. At one stage it was estimated that 90 'runners' were operating on the 9th Division's front.

On the night of 23rd October 1942 a massed barrage of artillery crashed into the Axis positions – the Battle of El Alamein had begun.

Montgomery's plan called for three stages of operations. First was the 'Break In' where minefields would be penetrated and the Axis defences engaged. Second came the 'Dog Fight' or 'Crumbling', which involved the destruction of enemy infantry formations along with any armoured reserves that came to their aid. Lastly was the 'Pursuit' where the last enemy armour would have been defeated and the remnants mopped up.

As the diggers advanced from their positions they had formidable defences to overcome. For two months the enemy infantry had been digging in. Minefields were often more than a kilometre deep and protected by well sited posts containing mortars, machine guns and anti-tank weapons. Wires, booby trapped with a devilish array of explosives, protected the emplacement. To the rear, massed artillery stood poised to bring murderous barrages down on the attacking infantry, while dug in deadly 88s could knock out any armour from a distance of two kilometres.

Over the next two days 30th Corps, which included the 9th, fought its way forward and seized all of the objectives assigned to it. New Axis defence lines were erected to hold them in check. Forces to the south received a drubbing from the defenders and had been stopped in their tracks. Montgomery ordered the Australians forward again on 28 October. So much German armour was drawn to their front that Montgomery decided to alter his entire plan. The Allied breakout was moved from the coast road to the centre of the battlefield.

On 30 October a salient was formed when the Australians seized a portion of the coast road, cutting off enemy troops to the east. Here they fought in what could only be termed a cauldron. A total of 25 attacks were beaten off as massed German artillery and armour sought to retake the terrain by attacking from all directions. Two whole German divisions launched furious attacks with the last of their runners.

Tiny features indistinguishable on any map became focal points for the carnage of battle. Thompson's Post, the Fig Orchard, the Blockhouse and the Saucer became the blood soaked target for a storm of bombs, shells and bullets as the Australians grimly hung on to their newly won real estate.

On 31 October more attacks were launched by the tired battalions. The losses to the Australians were horrendous. The 2/48th had entered the battle with almost 700 men. By this date it had 41 men combat ready.

Not only the infantry suffered. The losses to 2nd/3rd Anti-Tank Regiment supporting the foot brigades illustrate their importance in holding off the Germans. In 13 days fighting they sustained 107 casualties, including 23 killed. Thirty-six of their anti-tank guns, more than half of their complement, were knocked out and 34 vehicles were destroyed on minefields or by shells and bombs.

Over the entrance way to the 9th Division's cemetery at Tobruk is an inscription by the British: 'They fought themselves and their enemy to a standstill until flesh and blood could stand no more, then they went on fighting.'

No truer words were ever spoken. But their sacrifice was not in vain. On 2 November an immense artillery barrage broke out to the south. Operation Supercharge, Montgomery's great breakout, had begun. With his mobile reserves committed to the salient near the coast road there was little Rommel could do; by 4 November the Axis lines were torn open and the Africa Korps, with 20 remaining tanks, began a retreat that would not stop until Axis forces surrendered in Tunis on 13 May 1943.

After the battle Montgomery declared that the Australians had been 'magnificent.' He visited Morsehead and gave his personal thanks. They were well deserved. In the time between 23 October and 5 November the Division had suffered 620 killed, 1,944 wounded and 130 taken prisoner – one fifth of the 8th Army's butcher's bill.

The 6th and 7th Divisions had already left the Middle East for the Pacific. After Alamein the 9th was withdrawn from the front and had a final farewell parade at Gaza airport on 22 December. By January the division was steaming for home.

Fortunately for the British Empire, the Australians had been able to go toe-to-toe with one of Germany's greatest fighters. They had stopped the German Blitzkrieg and had then been instrumental in smashing it. The tide had turned and the Germans would never again regain the strategic initiative in the Mediterranean.

CHAPTER 9

WORLD WAR II –
PACIFIC ONSLAUGHT

While the threat from the Fascist powers of Europe seemed somehow remote from Australia's shores, there was a much more tangible danger to the north. As early as 1933 the world had been hearing of the dreadful atrocities carried out by the Imperial Japanese armed forces in China.

Once seen as an ally of the Entente powers in World War I, Japan's government had fallen under a military junta which was becoming increasingly aggressive. All aspects of Japanese society had become militarised and the warrior code of Bushido was fiercely adhered to by millions of men in the Japanese military.

The 'warrior's code' put military glory above all else. Japanese soldiers seemed like automatons who were conditioned to follow whatever orders were given by their superiors. This fanaticism, combined with a savage racism, had led to incidents such as the Rape of Nanking (1937) where up to 300,000 innocent civilians and captured Chinese soldiers were brutally massacred. The Japanese press had revelled in the 'heroic' actions of their military. Officers had indulged in competitions to see who could decapitate the most Chinese in an hour. Infantry privates had used countless numbers of Chinese in live bayonet practice.

The League of Nations, a body supposedly set up to preserve peace, had been powerless to stop this oriental fury.

In the late 1930s the Australian government became aware that Japan's military ambitions were trending southward. It had been reluctant to send too many troops to the European theatre due to the impending threat from Japan. Under pressure from the British government after the catastrophic defeats in France in 1940, four divisions of the AIF were sent to do Churchill's bidding. This left Australia almost denuded of quality military formations and its possessions to the north had only poorly equipped and trained units.

Then in December 1941 the Japanese storm broke. In a Pacific Blitzkrieg that almost eclipsed the Wehrmacht's achievements, much of South East Asia fell.

Vietnam, Cambodia, Laos, the Philippines and the Dutch East Indies (Indonesia) were among the countries conquered. Woe betide any inhabitants of Chinese descent in these territories; hundreds of thousands felt the full racial hatred of the Japanese conquerors.

The British possession of Malaya and Singapore fell, with upwards of 15,000 Australians going into the bag. Treated with contempt by their Japanese conquerors, almost a third would never make it home. Years of brutal treatment and deprivation would break many of the survivors, both physically and mentally.

There was a worse fate for the defenders of Rabaul. In a catalogue of unbounded horror almost all were executed or drowned at sea. Whispers of these fouls atrocities reached Australia.

That was not all that reached Australia. Rabaul became the heart of Japanese plans to conquer the rest of the Pacific. Bombers launched from the base began terror raids across the top end of Australia.

Submarines set out from Rabaul to patrol off the coastlines of Australia attacking shipping and even penetrating into Sydney Harbour.

It could only be imagined, with dread and loathing, what would happen should Australia fall to the 'ravening oriental horde' to the north! Allied propaganda managed to further stoke the fears of the Australian public.

In early 1942 it seemed they were unstoppable. Australian society would have to rapidly industrialise this meet this threat. Two home grown inventions were built to fight the Japanese menace: the Sentinel tank and the Owen machine gun.

AUSSIE INITIATIVE: THE SENTINAL TANK

As war clouds gathered over Europe, the Australian Government realised that it had no armoured capability or the means to produce it. It was equipped with four Vickers medium tanks built in 1928, and ten Vickers light tanks armed only with machine guns. The government also realised that it was unlikely that our greatest ally, Great Britain, would be in a position to supply the Australian Army with any tanks in the near future.

Undaunted, it was decided that Australia needed its own home grown tank, and in a remarkable display of ingenuity the Sentinel was produced within 22 months. Although the tank never saw action, it would have been more than a match for any Japanese tanks it might have encountered on the battlefield. The Sentinel AC 1 (Australian Cruiser 1) was, in many ways, ahead of its time.

An engineer was sent to America to examine their tank industry and an experienced designer was obtained from England. The two experts then took the army's specifications and began designing the Sentinel. This excellent vehicle had a cast steel turret and hull with a relatively heavy armour of up to 65mm. Not only was the casting process state-of-the-art but the faces were well sloped, something that many other nations did not build into their designs until 1943. A reliable suspension system was adopted and three car engines were linked to provide a cost effective power plant. The British 2 pounder AT gun was mounted in the turret along with two .303 machine guns. By January 1942 the first tanks were rolling off production lines specifically built for them. New versions were soon produced, mounting the devastating 25 pdr howitzer and even the 17 pdr anti-tank gun. The designers had built a wide superstructure allowing the up gunning to take place without affecting the performance and stability of the vehicle. One particularly lethal version had two 25 pounders mounted in the turret. Just over 60 vehicles were built.

Sadly, this little gem of Australian design never got to the battlefield as American armour and the British Matilda began to arrive in large numbers. No doubt the Sentinel would have made short work of any lightly armoured Japanese tanks, and given them a healthy respect for Australian wartime manufacturing.

TWIN DISASTERS – RABAUL AND SINGAPORE

Rabaul, on the easternmost point of the Island of New Britain, was the perfect location for the Japanese to set up a base to launch their attacks towards Australia. By the time the war ended 100,000 Japanese naval and army personnel were stationed there.

But first the Japanese had to take the port, and on 23 January they did just that. The Australian government had one battalion – named Lark Force, of approximately 1,400 men – to defend this vital location. The Japanese sent in upwards of 9,000 men along with a carrier fleet to seize the vital territory. After patchy resistance the Australians were given the command to scatter – every man for himself.

Over the next few weeks the Japanese managed to round up most of the fleeing garrison.

The fate of the captured Australians proved that this was no gentleman's war. After about a week wandering through the jungle, approximately 140 prisoners were seized by Japanese soldiers as they emerged onto the coast near a settlement known as Tol Plantation.

At first it seemed that the Japanese would treat their prisoners honourably. This illusion did not last for long. Over the next few days the captives were killed in a range of bestial executions. Medics had their Red Cross brassards ripped off and badges of rank were cut from uniforms as souvenirs. Batches of prisoners were tied together in small groups and herded into the jungle, where they were tortured and killed with bayonet or bullet. Groups of Japanese would emerge from the jungle, wiping their bayonets, before

Bren gunner Private S. Henry of King Island, Tasmania, a member of the 3rd Battalion, the Royal Australian Regiment, waits with his platoon for a briefing from his Company Commander during a night patrol into the Chinese lines in Korea, 1951.

A cheery South Korean interpreter carries his nation's flag as he advances with Australians of the 3rd Battalion, Royal Australia Regiment (RAR). The Australians are shown wearing the American winter-proofed clothing which they adopted as the cold became more intense.

Military Police of the main body of Australian troops bound for Malaya boarding the troopship Georgic, October 1955. All carry revolvers and are dressed in khaki drill.

Australian Prime Minister Harold Hold (left) walks down the steps of Old Parliament House with his special guest, US President Lyndon Baines in October 1966. Johnson became the first sitting President to visit Australia when he honoured an invitation from Holt after Australia supported LBJ's decision to send troops to the Vietnam War.

Anti-Vietnam War protesters lay down in the streets of Sydney to stop the motorcade carrying US President Lyndon Johnson, 1966. NSW Premier Robert Askin, who was sitting beside Johnson, famously told the driver to 'run the bastards over.'

Australian troops waiting for word of their movement, Vietnam, late 1960s.

Troops of the 1st Battalion RAR in Vietnam.

Entertainer Lorrae Desmond entertains Australian troops in Vietnam. While an entertaining diversion, the thought that the conflict was still uncomfortably close was forefront in everyone's minds.

The funeral of Private Errol Noack, the first Australian conscripted soldier to be killed on the battlefields of Vietnam. Noack, from Adelaide, was conscripted with the first wave in 1965. He was killed after just serving 11 days in Vietnam.

An Australian soldier investigates a Viet Kong escape tunnel, Vietnam.

Hercules crewmen feeding South Vietnamese war orphans at Son Nhut airport in Saigon in April 1975. A total of 288 war orphans were evacuated to Australia as South Vietnamese resistance to the Viet Cong collapsed.

Signalman Anthony Colbert, a member of the 40-strong Australian Army Communications Contingent, provides a vital communications link between arriving French United troops and their headquarters in the Cambodian capital Phnom Penh as part of the United Nations advance mission in Cambodia (UNAMIC), early 1990s.

An Australian soldier of 1RAR guarding food supplies on their way to starving people in Somalia, 1993.

Smiling Somali children welcoming Australian soldier Sergeant Peter Watson. The Australian Army, which included a reduced squadron of armoured personnel carrier (APC's), was committed to a 17-week tour of duty in Somalia in the 1990s.

Australian soldiers with 'Operation Solace' in Somalia, which ensured starving people received food supplies, fly the flag in their camp, 1993.

After more than 75 years, one of the 60,000 Australians who lost their lives in the First World War leaves France for his final resting place in the Australian War Memorial, 1993. The body of the unknown Australian soldier was recovered from Adelaide Cemetery near Villers-Bretonneux in France. This photograph was taken by Corporal Robyn White, of Army Public Relations, and won the Damien Parer Photographic Award for 1994.

WORLD WAR II – PACIFIC ONSLAUGHT

returning with more captives. Many cruel games were played. Australians were asked if they preferred the bayonet or the bullet, before being killed using the opposite method to their request. Several who tried to escape were covered in pig lard and burnt alive in the humpy where they had sheltered.

Remarkably, some survivors emerged from the bloody jungle. Private Billy Cook was bayoneted in the back at least six times. He continued to breathe and received four more wounds, one of which went through his ear into his mouth.

Word gradually trickled back to Australia – any illusions about the horror that the Japanese would inflict on their defeated enemies were demolished forever.

The fate of the other captives and civilians was perhaps worse. Locked into the hold of a tramp steamer, approximately 1,000 died when the ship was torpedoed while they were in transit to Japan to serve as slave labour.

SINGAPORE

The Australian public had no real idea of the strategic importance of Rabaul. They did know full well the importance of England's largest military base in the East – Singapore. The fall of Singapore on 15 February 1942 was a serious blow to Australian morale. Years of British propaganda had painted a portrait of an invulnerable 'Gibraltar of the East.' The problem was Singapore's defences were built to resist a seaborne attack. The Japanese attacked from the landward side.

The ill-fated Malaya campaign began with the sinking, on 10 December 1941, of the battleship *Prince of Wales* and the battle cruiser *Repulse*. The two capital ships, the cream of the British Navy, had been steaming north of Singapore with the intention of engaging the Japanese invasion fleet, which had been landing Japanese troops in the north for several days. In several well coordinated waves, the Japanese torpedo bombers sent both ships to the bottom of the ocean with massive loss of life. The British Eastern Fleet was neutered, giving the Japanese a free hand in Malaya.

They deployed their hand brilliantly. Pouring down the peninsula, the battle hardened Japanese proved more than a match for the ill-led Commonwealth forces. The British were bound to the roads of the peninsula and their defence largely rested on setting up roadblocks to combat the Japanese. Being old hands at jungle warfare, the Japanese would fix the Allied roadblocks with tanks and artillery while units moved to outflank the British, who were then forced to withdraw.

Remarkably, the Japanese used the bicycle as a weapon of war. Their bike mounted troops created an oriental style Blitzkrieg.

The Japanese had total air superiority and reduced Singapore to a blazing, demoralised wreck. When the Japanese closed up to the Johore Strait on 31 January, their remorseless pressure had already broken the will of the British to resist, even though they vastly outnumbered their oriental foe. Eighty-five thousand combat troops, including the Australian 8th Division awaited the inevitable attack.

On 8 February the Japanese launched consecutive attacks across the Johore Straits. The Australian 22nd Brigade managed to hold off the attacks in their sector but, as units on their flank caved in, was forced to withdraw.

On 15 February General Percival surrendered; 140,000 Empire troops had been defeated by half that number of Japanese.

Fifteen thousand Australians went into the bag. A third of those would die in Japanese captivity.

DEFENDING PAPUA NEW GUINEA

When the Japanese struck at Pearl Harbour in November 1941, the Australian government was worried. When Singapore fell soon afterwards they were mortified. The best troops that Australia had to offer were either fighting the Germans in the Mediterranean theatre or stewing in German and Japanese POW camps thanks to the bungling of the British High Command.

Prime Minister John Curtin was determined to bring back the troops to defend Australia. The 6th and 7th Divisions were pulled out of combat and began steaming towards the Pacific. Incredibly, Winston Churchill decided that the Australians would be best employed defending Ceylon and the Indian border with Burma. The American and British administrations had both agreed that Britain's war aims should take precedent over all other considerations. Curtin sent an urgent telegram to Churchill rerouting the divisions back to Australian waters.

Churchill said Curtin should sleep on it for five or so days and get back to him. Thankfully for Australia, Curtin refused to bow to Churchill's will, and soon the experienced troops were heading for home.

It is fortunate that they were. Australia was basically defenceless. A company of rusty mid war tanks, some squadrons of Wirraway trainers designated 'interceptors' and a brigade or two of 'choccos' was all that stood before the Asiatic horde descending from the north.

With the outbreak of war, the Australian government had embarked upon a two army policy. The Australian Imperial Force (AIF) would get the pick of the professional military personnel and equipment. It was intended to fight overseas, as the name suggests, for the defence of Australia's Imperial 'masters'. The best and brightest recruits over 21 were able to join this elite force.

Staying at home and intended as a reserve force were the militia. They were perceived as second stringers, callow youths from 17 to 20, pensioned off officers and patriotic wanabees who could only be dragooned into enlisting. The experiences of the 39th Battalion raised in Melbourne were perhaps typical of this service. Young men were convinced to join up and promised action, adventure and girls. Despite this prejudice, many militia units proved to be some of the finest fighting units in Australian history.

The militia received rudimentary training and even worse equipment. When the 39th first faced the Japanese, on the ridge above Kokoda, they did not even have entrenching tools! Many platoons were issued with World War I vintage Lewis machine guns and only managed to get modern Bren guns by purloining them.

The AIF called these militia battalions 'choccos'; it was presumed they would melt like chocolate once exposed to the heat.

Not many recruits read the fine print, which stated that as a militia force they could serve anywhere in Australian territories – including the 'Territory of Papua' taken from the Germans in World War I.

On 3 January 1942 the 39th and 53rd Battalions joined the 49th Battalion at Port Moresby. An insignificant town on the southern side of the Australian territory had suddenly assumed tremendous strategic significance. From its airfields the owner of this rare piece of flat ground could dominate the sea routes to Australia's eastern seaboard. The militia found that, rather than being engaged in glorious conquests, they were to be employed as navies. Hauling supplies and building airstrips in the baking tropical sun became their sole purpose in life. The Australian teenagers had been thrust into one of the most inhospitable environments on earth. One journalist picked up a militia man thumbing a ride. He was disgusted to see that the private's knees, elbows and ankles were covered in livid red insect bites that wept puss and blood. He advised the young man to stop scratching the sores. That was fine, explained the youth, he could stop scratching during the day – but he had no control over his hands while he was sleeping!

Japanese forces were getting closer and closer to Australia. On 23 January, Rabaul fell. Bombers from the newly captured territory bombed Port Moresby on 2 February. On 15 February 1942, Singapore fell.

The Japanese bombing of Port Moresby was a rude awakening for the choccos. They had been ordered to dig in previous to the attack but had been remarkably reluctant to do so. The sight of body parts being strewn across the airfields and dock areas led to the sudden realisation that they were at war. This message was rammed home with the bombing of Darwin.

THE BOMBING OF DARWIN

The shell-shocked Australian public hadn't even begun to digest the traumatic news out of Singapore when even worse arrived: the full fury of the Imperial Japanese Air Force descended on Darwin on 19 February 1942.

The consequences of the Australian government's acquiescence to British strategic demands were apparent in Darwin. Despite its immense strategic importance, the defences were seemingly inspired by the Keystone Cops. There were only 18 heavy AA guns manned by troops with poor training due to their limited ammunition. These were supported by a small number of World War I vintage Lewis guns for low flying targets. The RAF fighter defence was even worse. No 12 Squadron was equipped with six Wirraway trainers that had recently been reclassified as fighters. Fortunately for the pilots of these antiquated jalopies, none were serviceable. Ten USAAF P-40s were available, because they happened to be stopping over en route to Java.

Facing this motley assortment was the cream of the Japanese Fleet, air arm. The dive bombers, torpedo bombers and fighters from the carriers *Akagi*, *Kaga*, *Hiryu* and *Soryu*, fresh from their triumph at Pearl

Harbour, were about to descend on Darwin. Fifty-four land based bombers, operating out of bases to the north, were to assist.

Newspaper reports from the time recounted the horrific effect of the attack. At about 10.00a.m. the first of the 188 carrier planes appeared over Darwin. No air raid alarm had been sounded despite several warnings of the impending attack.

These attacks concentrated on the shipping in the harbour and the town infrastructure. Only when the first ships were hit did the alarm finally sound. Six ships were sunk in Darwin Harbour, and at least ten others suffered severe damage. Dock workers were killed and all of the P-40s were shot down or destroyed on the ground.

Journalists reported that seemingly every administration building in Darwin was destroyed and early estimates put the losses at 250 people. Hundreds were wounded and, even four days later, at least 400 military personnel were missing. They had not of course been captured but had taken to the bush. One got as far as Adelaide. Many presumed the attack presaged an invasion and the single road south of Darwin was filled with fleeing civilians. Those who remained began looting deserted stores and pubs. The night soil carts were included in the rout and for more than a week those who remained in Darwin were without this precious service.

The second raid, that came in at approximately noon, concentrated on the RAAF base. Three hundred thousand rounds of ammunition, bombs and fuel dumps were destroyed as well as any remaining planes.

These were the first of 58 raids that occurred over the next two years. But none had the psychological impact of the 19 February raids.

THE INVASION OF PAPUA

13 March 1942 saw the Japanese get their first foothold on the island of Papua. Lae and Salamuau were captured and immediately converted into strategic assets by the Japanese.

Soon after, General Douglas MacArthur arrived in Australia and was given the strategic command of the theatre. Nestling into the bridal suite of a top Melbourne hotel, his first objective was to arrange for a piano to be delivered for his wife!

One of the most remarkable decisions of the war was made by MacArthur and his subservient Australian Subordinate General Blamey. The first AIF troops steamed into their homeland in March 1942. Rather than sending them north, the battalions began training north of Brisbane and were ordered to create the Brisbane Line, ready to ward off any invasion on the mainland.

MacArthur's folly was plain to see when the Japanese invasion fleet steamed from Rabaul with the intention of capturing Port Moresby. Fortunately, the fleet, with its hardened Japanese infantry ensconced in the bellies of their transports, was stopped at the Battle of Coral Sea.

The Royal Australian Navy played a big part in the fleet action that stopped the seaborne invasion of Port Moresby.

There is still confusion about Japanese intentions for the invasion of Australia. Millions of dollars of occupation notes were printed, and contingencies were put in place for the occupation of the north. The Australian Government had its own contingency plan ready, drawn up, and issued to all government departments. It was prepared to set up the so called Brisbane Line and defend the East Coast from that city while torching all infrastructure to the north.

There is no doubt about the Japanese intentions for Papua New Guinea. The Japanese were determined to seize the archipelago. They would use bases there, particularly Port Moresby, as a springboard for further conquests into the Solomon Islands, the New Hebrides, Fiji and ultimately as far east as Samoa. This would allow them to interdict supplies coming into Australia from America and England, and force her out of the war.

CORAL SEA

The Battle of the Coral Sea is of historical importance for two reasons. It was the first fleet action where there was no direct gunfire between opposing fighting ships. Land based and seaborne planes mounted all of the attacks. It was also the first time that the IJ (Imperial Japanese) Navy was fought to a standstill since the Russo-Japanese war of 1905.

The Japanese gave command of the operation to seize Port Moresby, codenamed MO, to Vice Admiral Shigeyoshi Inouye. He had at his command several carrier divisions which included the Japanese carriers *Shoho*, *Shokaku* and *Zuikaku*. Their role was to operate around the Solomon Islands and defeat any Australian or American naval assets that sought to impede the Port Moresby Invasion Group, which was to proceed from Rabaul, New Britain, through the Jomard Passage and on to the weakly held capital of Papua. This Port Moresby Invasion Group consisted of 11 transports with a heavy destroyer screen. Bombers operating out of Rabaul were to support this group.

Task Force 17, under the command of Rear Admiral Fletcher, was given the job of stopping the seaborne invasion of the Port Moresby. He had two carriers, the Yorktown and Lexington, with supporting cruisers and destroyers. Several hundred American bombers were also operating out of Australia and Papua. The carrier groups were tasked with derailing the rather complex Japanese battle plan.

On 3 May 1942, MO was kicked off. Over the next four days Japanese and American carrier groups launched repeated air attacks against each other. Inouye's intelligence had predicted there would be one carrier at the most to oppose his forces, so it came as something of a shock when Task Force 17 proved to be much stronger than predicted.

Crucial to Fletcher's plan was the role of the Support Group under the Australian Rear Admiral John G Crace (b. 1887 d. 1968). The heart of this group were the Australian cruisers *Australia* and *Hobart*, and the USS *Chicago*.

On the morning of 7 May, Fletcher sent Crace and his command south to guard the Jomard Passage past the east coast of Papua and ensure that the Japanese Port Moresby Invasion Group didn't get to Port Moresby. This was a risky move as the group was without air cover. Fletcher had picked the right man for the job.

Crace immediately ordered his ships to take up a diamond shaped anti-aircraft formation and adopted a policy of shoot first and ask questions later. On 7 May one attack was seen off without loss before another larger group of Japanese aircraft attacked at 1500 hours. Crace ordered his ships to steam directly at the incoming aircraft to give them as small a target as possible. They then began evasive maneuverers while pouring intensive ack ack salvoes onto the Japanese bombers. The Japanese were taken aback and released their torpedoes too early, to no effect. The torpedo bombers then strafed the cruisers, but were seen off with heavy loss. Crace's small task force had acted as a decoy and drawn the bulk of the Japanese carrier planes away from the American carriers, in futile attacks

The threat was not over. Waves of high altitude bombers out of Rabaul attacked and concentrated on HMAS *Australia*. Crace's expert handling prevented any damage.

His fluid handling of his fleet had also unnerved the Japanese high command. The returning Japanese planes returned with claims that a large battleship group was patrolling the Jomard Passage.

On the same day there was another blow to Japanese ambitions. The *Soho* was sunk by American carrier borne aircraft.

These pressures were too much for Admiral Inouye. He ordered the Moresby Invasion Force to turn away back north until Crace's 'battleships' and the American carriers had been dealt with. This was never to happen. Although *Lexington* was sunk, the rest of the Allied forces had extracted too heavy a toll on Japanese planes and ships for the action to continue. Both sides retired to lick their wounds. Strategically, the Japanese seaborne assaults had been halted.

There was another strategic impact of the Battle of the Coral Sea. The two surviving Japanese carriers were not able to replenish their air wings in time for the Battle of Midway. They might have made the difference between Japanese victory and defeat in this crucial battle.

The Japanese realised that they could not launch a seaborne invasion of Port Moresby and would have to go over the Owen Stanley Mountains across the Kokoda track. The Allied commanders were keen to ignore this threat.

Finally, in late June, Macarthur did make one concession to the Japanese threat to the north: one militia battalion, the 39th, was ordered to cross the Owen Stanley ranges, fortify Kokoda and then move on to seize Buna on the coast. From here MacArthur intended to raid Japanese possessions to the north.

It was lucky that he did make this decision.

The Japanese naval command decided that the army could take Port Moresby by advancing over the Kokoda track.

On 20 July, two thousand elite Japanese jungle fighters, the 144th Regiment, with a company of marines from the 5th Sasebo Naval Landing Force, were dispatched from Rabaul to seize three towns adjacent to the northern end of the Kokoda track. Buna, Sanananda and Gona were small missionary towns. The Japanese seized them without opposition and began unloading.

These troops of the South Seas Force, under the overall command of General Tomitaro Horii, were perfectly suited to their task. Each man was a veteran and had the latest equipment designed for jungle warfare.

The 70mm Battalion Gun Type 92 was one of the most successful infantry support weapons of the war. With its outsize wheels and short barrel, the gun looked almost conical. Its simple appearance belied the sophisticated nature of the piece. It could be broken up into small loads for transportation through the roughest terrain, while numerous holes and brackets on the carriage through which long poles could be inserted meant it was perfect for shoot and scoot missions. The crew would fire off a volley of harassing rounds and pick up the entire weapon before moving it to another position. The high elevation allowed it to give close support up to 100 metres, and the effective HE shells were particularly damaging with plunging fire through jungle canopies. The shrapnel shell was lethal when used to break up close assaults. Another remarkable feature was the cranked axle, which allowed the wheels to be folded under the belly of the weapon so it could be fired from ground level. With the shield removed it was almost impossible to detect. Light pack mounted howitzers could be hauled, disassembled, through the harshest terrain. Once called upon, the 70mm guns were rapidly assembled and could pour high trajectory shells onto any defenders.

The other battle winning device was the so called 'knee mortar'. This fine piece of hardware could throw smoke bombs, shells and flares out to 650 metres as soon as contact was made. Weighing in at four and a half kilos, it gave each section immediate fire support. Several Australian troops were injured using captured examples. While the base plate looked as if it was intended to be fired from the thigh above the knee, any soldier foolish enough to give it a try was soon on his way to the rear with a shattered leg bone.

At least the Australian Bren Light Machine Gun (LMG) built in Melbourne was far superior to the Japanese variants. The type 11 Nambu and the Type 96 machine guns fired a smaller calibre bullet (6.5mm), although they were prone to jamming. At least they both had a bayonet lug so they could be hoisted up by the gunner to use like a spear if it jammed!

Each man was dressed in camouflaged uniforms with netting over the helmet and often around the body. Australians testified that approaching Japanese would often be seen marching in column before suddenly melting into the terrain.

Any Europeans unfortunate enough to be caught once the South Seas force landed on 21 July faced almost certain death. Two missionaries, Nurse May Hayman and teacher Mavis Parkinson, fled from their lowland mission towards the inland mountains. They were soon rounded up and interrogated. Shortly afterwards the women were taken into a small clearing by four soldiers who dug a shallow grave. Mavis made an attempt to run, but got a bayonet in her side before being bundled into the 3 foot hole. May, incapacitated by fear, had a towel wrapped around her head before having her throat cut.

These seasoned warriors, victors of countless campaigns, firmly believed in the concept of Senjinkun; the Japanese soldier was ordered not to surrender or retreat. They, and the following 10,000 men, had no doubt that they would be able to march to Kokoda, fight their way over the Owen Stanley mountains and seize Port Moresby. Hori expected it would take eight days, and as the first wave of 900 men moved off from the coast they all had eight days ammo and rations strapped to makeshift frames.

There was however one hitch in Hori's plan: the 39th Militia Battalion of approximately 490 poorly armed, green teenagers. For the past few weeks they had been straggling over the Owen Stanley mountains and only one company was up front on 23 July ready to meet the advancing Japanese. The 39th did have one advantage. At the end of June, 18 veteran combat officers from the 7th AIF Division had been posted to the battalion. They took up command positions within companies and their experience proved crucial in the coming weeks.

On 23 July the Japanese marines' advance party were marching along the lowlands out of Gona. Lying in wait were elements of D Company 39th Battalion. As soon as the Japanese came in range, walking in column while pushing their cycles, the Australians let fly. The leading elements of the Japanese were knocked for six. Maybe fifteen went down, while the rest scattered into the tall Kunai grass on either side of the track and returned fire.

Almost immediately mortar shells started exploding around the Australians. These were followed by the whistle of heavy artillery. While the lead elements were pinned down, other parties began working around the flanks of the diggers. Knowing the score from experiences in Malaya, the platoon pulled out down prearranged escape routes and withdrew behind the next ambush site.

This set the scene for the days to come. Japanese columns would advance, with one or two men up front, to draw the enemy fire, before pouring down fire on the Australians. But it was no walk over for the veteran Nipponese fighters as they gradually pushed the choccos towards Kokoda. The militia battalion which had been treated with such scorn soon proved adept at jungle warfare. Crossings over water features were destroyed, holding up the pursuers. Troops would defend a position and pull out when artillery concentrations became too much. The choccos would then launch savage bayonet attacks to recapture the positions. The Australians had learnt that the Japanese would blanket suspected defensive positions with fire, seeking to tempt them to fire and reveal their positions. The diggers learnt to withhold their fire until the last moment. The thick jungle reduced visibility to less than a meter, perfect for a successful shot.

They had also become acclimatised to the rugged jungle conditions. Underwear were a thing of the past. Hot air built up in the crotch, causing abominably itchy rashes. Kit was trimmed to a minimum, with men sharing half a towel and a shaving kit. Beards were worn; it allowed at least one part of the face to be protected from the interminable flying biting insects. Why have a mess tin each when five blokes could eat in relays?

One example is illustrative of the 39th's burgeoning confidence in the once hostile environment. When the Japanese finally took Kokoda, with its precious airfield, on 28 July, the defenders managed to withdraw under the cover of a clinging mist. One Bren gun team, privates 'Snowy' Parr and 'Rusty' Hollow, decided to stay behind in defiance of orders and give the Japanese a parting gift. In the pre-dawn light the two men saw the Japanese gathering around the settlement's flag pole to haul up the Rising Sun flag. Picking their moment, the men fired off their magazines of .303 bullets into the close packed Japanese. They brought down at least a score.

The two men faded into the mist and rejoined their retreating comrades. Remarkably, while Maroubra Force, as it was known, only had a small number of men holding back the Japanese, the 144th estimated they were faced by 6,000 men who had inflicted 'unexpectedly heavy casualties.'

On 8 August the battalion even managed to retake Kokoda, sending the Japanese into a panicked, if temporary, retreat.

The Japanese were taking the offensive seriously and finally, with their entry into Kokoda on 28 July, the Allied high command did too. On 3 August the 21st Brigade from the 7th Division were finally ordered to Port Moresby.

There was still much hard fighting in store for the 39th. On 14 August they were forced out of Deniki and began a withdrawal to the next line of defence – Isurava.

This mountainous location thousands of feet above Deniki was almost impossible to reach for the exhausted militia men. When they finally arrived, the battalion was down to 250 men. Many were suffering from dengue fever, dysentery or malaria – some from all three. As the exhausted men scraped new defence positions, 6,000 Japanese, now commanded by General Hori in person, closed in to finish the job.

His one week plan had now stretched into three weeks, and the Japanese were not even half way to their objective. The Japanese general knew that his men were beginning to tire. Supplies were running low. Hori needed to get to Port Moresby in five days.

He launched what he thought would be the final offensive. In the nick of time, 2/14th Battalion of the 7th Division arrived. Other elements from the brigade came up and the militia and AIF forces united to fight together. There was no more talk of 'choccos'. The Victorian Militia had earned their comrades' undying respect.

In the days that followed, 1,700 Australians fought off 6,000 Japanese. Artillery supremacy and flanking moves proved the difference and the Australians withdrew on 31 August.

Little did the exhausted Australians realise that, as they were retreating, another brigade of the 7th Division was whipping the Japanese at Milne Bay. It was the first time in the war that a Japanese land assault was halted.

THE BATTLE OF MILNE BAY

Just as the Australians at Tobruk derailed Rommel's strategic plan, so the Australians at Milne Bay inflicted a strategic defeat on the warlords in Tokyo. The British General Slim said it best, with the observation that the Australian defenders 'first broke the spell of the invincibility of the Japanese Army.'

The Australians didn't only defeat the Japanese landing force – they destroyed them.

The Japanese high command was concerned with the slow progress of the Kokoda operation. When intelligence revealed that the Allies were building air strips in the Milne Bay area, it was decided to seize the position and use the airstrip to outflank the Allied defences. Milne Bay experiences some of the worst weather possible. Continuous soaking rain and extraordinarily high humidity were constant features of the landscape. Surrounding the bay were high mountains and a small flat coastal fringe that combined deep forest with glutinous mud. Numerous streams crossed the terrain, making movement difficult at the best of times. Only at the western end of the bay was there enough stable flat land to allow the airfields to be constructed.

The Australians realised the importance of the position. The 7th Militia Brigade had been reinforced with the elite 18th AIF Brigade – newly shipped to the Pacific after seeing off Rommel in Tobruk as part of the 7th Division. As well as some American Ack-Ack and engineers, the 75th and 76th RAAF Kitty Hawk Squadrons were operating on the air base. Milne Force was poised to give the Japanese a bloody nose.

Both the 75th and 76th RAAF Squadrons were decisive in the defence of both Port Moresby and Milne Bay.

The P-40 Kittyhawk was a rugged fighter with six 12.7mm guns in its wings. It also could carry a 454 kg bomb, making it a lethal ground attack plane.

The RAAF was initially expecting Spitfires from Britain, but with the urgency of the Papua invasion the 75th and 76th Squadrons were fortunate to be equipped with 25 P-40s originally destined for the Philippines. Rushed to the theatre with only seven days of training under their belts, many Kittyhawks were lost to accidents. It also appeared that they were outclassed by Japanese planes such as the Zero.

With experience, the aircrew began to appreciate the tough Kittyhawk and many successes against Japanese bombers and fighters were achieved. They were the decisive factor against the Japanese at Milne Bay and were able to negate the Japanese naval dominance, shooting up supplies and interdicting reinforcements. Eventually, eight Australian squadrons were equipped with the robust fighter; 840 were supplied to the RAAF.

THE ATTACK

On the night of 25 August, 2,000 veteran Japanese marines landed on the north coast of Milne Bay. Supported by naval gunfire and with armoured support, the Japanese began a rapid advance westward towards the airfields.

Using practiced tactics of outflanking and night marches, the Japanese were able to bring their localised superior numbers to push some of the Australian militia battalions back. But where the Japanese expected a swift assault to rapidly break through the Allied lines, continued heavy resistance from the Australian militia caused heavy casualties. P-40s from 75th and 76th Squadrons made daylight movement difficult. Several Japanese supply dumps were destroyed by the fighters and, most importantly, the Kittyhawks were instrumental in destroying the Japanese landing barges, preventing them from outflanking the Australian defence lines.

The fighting wasn't by any means one-sided. The Japanese were veteran jungle fighters. They could also call on a destroyer flotilla, which regularly poured heavy shell fire into the Australian positions.

On 28 August it seemed to the Japanese that they were on the cusp of victory. The marines had reached the eastern end of the airstrips, forcing the 75th and 76th Squadrons to pull out to Port Moresby. Over the next night 800 more infantry were landed for the final push.

Before dawn of 31 August, with artillery and mortar support, the Japanese unleashed successive banzai charges. In the past few had been able to resist these fanatical attacks. The Australians poured fire over the open terrain, decimating three charges. They were supported by American halftracks mounting 50cal machine guns, and ack-ack guns firing over open sights.

Faced with this storm of lead the attackers tried to outflank the Allied positions, but they were met by a dug in platoon that chewed them apart with well aimed Bren gun fire.

By dawn, bugle calls indicated that the Japanese were withdrawing. In just three hours, the last chance for Japanese domination of the Pacific had been destroyed.

The shell-shocked Japanese began a steady withdrawal to their original landing positions. They defended doggedly all the way and the Australians got their first taste of the fanatical code of bushido.

As the Australians walked across the scene of the Japanese repulse, they saw dozens of dead 'Japs' strewn across the airstrip. One man, apparently wounded, cried out to an Australian officer to help him. As he did, the Japanese sprang to life and hurled a grenade at the Australians, wounding several. After that the diggers took no chances. Any 'wounded' Japanese who gave the slightest twitch was dispatched with a bullet or bayonet. Dead Japanese were systematically bayoneted even if they appeared to be decomposing.

On the evenings of 5 and 6 September the last Japanese troops were evacuated. Out of 3,000 landed, slightly more than 1,000 unwounded soldiers escaped. The Australians and Americans suffered around 400 casualties.

PORT MORESBY IN SIGHT

Unaware of this reverse, Hori whipped his men into the pursuit of the retreating Australians. Any commander who dallied was removed in disgrace.

The seasoned Japanese General's dogged determination was to bear fruit in the next major confrontation. As the Japanese closed up on Brigade Hill (Efogi), Allied air supremacy began to take a toll on the Japanese. Undaunted, they once again sought to get behind the Australians, and very nearly succeeded in cutting off the entire Maroubra force. One company of Japanese got lost – and found itself looking over the Australian command post. FOOs called in Japanese artillery on the Australian positions, while one regiment lay astride the track to the Australian rear. The order to retreat was given and the Australians were hurled back pell-mell. More than 500 men had to seek refuge in the jungle and many did not return to the Allied lines until a month later.

On 14 September the Japanese attacked Ioribaiwa Ridge. After four days of fierce fighting, the Australians withdrew and the Japanese occupied their positions. They were less than 40 kilometres from Port Moresby, and as they ascended the ridge line the jubilant Japanese could see the sea, their objective, on the horizon. Several probing attacks were launched on the new defences at Imita ridge on 16 and 17 September, but they were thrown back.

The Japanese commander was still optimistic. Hori's South Seas Detachment had fought a gruelling campaign for eight weeks. He could see the end in sight and gave an inspirational speech to his soldiers: soon all their woes would be over and they would be refitted and replenished. Victory was theirs. He launched several probing attacks on the last line of defence before the lowlands of Port Moresby.

It was not to be. Low on supplies, his soldiers were being increasingly targeted by the resurgent Allied air force. Ammunition was running short and the Australians were well dug in on the final obstacle at Imita ridge. Eight weeks earlier Port Moresby had been a sleepy town with a brigade of ragged militia digging makeshift defences. By September 1942 it was filled with depots crammed with supplies and weaponry. A small unit of Kittyhawks had been reinforced by American and Australian fighter bomber squadrons, while a fleet of transports flew missions back and forth. On a high crest at Imita ridge, the Australians finally managed to get some specially modified 25 pdrs into firing positions. These 88mm guns had been crucial in stopping Rommel at Tobruk and Alamein, and at long last the tired diggers had artillery of their own. The modified 25 pdrs had a cut down barrel and platform, with a large muzzle break to limit recoil. Many diggers wept when they heard the first shots arcing over the last valley before Port Moresby, to smash into the Japanese positions on Ioribaiwa Ridge.

While it is unlikely Hori could have got his tired troops into Moresby (many consider the battle of Ioribaiwa to be a draw, with the Australians only withdrawing due to Japanese artillery superiority) other strategic factors proved to be his ultimate undoing.

Milne Bay had been a disaster for the Japanese and the hard fought battle of Guadalcanal was draining Japanese resources. The high command was reluctant to feed more resources into the Moresby battle until the situation had clarified.

On 24 September Hori was ordered to make a tactical retreat to the Eora region. The retreat soon turned into a rout.

It was unthinkable to the Japanese soldiers that they could turn their back and retreat. Morale collapsed. Cannibalism became rife. Pursuing Australian troops found butchered cadavers of both friend and foe with meat steaming on recently abandoned campfires. Prisoners of the Japanese were found tied to trees where they had been bayoneted to death or tortured. An overwhelming stench of starving and unwashed bodies made the Australians hate the Japanese even more and, now seeing them as subhuman monsters, would grant them no mercy. 'No quarter' became an unwritten rule followed by all. Some emaciated Japanese tied themselves to tree trunks, determined to die fighting. Many fleeing Japanese drowned in the Kumusi River. Some fought on with bare hands and were shot in what became known as 'the Death Valley Massacre.'

The Japanese sought to make a stand at Eora Creek in October, but suffered a significant defeat. By 1 November the pursuing Australians marched unopposed into Kokoda.

A great victory had been won. By 11 November the campaign had ended. Six hundred and seven Australians had been killed and 1,015 wounded. Many more were 'hors de combat' with malaria and jungle rot.

The Japanese lost many more thousands.

THE OWEN MACHINE GUN

In the steamy jungles of Papua or on a frozen hill in Korea, many an Australian owed their life to the trusty Owen machine gun. The rugged, reliable and light submachine gun functioned in the harshest of conditions. Many enemy attacks were broken up by a hail of 9mm bullets issuing from the Australian made gun. The weapon could be dropped in mud, slime and seawater, but nothing could stop it pumping out heavy 9mm slugs at a rate of 700rpm from its unique 33 round vertical magazine – a perfect weapon for close-in trench warfare or jungle fighting.

The Owen only came into existence through the most remarkable set of circumstances. The gun was only produced after its inventor abandoned the prototype on a doorstep; it was almost the gun that never was.

The gun's inventor, Evelyn Owen, was a compulsive tinkerer who developed a simplified .22 calibre submachine gun as a teenager. His prototype simplified the blowback system of most submachine guns (where the recoil ejects a spent bullet casing while loading a new round) and utilised fewer moving parts than contemporary weapons.

Owen shopped his weapon around without success and enlisted on the outbreak of the war. Invited to the pub with some chums, Owen dumped his prototype at his front door and headed off for a drink. Owen's next door neighbour, who happened to have ties with defence contractors, came home to find a hessian bag next to his doorstep with a submachine gun barrel sticking out of the top! Vincent Wardell immediately saw the potential of the weapon that he had stumbled upon and, with Owen's agreement, modified the design from a drum magazine to an upright magazine and increased the calibre.

The upgraded version was included in Australian Army trials which compared the performance of the British Sten (in Australia called the Austen), the Owen and the Thompson machine gun. In all trials the Owen proved superior, but it was only when wartime pressures prevented Allied governments from supplying Australia that the Owen was put into mass production.

There were 45,500 produced for the grateful Australian troops, who received them from July 1942 onward. It was the perfect weapon for jungle fighting and was extensively used in the Pacific, Korea, Malaya and Indonesia.

It fell out of favour in Vietnam because Australian soldiers thought it lacked penetrating power. No wonder – the ammunition was 20 years old!

ENDGAME

There was much more fighting to be done. As the Australians pursued their foe over the ranges towards the north coast of Papua, the Japanese dug in on a 15km plot of land surrounding the three small townships of Buna, Gona and Sanananda.

4,000 survivors of Hori's original 12,000 men were joined by 5,000 reinforcements from Rabaul. They were determined to hang on to their possessions for future counter strikes.

By 22 January these insignificant settlements on the muddy, pest ridden shores of one of the most inhospitable places on Earth had been captured. The Japanese had enjoyed excellent fields of fire and it had taken almost suicidal attacks to winkle them out of their positions.

The 7th and 9th Divisions then fought hard to eject the Japanese from Salamuau and Lae, before bundling them out of the Huon peninsula at great loss of men and material.

There was no glory in this war. The sweeping movements of the desert war had been replaced by attack after attack against a dug in and fanatical opposition in pestilential conditions. Although they did not win many plaudits in the public eye, the soldiers fighting these battles performed remarkably in what can possibly be called the worst conditions Australians ever fought under.

Papua was not cleared until December 1943. In the final stage of the war the Australians were engaged in mopping up operations from Borneo to Bougainville. Set piece battles alternated with what amounted to police actions as small detachments hunted desperate fugitives from the Japanese Army.

These vital actions did little to add to the Australian Armed Forces' reputation but, by the time the Japanese surrendered on 15 August 1945, there was no doubt that the heroic actions by the Australians around Papua had significantly contributed to their surrender.

It must be noted that women made a huge contribution to the Australian war effort and were absolutely necessary for the ultimate victory against the Japanese.

Australia could not have maintained its forces in the field without the contribution of women. The industrial effort relied on a large female workforce producing munitions and optics. Eighty thousand women enlisted in the armed forces; eighteen thousand were members of the Woman's Auxiliary Australian Air Force (WAAF) responsible for wireless communication, teleprinter operations and mechanical repair work. Similarly, thousands joined the Women's Royal Australian Naval Service (WRANS). The Australian Women's Army Service (AWAS) had 31,000 recruits by the end of the war. These not only served rear echelon duties but were trained in combat techniques. One hundred were technically front line troops when they helped suppress the Cowra breakout, which was designated a theatre of war.

The women who paid for their effort in the war with blood were the Australian Army Nursing Services (AANS). They were the only Australian females to serve overseas and were subject to hostile strafing and artillery fire in front line hospitals, or clusters of torpedoes while serving aboard hospital ships in the Mediterranean or Pacific.

In one instance they also had to face Japanese soldiers bent on murder.

Just before the fall of Singapore, thousands of nurses, wounded soldiers and civilians were evacuated by boat. One of the ships was the *Vyner Brooke*, which left with 65 nurses and many injured soldiers in their care. The coastal steamer was sunk by Japanese planes near Sumatra and many survivors were packed into lifeboats. Even these were strafed, and it was a sadly depleted group who finally staggered ashore on Bangka Island.

One group of 22 Australian nurses included Sister Vivian Bullwinkel. They set up a Red Cross station to look after some wounded soldiers and some civilians. It was decided that they would surrender, so a party of civilians proceeded to a nearby town to find the Japanese commander in the area. A group of Japanese soldiers quickly arrived. They ordered the fit British to move around a headland. Bullwinkel and her fellow nurses soon heard shouting and rifle fire. The Japanese returned with bloodied bayonets.

Despite the fact that all of the nurses had Red Cross insignia on their uniforms, a feature which should have protected them, the 22 were formed into a line and ordered to walk into the surf. The Australian nurses walked into the ocean with heads held high. They knew what was coming and didn't deign to plead for mercy from the callous war criminals. Once the water was waist deep, the laughing and shouting Japanese shot the defenceless women in the backs. Sister Bullwinkel was knocked into the surf by a bullet. She was only wounded and played dead. She did, however, hear the rest of the wounded on the beach being finished off by the Japanese.

Remarkably, Bullwinkel survived the war to testify at war crimes trials.

HMAS *AUSTRALIA* AND THE FIRST KAMIKAZE ATTACK

HMAS *Australia*, known, not surprisingly as the *Aussie* was perhaps the first Allied ship to suffer from a Kamikaze attack – the Divine Wind.

The County-class cruiser was the Australian flagship and did sterling service in the Mediterranean against the Germans, and at the Battle of the Coral Sea and the Battle of Guadalcanal against the Japanese.

No doubt Japanese Intelligence knew that the distinctive three funnel cruiser was the Australian flagship and any pilot would have considered it a great honour to send her to the bottom.

They almost did.

By 1944 the Allies had wrested air and naval supremacy from the Japanese. In a desperate last effort to stop the American and Australian fleets from closing in on the home islands, the Japanese Imperial Headquarters tasked Admiral Onishi Takajiro with the creation of the kamikaze tokkotai (Divine Wind Special Attack Unit). Pilots were given basic training and, with petrol or bomb laden planes, were ordered to attack the base of the bridges on enemy ships.

On 21 October 1944 the RAN were engaged in supporting the landings at Leyte Gulf as the Americans began the reconquest of the Philippines. A Japanese Val dive bomber suddenly appeared out of the morning mist at low altitude and, after taking some Ack Ack hits, flew into the port side of *Australia*'s bridge. This attack was lethal. Gasoline was sprayed to all corners of the bridge before igniting with fatal consequences. Thirty crew and officers were killed while 60 were wounded, many seriously. Some victims were charred so badly they were unrecognisable. Included in the casualty list was Squadron Commander John Collins, who was severely burned, and the captain Emile Dechaineux, who died from shrapnel wounds.

The flagship's ordeal had only begun. The *Australia* was repaired and back in action by November. On 5 January another kamikaze smashed into the ship. This plane was laden with bombs, causing 55 casualties, many of which were among the gun crews. Despite newly installed AA defences another attack saw a 'Val' dive bomber crash into *Australia*'s upper deck. The resulting fire ball caused another 40 casualties while taking out many of the cruiser's defences.

On 8 January things got worse. Waves of kamikaze targeted the *Aussie*. One dropped a bomb piercing the hull at the waterline. Another exploded above the ship, showering aviation fuel and lethal debris on the sailors. Even though the plane disintegrated, its engine carried on and smashed through a bulkhead, ending up in the captain's cabin. Another was destroyed just 15 metres from the hull side, but its propellers destroyed a life raft while the aircraft smashed into the hull side, rupturing one of the ship's fuel tanks and destroying two mess decks.

Despite having to reduce speed to 15 knots, the *Australian* refused to leave the Allied battle line. The next day the Japanese determined to finish her off. One more plane penetrated the fusillade of defensive fire and took off the foremost funnel. Unable to generate sufficient updraft for two of her boilers, the *Australia* limped out of the battle line and headed home for repairs. The kamikaze had thrown everything they had at the proud ship but failed to sink her.

Other ships were not so lucky. At least 55 were sunk by this bestial tactic and more than 200 knocked out permanently from the war effort.

JAPANESE ATTACK SYDNEY HARBOUR

Early one morning in late May 1942, some astute observers noticed a single prop sea plane taking lazy circles around Sydney Harbour before heading out to sea, flying over Manly. Nobody knew it yet but World War II had come to Sydney.

A few days later, during the evening of Sunday 31 May, five unwelcome visitors gathered just outside Sydney Harbour.

Two were B1 type submarines that could launch an amphibious reconnaissance plane, while the other three had mounted on their hulls a type A midget submarine. These made up the Eastern Attack Group of the 8th Submarine Squadron of the Imperial Japanese Navy. The group had been scouting the South Pacific for several months and had decided that Sydney Harbour was the easiest and most fruitful location to launch an attack. It was from one of these subs that the unknown and almost unnoticed scout plane had been launched. It had returned to report that the harbour was chock full of likely targets, including the heavy cruisers USS *Chicago* and the HMAS *Canberra*.

Conditions were perfect; the flotilla would launch an attack that evening.

The Australian public was already reeling from the successes of Japanese arms. Pearl Harbour had been attacked, Singapore had fallen and Darwin had undergone a relentless bombing campaign. The Japanese were about to prove that nowhere was safe by striking in the heart of Australia's largest city.

Ten kilometres to the east of the harbour, three of the mother ships disgorged their midget submarines. Each of these battery powered subs could travel at 24 knots and was crewed by two men. Their armament was two Type 97 torpedoes.

The 97 torpedoes were a smaller version of the famed type 93 'long lance' torpedo that wrought havoc with its speed and accuracy in the Pacific War.

The first of the submarines – *M27* – entered the harbour mouth at 8p.m. Her commander managed to get through the heads but blundered into a partially completed anti-submarine boom net that was emplaced just beyond the heads. As the commander desperately sought to free his submarine from the nets, turbulence was noticed on the water's surface at 9.30p.m. A converted leisure craft approached the net and dropped several of its equipped depth charges. They failed to explode. Aware that it was only a matter of time before he was captured or destroyed, the commander of *M27* – Lieutenant Chuma Kensi – decided to scuttle his craft. A 35 kilo charge was detonated, which killed both men and sent the submarine to the harbour floor.

A general alarm was sounded. Sydney was at war.

Avoiding all of the distractions was *M24*, which passed to the south of the submarine boom and made its way towards Pott's point. Sub-Lieutenant Ban Katsuhisa was obviously made of stern stuff, and although his tiny craft came under fire from several warships, he lined up to deliver a volley of torpedoes at the heavy cruiser *Chicago*. If his aim was as good as his bravery, Katsuhisa would have achieved a famous victory. Instead, both torpedoes went wide. One ran ashore on Garden Island while the other hit a sea wall to which a converted ferry was moored. HMAS *Kuttabul* rapidly settled and the blast killed 19 Australian and two British seamen on board. Eyewitnesses reported that the whole ferry seemed to lift almost out of the water, as if on the crest of an enormous wave, before sinking by the stern. Wood and debris was thrown for hundreds of metres around the dock area.

Soon small and large craft were zooming around the harbour, firing off flares and dropping depth charges on anything that looked suspicious. *M24* managed to avoid all of the strife and most likely skulked out of the harbour at 2a.m.

It seems that some damage may have been inflicted on the sub; it couldn't rendezvous with its mother ship. The whereabouts of *M24* was unknown until 2006, when a group of divers came across the sunken hull in 55 metres of water, 5 kilometres offshore. The sub is shrouded in nets and the two crew remain entombed in the rusty wreck.

The third midget submarine, *M22*, probably entered the harbour at the same time as the other two. She too slipped around the southern tip of the submarine netting and penetrated deep into the harbour. *M22* was spotted by HMAS *Yandra* and subjected to a depth charge attack that forced her to the harbour floor, where she lay low for several hours. At 5a.m. the submarine was spotted again and several ships converged on her location, laying down a deadly pattern of depth charges. *M22* was forced to the surface and it was discovered that the two crewmen had committed suicide with pistol shots to the head to avoid capture.

The attack could not really be seen as a success from a military point of view. If anything it strengthened Australian resolve to pursue total war.

The Japanese flotilla was by no means finished with Sydney. On Monday 8 June, two of the submarines fired shells at Newcastle and Sydney. They had also begun a campaign against merchant shipping, moving along the east coast. On 3 June, the merchant ship SS *Iron Chieftain* was the first Allied casualty.

In one of the greatest tragedies of World War II, the hospital ship *Centaur* was torpedoed by a Japanese submarine in the early hours of 14 May 1943.

Despite displaying clear Red Cross markings over a white painted hull, and being brilliantly illuminated, the helpless ship was sunk – likely by *I-177* under Lieutenant Commander Nakagawa – causing massive loss of life. Only one of the twelve nurses on board at the time survived. Nakagawa had earned his stripes as a war criminal earlier in the war, by machine-gunning escaping sailors of other ships he had sunk in the Indian Ocean.

The ship was 50 miles northeast of Brisbane. The survivors spent 35 hours clinging to rafts before they were rescued.

As the war turned against the Japanese, many submarines were taken from offensive actions and used to ferry supplies and reinforcements to garrisons that were isolated by superior Allied naval and air power. The last Japanese submarines left Australian waters by the end of 1943.

Only one of the twenty B1 submarines survived the war. Having a large, pressurised compartment on the front of the hull made it difficult for them to submerge rapidly and reduced the depth they could penetrate to.

CHAPTER 10

COLD WAR WARRIORS

INTRODUCTION

The promise of a brave new world free of conflict was already an impossible dream, even as the rubble settled in Germany in 1945. Tensions between the USSR and the Western Powers escalated, with Winston Churchill declaring an Iron Curtain descending over Europe in March 1946.

Nascent communist movements throughout Asia were given a huge boost with Mao Tse Tung's founding of the People's Republic of China on 1 October 1949. Rather than being a benign and moderate regime, the rulers of the most populous country in the world embarked upon a violent and radical programme of class warfare. Chinese equipment, advisors and doctrine were sent south to spread the Revolution.

Both the British and Americans set out to stop the insurgencies. In Malaya and Korea, the communists were halted, in no small part because of the assistance given by the Australian Army.

In 1948 it was decided to reform the structure of the army. Replacing the plethora of numbered infantry battalions was a new command structure given the title the Royal Australian Regiment (RAR). Three battalions were originally formed, but numbers were increased or decreased as the need of the army changed. The 3rd Battalion Royal Australian Regiment (3 RAR) was the first unit to be committed in the Cold War.

KOREA

Peter Cundall (b. 1927) is well known in Australia as the avuncular presenter of an ABC gardening show. Retaining this cheerful demeanour is a testament to his character. Once on ABC radio he gave an amazing description of how he ended up in the Korean War. Cundall was in the British Army and, in the closing stages of World War II, he was exposed to the horrors of the German concentration camps before being held for six months in solitary confinement in Tito's communist Yugoslavia.

Soon after his release, the young man was back in gloomy old England wondering what to do with his future. One shop front caught his eye: an Australian Army recruitment office. He went in and the recruiting sergeant opened up his files to 'discover' that there was an opening which would be perfect for the ex-squaddie. The Australian Army, explained the friendly Aussie, maintained a library on Main Street Bondi, just opposite Bondi Beach. It was in desperate need for a young volunteer with a literary bent to man the desk; no doubt Peter Cundall would fit the bill. The sergeant had some pictures of the beach, with its sun, surf and sheilas, and Cundall joined up straight away.

Soon after Cundall was the number one Gunner on a Vickers MKIII tripod mounted machine gun, fighting in a defensive action as thousands of communist soldiers poured over the rain sodden hills of Korea in the first major conflict of the Cold War. His unit, the Third Battalion, Royal Australian Regiment, fought many battles against desperate North Korean and Chinese soldiers.

Cundall was perfect fodder for any savvy recruiting sergeant. As a veteran of World War II he would have been trained on exactly the same weapons that were used by the battalions of the RAR.

Along with many Australian soldiers who found themselves fighting a desperate battle to survive in Korea, Cundall may have wondered what convoluted fate had brought them there.

The roots of the war extended back to 1945 when Russian troops, who had just bundled Japan out of Manchuria, occupied the northern half of Korea and established a capital at Pyongyang. American troops occupied the south and established a capital at Seoul. The demarcation line was the 38th parallel north, which split the country in two. Attempts were made to unify the country, but the Russians refused to cooperate and two new states were formed: the Republic of Korea (ROK) in the south. and the Korean Democratic People's Republic in the north. Not surprisingly, North Korea under Kim Il Sung was not democratic, and he was determined to unite the two countries through force. By 1950 the USSR – as well as the USA – had all but withdrawn from the country, but the Korean People's Army (KPA) had been trained by USSR specialists and was equipped with reliable Soviet equipment such as the T34/85.

On 25 June 1950 the KPA poured over the 38th parallel, sweeping all before them. The poorly trained and ill equipped ROK armed forces fled before the onset and it seemed that the war would be over in a matter of weeks. But on 4 August the remnants of the shattered army reached the hills around Pusan, in the southern tip of Korea, and with United Nations help was able to halt the Northern onslaught. The United Nations had reacted swiftly to Kim Il Sung's aggression and, within the space of a few weeks, detachments from at least fifteen nations had embarked to assist the ROK.

The Australian involvement in the Korean War can be divided into three phases. The first phase saw the Australians with American allies break out of the Pusan bridgehead and push the North Korean forces back towards the Chinese border.

The second phase opened when 300,000 Chinese soldiers poured into North Korea. The UN forces were overwhelmed by the Chinese assault tactics and retreated past the 38th parallel. The war degenerated into a seesawing brawl, with UN forces and communist troops seeking to free Seoul and regain the 38th parallel.

The war then settled into an almost static front, reminiscent of the trenches of World War I. Australian troops had to fight against the elements for survival as well as against their tenacious communist enemies.

PHASE ONE

The 3rd Battalion RAR was the first Australian unit deployed to Korea, just after the United Nations forces had broken out of the Pusan bridgehead.

The UN Commander-in-Chief, American General Douglas MacArthur, managed to turn the RKO flank with an amphibious landing at Seoul. At the same time a tremendous array of military hardware had been marshalled in the Pusan bridgehead, giving the UN forces superiority in the air and on the ground. The combined offensives bundled the North Koreans over the 38th parallel and drove them northwards, towards Manchuria.

Arriving in September 1950, the Australians were joined by the 1st Battalion Middlesex Regiment and the 1st Battalion Argyll and Sutherland Highlanders to form the 27th British Commonwealth Infantry Brigade. Attached to the brigade was the US Army's 89th Medium Tank Battalion, equipped with late model Sherman's mounting an effective 76mm cannon.

In the pell-mell pursuit that followed the collapse of the communist forces, the Australians were often given objectives but arrived to find that they had already been seized by other allied units. Friend and foe frequently became intermixed.

One of the greatest coups of the war was when Major Ferguson and Major Thirlwell of the 3rd RAR founds themselves isolated in the midst of a North Korean battlegroup. Standing on top of a Sherman the officers announced, through an interpreter, that the KPA troops were surrounded and were advised to surrender. After two minutes of almost unbearable tension the Northerners gave themselves up. Almost 2,000 men went into the bag along with anti-tank guns, machine guns and mortars.

The motorised brigade was carried along with the victorious UN forces as they pursued the beaten North Koreans past the capital, Pyongyang, towards the Chinese border. The headlong advance was finally halted at the Chongchon River, where the North Korean forces strung together a defensive line on the higher northern bank of the river. They blew the crossings and were reinforced with at least fifty T34/85s. After several days fierce fighting the brigade crossed the river and, by 29 October, they were preparing for the final push north. During this action the Australians had suffered 8 killed and 22 wounded. Perhaps many diggers thought the war was almost over before they had really had a chance to get stuck in. It was not to be.

PHASE 2

The Chinese communist regime under tyrannical Mao Tse Tung had warned the UN that, if troops closed up on the border with China, he would be forced to intervene and commit the PLA (People's Liberation Army) to the conflict. On 26 November MacArthur ordered a final campaign to drive the remaining North Koreans into the Yalu River.

Mao was not making idle threats. Since October, Chinese divisions amounting to more than 300,000 men had been massing, and by 1 November a sequence of rolling offensives had shattered the UN lines. Bitter winds howling down from the north were accompanied by Red Army troops, who used their overwhelming numbers to burst through the ROK forces in the centre of the line. The Red Army was a well equipped and unified force with a record of success going back decades. Between 1937 and 1949 they had countered everything the Japanese Army and Nationalist forces under Chiang Kai-shek had thrown at them. Many of the troops committed to Korea were ex-Nationalist soldiers determined to show their allegiance to the new regime.

Whole allied divisions were forced to break out of encirclements. The Australians fought many bitter rear guard actions before the UN forces regrouped south of Seoul. Another counterattack by the allies saw them push back north of the 38th parallel and recapture Seoul. The Australians were instrumental in many of these offensive actions. In late March they found themselves in reserve, 40 kilometres north of Seoul, enjoying some well deserved rest.

Little did the tired diggers know that soon they would feel the full weight of the Chinese Spring Offensive designed to seize Seoul one last time and eject the UN from the peninsula for ever.

THE BATTLE OF KAPYONG

On the eve of Anzac Day, 24 April, the 3rd RAR found itself dug in on a range of hills overlooking the Kapyong River valley. Streaming around them were the shattered remnants of the 6th ROK Division, which had been thrown out of their positions by the Chinese 64th Division. More than 330,000 men had been committed to the PLA (People's Liberation Army) offensive and they were determined to throw the UN out Korea once and for all.

For thousands of years the Kapyong valley had been used by invasion forces as a route to or out of Seoul; the position had to be held to protect the South Korean capital. All that stood before the rampaging Chinese was the 27th Brigade. Holding the shoulders of the valley were the Australian 3rd RAR on the right flank. Opposite them were the Canadian Light Infantry, while in reserve were the British Middlesex Regiment, a regiment of New Zealand Field Artillery and a company of the American 72nd Tank Battalion equipped with 17 Shermans.

The brigade had to hold 7 kilometres of broken terrain. A continuous front could not be formed, so the troops began digging company strongpoints. Companies B, A and D were thrown forward, with C in reserve.

As the night progressed, the trickle of retreating ROK troops became a flood, and following on their heels came the Chinese 10th Division. The Australians were about to experience the full fury of a Chinese human wave attack.

The Chinese used to attack in human waves similar to those used in the Chinese Civil War. They were experts at camouflage and, aware of the United Nation's air superiority, they usually only moved at night. During the day their dun coloured cotton jackets blended in perfectly with the grey soils of Korea, while tanks and trucks would hide in buildings or under haystacks.

The Australians perched on their rocky hilltop later reported that it seemed as if entire hills around Kapyong were moving in the fading dusk light. Landscapes seemed to change colours as the mass of Chinese infantry moved over the terrain towards the hastily dug positions. The veteran 3rd RAR – some considered it to have been the finest battalion in the whole theatre – waited with their World War II weaponry as the Chinese hordes approached.

At nightfall the first intimation many soldiers had that the Chinese were close was the overwhelming smell of garlic; Chinese soldiers used to chew raw garlic cloves instead of chewing gum. At 10.00p.m. all hell broke loose. Columns of PLA troops closed up on the positions and began their attacks.

There is a perception that the Chinese used mindless 'human wave' attacks without any tactical finesse. Nothing could be further from the truth. Rather than spreading attacks along a continuous front, Chinese commanders were trained to identify likely weak points in an enemy line and throw consecutive attacks on that point until it broke. Successive waves of men armed with 'burp guns' and grenades would hurl themselves onto a selection of points until a lodgement had been made. Machine guns were then set up on the new positions, which were used as a launch pad for further assaults into the flanks and rear of the defences. The Chinese particularly liked to attack at night. Not only did this lend a nightmarish quality to the battles, but it also negated to some extent the UN forces' superiority in artillery and airpower.

The Chinese would move, silently, as close as they could to the enemy trenches; often only a metre separated the attackers from their unsuspecting foes. LMGs would infiltrate the position while others set up ambushes behind the enemy defence lines. At a given signal the assault would go in. Concentric arcs of fire from the infiltrators were often enough to shatter the morale of the defenders, sending them panicked to the rear, where they would be cut down by the waiting ambushers. Only the best troops could hold their positions and fight on to victory. The human wave flowed around the enemy positions, using the ground in a sophisticated manner. This is at odds with the idea that they advanced in a succession of waves reminiscent of the British on the Somme.

Thousands of Chinese threw themselves at the Australian strong points. The battalion commander refused to fire flares as that would strip his soldiers of their night vision. The veteran Australian troops cut down swathes of Chinese with rifles, Vickers and Brens. The Chinese kept coming. Marshalled by bugles and whistles they seemed like an unstoppable torrent supported by mortar fire and barrages of grenades. A and B companies held off nine set piece assaults that night. Chinese soldiers infiltrated between company and platoon positions and had to be ejected at bayonet point. The command company was almost overwhelmed and only support from the Middlesex Regiment saved their bacon.

In the early hours of Anzac Day, a bright full moon broke from the clouds and illuminated the fighting. It seemed to the defenders that their entire position was like a mound boiling with angry ants. As dawn broke, the allied troops took a terrible revenge. The Chinese were out in the open between A and B company and the defenders poured fire from mortars, tanks and machine guns into the withdrawing formations, causing heavy losses.

The Australian battalion had fought off what may have been the entire strength of a Chinese division for a crucial 24 hours. Thirty-two Australians died and 59 were wounded, along with three taken prisoner. More than 600 Chinese died and an unknown number were wounded.

The Chinese switched their attention to the Canadians on the left shoulder of the valley, but their blown troops could make little headway. Despite these reverses the Chinese offensive, intended to take Seoul by 1 May, broke through in other sectors, necessitating the phased withdrawal of the Commonwealth Brigade. They continued to inflict casualties on the pursuing Chinese until, on 30 April, the Spring Offensive was finally halted 9 kilometres north of Seoul.

Even the communists were appalled by the loss of life and, seeing that their last throw of the dice had been stymied by the allies, they entered armistice negotiations in July 1951.

PHASE THREE

For two years the Australians held their section of the UN line. It wasn't until 27 July 1953 that a truce was signed between the warring parties. While lacking the dramatic to and fro movements of the previous year, there was nothing easy about holding the front line.

Veterans remember the freezing nights perched up in their defensive positions looking over no-man's-land. Freezing winters gave over to broiling summers. The Korean peasants used human waste to fertilise their fields and the reek of decomposing faeces seemed to permeate even the pores of men behind the front lines. Men built 'huchis' (pronounced hootches) on the hillsides of their positions. Those on rear slopes could be quite established, with thick sandbagged walls and stout roofs. Camp stretchers and oil lamps made them almost comfortable. Those facing the enemy were more rudimentary and were sometimes just shallow foxholes scraped into the frozen, stony soil. Neither type could keep out the elements and in the depths of winter it was impossible to hoard beer – the bottles exploded in the cold.

Soldiers had to scrape icicle beards off their faces before they could eat or drink. Supplies had to be humped up the side of mountains and hills where only donkeys could get traction.

But this was no cold war. Australians soldiers had to stand to at dawn and dusk for at least an hour; that was the time the Chinese were most likely to launch a surprise attack. Both sides constantly lobbed shells and mortar bombs at their opposition, leading to a constant trickle of casualties. At night, patrols roamed no-man's-land, launching lighting raids to kill or capture.

As negotiations continued, both sides jockeyed for the best positions, hoping to influence the final terms of any treaty. In October 1951 Operation Commando was launched, and the Australians were given the objective of Hill 317, a feature that dominated the communist positions. Allied jets and artillery pounded the position before the Australians took it at the point of the bayonet. The next day Hill 217 was also taken. Twenty Australians lay dead and 104 were wounded. Two weeks later the Chinese reclaimed the features.

When the Australians were finally pulled out of Korea they had enhanced their reputation as a crack formation. A total of 1,068 had been wounded and 278 were killed.

THE RAN IN KOREA

Most ships of the Australian Navy saw some service in the Korean War. The two Australian ships – the frigate *Shoalhaven* and the destroyer *Bataan* – were among the first to steam to the peninsula after being ordered there by Prime Minister Robert Menzies, just four days after the invasion.

The frigate *Shoalhaven* was the first Australian unit to carry out an operation in the Korean War. On 1 July she sailed into Korean waters as an escort to an American ammunition supply ship, and was berthed in Pusan harbour the next day. As she left that evening, the first American transports laden with GIs steamed into the harbour: the Korean War was about to become a much bigger conflict.

The *Bataan* was the next Australian ship on the scene, and between 6 and 13 July helped escort another three convoys into Pusan. *Bataan* was a state-of-the-art destroyer. One of three Tribal-class destroyers, it was built during the Second World War and had valuable upgrades using information from the opening years of that conflict. It could achieve a cracking speed of 36.5 knots (67km/h) and was armed with six 4.7 inch (120mm) Mark V-II guns in three centrally controlled turrets, as well as multiple bofors, pom poms, torpedoes and depth charges.

Bataan fired the RAN's first shots in the war when she was surprised on 1 August 1950 by a North Korean shore battery. The destroyer had been enforcing a coastal blockade on communist territories and was intercepting some suspicious junks making for the coast. At 6p.m. a salvo from some concealed artillery positions straddled *Bataan*. She was able to return fire and, after a brief but fierce gun battle, made good her escape.

These two ships were the first of many and the RAN spent the war shelling communist positions, evacuating refugees and blockading the coast as part of their duties. During the war two aircraft carriers, five destroyers and four frigates operated against the communists.

The aircraft carrier HMAS *Sydney* served off the coast of Korea for two tours. The first was between October 1951 and January 1952. The second tour extended from November 1953 to January 1954.

Mounted on the carrier were three RAN air squadrons. They were No 805 and No 808 Squadrons, flying the Hawker Sea Fury, and No 817 Squadron, operating with the Fairey Firefly. The *Sydney* patrolled off the coast of Korea and her air armada was crucial for giving support to allied ground forces. This support included launching ground attacks on enemy forces, destroying bridges, closing tunnels, attacking logistic centres and taking out airfields. Such was the success of the allied naval air efforts that in coastal regions the enemy was forced to move supplies at night, lest they receive the deadly attentions of the RAN air wing.

In addition, the planes performed reconnaissance duties with high and medium altitude photography runs. At times they were required to act as aerial spotters for offshore naval bombardments – a dangerous task. The three squadrons flew 2,366 sorties and during their tour of duty lost 13 planes to a combination of causes, including enemy fire, deck accidents and rough weather.

The Hawker Sea Fury was an exceptional carrier borne aircraft. One of the fastest piston driven fighters ever developed (it could attain 740km), it was initially designed as a fighter interceptor. Its robust construction allowed it to be equipped with 16 rockets under the wings, or several 250 kilogram bombs to add to the four 20mm cannon mounted on the wings. In a rare feat for a propeller driven plane, one Hawker Sea Fury was credited with bringing down a MIG 15 in 1952.

Mines were a constant threat to ships operating off Korea, but the real danger was the weather. Freezing cold conditions led to aircraft on deck being rendered unserviceable, and ice made taking off a hazardous operation. During the nights of 14 and 15 October 1951, Cyclone Ruth struck HMAS *Sydney* and her escorts. Huge seas and winds of 100 knots (185km) led to tremendous damage on the flat-top. Sea water entered the ship's ventilation systems, causing a number of electrical fires. Several aircraft were washed overboard and for three days the aircraft carrier was out of action.

Working day and night in extremes of weather while maintaining air cover over significant parts of Korea was a real challenge for the crew of *Sydney*. On average, 38% of planes returned from combat in a damaged state. These required a tremendous effort from maintenance crews in cramped conditions far removed from spare parts depots. Ninety-nine planes were hit by Flak and nine were shot down.

Destroyers and frigates served several rotations. As the workhorses of the Australian Navy they had many tasks. HMAS *Warramunga* had two tours, with the first extending from September 1950 to September 1951. During this 12 month tour the *Warramunga*: was part of the screen that protected the Australian carrier HMAS *Sydney*; she and *Bataan* provided fire support for the Inchon landing; she escorted an American dredger for inshore operations; she helped enforce the naval blockade off the North West Coast of Korea and she bombarded enemy coastal positions. In 1951, when the Reds were resurgent with the Chinese intervention, *Warramunga* and *Bataan* were tasked with evacuating refugees from the coastal town of Chinnampo. Due to faulty naval charts *Warramunga* ran aground. A dicey few hours were spent trying to pull the ship back into deep water while Chinese forces approached. Fortunately, she managed to free herself in time.

AUSSIES CAUGHT SHORT – RAAF IN KOREA

Just as the digger marched to meet his communist foes in the mountains of Korea equipped with World War II weapons and support services, so did the RAAF. In 1945 the Mustang was a state of the art fighter and proved instrumental in paving the way for the huge bomber formations that brought the Nazi state to its knees. In Korea it was still an excellent ground support fighter, especially when it was equipped with High Velocity Aerial rockets (HVAR), that could take out a Soviet tank or bunker with absolute precision.

The 77th Squadron RAAF was the first Commonwealth air formation to find itself in Korea. General Douglas MacArthur had specifically asked for the squadron to be committed to the new conflict. As the North Korean troops surged southwards, the American forces were lacking fighter bombers that could spend a lengthy amount of time in the air strafing ground formations and interdicting supplies. All of the American units available were jet powered and lacked the necessary range to be effective ground attack planes. On 30 June the 11th, which was stationed in Japan, got its marching orders. Soon the squadron was a vital part of the defences of the Pusan perimeter. After the Inchon landings, the Australians helped pave the way as the UN forces pursued the retreating North Koreans.

The Mustangs were particularly lethal when delivering napalm. Suspended under their belly were bright yellow bombs that looked like large bananas or mangos. The communist forces were terrified of these bombs. They would – almost gently – tumble to the earth once released, but upon impact would burst into a huge fire ball which at its heart reached 1,000 degrees Centigrade. Fiery fingers of jellied petroleum would reach out from the blast and whatever they touched – tanks, blockhouses or infantry in trenches – would burst into flame and be destroyed.

The Chinese, on the other hand, tried some novel bombing techniques. Once they spread a black smoke like substance over allied lines. On inspection it appeared that they had dropped millions of flies and fleas infected with bubonic plague. The problem was they were dropped in winter when there was still snow on the ground, killing the insects immediately.

On 1 November 1950 a new player entered the war. Five MIG-15 Soviet jet fighters from the 72 Guards Fighter Aviation Regiment swept into US airspace south of the Yalu River and broke up a formation of USAF Mustangs, bringing one crashing to earth.

The Cold War was not only an ideological war but also a technological race, and with the MIG-15 Russia was in the lead with cutting edge fighter technology. The MIG-15's swept wing design gave it an edge over most fighters of its day. What's more, it had a higher rate of climb, a higher ceiling and far better acceleration than any of its rivals. Like most Russian planes it could take lots of punishment, and its heavy weaponry allowed it to knock USAF bomber formations out of the sky at up to 2,000 metres. The MIG-15 was armed with one 37mm cannon and two 25mm machine guns. One high explosive bullet from the 37mm could destroy a plane, while a shell from the 25mm would rip a metre-wide hole in any plane, making recovery almost impossible.

The Americans quickly introduced the F-86 Sabre, which able to achieve some parity with the MIG-15.

The Australian 77 Squadron, equipped with Mustangs, was not so fortunate. No Sabres were available and the Australian government made the decision to convert 77 Squadron to the British Gloster Meteor. This was another bit of kit from World War II; the first operational British jet fighter.

It couldn't stand up to the MIG.

On July 1951 the squadron resumed operations in Korea, where its new aircraft were soon proved to be outclassed by the Soviet fighters. On 29 August one Meteor was downed and two damaged, while their opponents were unscathed. On 1 December a massive dogfight involving up to forty planes took place in 'MIG Alley'. A large formation of MIGs jumped the Australians from the rear and, in the desperate dogfight that followed, three Australians were shot down. Two pilots were captured and one man killed. An optimistic pilot claimed one 'probable' hit, but later investigations revealed the MIGs were unscathed.

This debacle led to the Meteors being taken from high altitude sweeps over North Korea and they returned to the ground attack role. This actually played in their favour, as at low altitudes the MIGs lost much of their performance and the two planes fought at parity. By the time the conflict finished, 77 Squadron had shot down six MIGs, flown 4,836 sorties and were credited with destroying 1,500 vehicles. During this time almost 30 Meteors were destroyed.

THE EVOLUTION OF AUSTRALIAN INFANTRY WEAPONS: COLD WAR TO TODAY

During the Korean War almost all of the kit and weapons were exactly the same as what the Australians used in World War II. By Vietnam they had almost all been replaced by more modern and lightweight weapons. While many of these Vietnam era weapons are still warehoused or issued to reserve units, Australian modern day infantry is equipped with state-of-the-art equipment.

Rifles

Lee Enfield Mark III

From the time large German assaults through Belgium were stopped by massed British rifle fire, the Lee Enfield has had a reputation for ease of handling, reliability and a high rate of fire. The Australians sent to fight in Korea still had the Lee Enfield as their basic weapon. It was produced in the Lithgow Arms Factory until 1953.

The SLR

The L1A1 SLR (Self-Loading Rifle) was adapted from a Belgian design and was much appreciated by the Australian diggers in Vietnam. Its 20 round magazine could produce 600 RPM when on full automatic, and the NATO standard 7.62mm round was both heavy enough to cut though dense jungle and effective to 700 metres. Each trooper carried 150 rounds.

The Steyr F88

The lightweight Steyr 88 was adopted in 1988. It possesses awesome stopping power and is noted for its reliability. The Australian version has a bayonet attachment for close combat and can be fitted with a laser sighted 40mm grenade launcher.

Machine Guns

The Bren

The Bren gun, with its top mounted forward curved magazine, is one of the most iconic weapons of the 20th Century. In Korea it was the basic light machine gun, manned by a gunner and a loader, and supported by the rest of an infantry section. Each magazine contained up to 30 rounds and, by firing in short aimed bursts, a rate of 120 rpm would be achieved. If the bipod was utilised it could take out enemies up to 1,500 meters away. Fired from the hip it was a devastating close combat weapon.

The Vickers Medium Machine Gun

The Vickers machine gun was a devastating weapon that could sustain a rate of fire of 450 rounds per minute for hours. It was a perfect weapon for fighting from entrenched positions against the Chinese human wave attacks of the Korean War, possessing an effective range of up to four kilometers. However, it required four men to move and was therefore unsuitable for mobile operations in Vietnam.

The M60

The M60 was an American post war design that was heavily influenced by the German MG 42. On a bipod it was a light section support weapon, and became a heavy position piece when mounted on a tripod. It was called 'the pig' by American soldiers due to its unwieldy size, but was generally considered a reliable weapon in Vietnam. Australian troopers referred to the weapon as 'the gun'. Each soldier within a squad helped carry 600-1,200 rounds for the MG in preloaded belts.

MAG58

After Vietnam the M60 was replaced with the MAG58. MAG stands for *Mitrailleuse d'Appui Général* – French for *general-purpose machine gun* – showing its Belgian origin. This remarkably successful gun is used by at least 80 other countries and is excellent for laying down sustained support fire out to a range of 800 metres. It can spit out 800 to 1,000 7.62mm bullets per minute and can be a light support weapon on a bipod, or be mounted on a heavier tripod. Troops appreciate its reliability and ruggedness in all conditions.

F89 LSW

The F89 Light Support Weapon is a state-of-the-art light machine gun. One user can lay down intensive fire of up to 700 rpm with high velocity light 5.56mm bullets. It is gas operated, fully automatic, air cooled and fed by a disintegrating link belt. As a section support weapon it can be equipped with night optics and can suppress opponents up to half a kilometre away.

Anti-Tank Weapons

The Boys Anti-Tank Rifle

The Australians adopted the Boys anti-tank rifle during the early stages of World War II. This bulky 17-kilogram weapon was issued to infantry and anti-tank formations. It was a conventional bolt action weapon which held five 14.3mm cartridges. The Boys was a beast to fire and often resulted in bruised shoulders or even broken bones. It saw some early success against Italian Tankettes but was soon phased out of service as it was useless against most tanks.

The Super Bazooka

This American tubular rocket launcher was adapted from the German Panzerschrek. It was first given to Australian forces in the Pacific theater in the closing stage of World War II. Australians in Korea were equipped with the M20 Super Bazooka. This 88mm weapon proved to be effective against the T34/85s. It was effective against tanks at 100 metres and could take out targets in the open up to a kilometre away.

The M72 Rocket Launcher

Experience in Malaya and Sarawak had proved that Bazookas were too unwieldy for long desert patrols. By the time of the Australian involvement in Vietnam the American M72 LAW (Light Anti-Tank Weapon) was available, and it proved ideal for use in the counterinsurgency. The 72, known by the diggers as the '66' due to its 66mm rocket, was a single shot disposable rocket launcher made of lightweight aluminum and plastic components. It was particularly effective at bunker busting and could take out targets at a range of 200 meters.

Karl Gustav

While the M72 has continued to be used up to squad level, heavier anti-tank weaponry was provided to the Australian troopers with the Karl Gustav. This 84mm hand held device is very accurate, and its 84mm rockets can take out most modern armour. It comes with anti-personnel rockets and high explosive anti-tank weapons, with an effective range out to 500 metres. The Australians are equipped with the M3 version, which is designed for the harshest desert or tropical conditions.

The Javelin

In 2016, the Australian Army received the Javelin Anti-Tank Missile. This absolutely lethal missile is effective to 2,000 meters and can demolish any known armoured vehicle. The firer sights the weapon on the intended target and discharges the missile. The initial soft launch creates almost no blowback before the rocket engine takes over. The missile roars upwards and then descends on the target, ensuring it hits where any armour is thinnest. Once locked on the target, the crew can disappear; it is a 'shoot and scoot' weapon.

MALAYA AND INDONESIA

The Malayan Emergency and the Indonesian Konfrontation laid the ground work for Australian success in the Vietnam War. Australians and their British allies, including crack Ghurkha units, excelled in the long jungle patrols needed to winkle out a hard core of communist insurgents seeking to create a communist state in the Malaysian provinces. Allied forces were supplied by prearranged air drops that allowed them to dominate large swathes of terrain. Meanwhile, ambushes were set by both sides in the difficult environment.

The lessons learnt by the Australian forces in Malay founded the techniques and tactics that allowed the Australians to drive insurgents out of Phuoc Toy Province; one of the few allied successes in the Vietnam conflict.

There were many similarities between the insurgency in Malay and Vietnam. The communist guerrillas in both countries were originally funded and supported by the allies during World War II. They were often better organised than other anti-Japanese insurgents and so were seen as a preferred option by the American and British Special Services. Both organisations moved among rural populations, making them elusive foes to combat, and both the Malay communists and the Vietnamese communists used Mao Tse Tung's playbook on insurgencies.

The main difference between the two revolutions is that the insurgency in Malaya was supressed. The Australian contribution to this victory was substantial.

In 1945 the British moved to repossess their colonial occupation of Malaya, Sarawak and Singapore. The British sought to unite the three in an independent state of Malaysia. Initially they met opposition from the indigenous Malays, who were wary that their Indian and Chinese minorities would dominate the new state. Seeking a peaceful exit, the British gave in to majority will and proposed a state where Malays would be able to dominate the economic and political framework.

The Chinese minority was not happy with this, and so began a civil war that lasted for almost 20 years. The Chinese guerrillas began a campaign of violence and destabilisation. On 16 June 1948, three English rubber planters were tied to trees and shot by the communists. Along with the execution of foreigners, 'collaborating' Malay officials were assassinated in their hundreds. The Viet Cong made this one of their key tactics of terror two decades later. This ongoing pattern of violence led the British to declare that Malaya was in a 'state of emergency', giving the conflict its name: the Malayan Emergency.

At first everything went pear shaped; the inexperienced British squaddies found it difficult to contain the growing insurgency. Resettling rural communities into closed villages and declaring the insurgents to be 'CTs' (communist terrorists) did little to stabilise the situation.

The British did the only logical thing: they called in the Aussies. The first unit to head north to help contain the threat was No 38 Squadron RAAF, which was equipped with Dakotas. For two years the Dakotas, operating out of Singapore, provided invaluable support ferrying troops and dropping supplies to columns patrolling hostile terrain.

One month later, the elite outfit No 1 Squadron RAAF arrived, equipped with the little known but effective Lincoln bomber. This was originally the last in the line of the Lancaster bomber variants, but was renamed the Lincoln. This was a long range and high altitude version of that redoubtable weapon, and most of those equipped to Australian squadrons were built in Australia. The Lincoln was just as tough and reliable as its predecessor and, with a crew of seven, could haul almost 7 tonnes of bombs at 500km/h, with a range of more than 5,000 kilometres.

This huge operational range was not required, as 1st Squadron RAAF operated out of Changi air base, right in the centre of operations. The communists had a healthy respect for the squadron. Time after time their supply bases, encampments and communications were pounded by the Australian flyers. In the seven years that the squadron operated in Malaysia it flew almost 4,000 sorties and delivered 35,000 tonnes of bombs: 85% of the ordinance dropped during the whole conflict. Mounted in both the nose and tail turrets were two .50 calibre machine guns that could strafe suspected enemy positions with two thousand 12mm bullets per minute. Other RAAF formations also fought in Malaya, including fighter squadrons Nos 3 and 77.

An example of the destructive power of the Lincolns was Operation Termite, mounted in July 1954. Five RAAF Lincolns made repeated bombing and strafing attacks of communist camps in Perak state. Paratroops were dropped by Dakotas and, with the aid of ground assaults, destroyed several communist units. The Bombers maintained operations for another ten days. By the end of the operation, 181 camps had been destroyed.

In October 1955 the first Australian infantry, 2 RAR, arrived in Malaya. This battalion and the formations that followed were a battle hardened groups, and many of their personnel had earned their stripes in some of the biggest battles in Korea. These veteran soldiers soon adapted their tactics to the needs of the new battlefield and excelled in long range patrols, where small groups of soldiers patrolled remote areas, hunting down and encircling known communist formations. Patience was the chief characteristic needed in this war and huge amounts of effort and ordinance were required to kill only a few CTs.

One of the most significant actions experienced by 2 RAR occurred on 22 June 1956. A patrol of five diggers was ambushed by insurgents, with three falling to semiautomatic fire. As other patrols converged on the site, three more Australians were casualties. Two CTs were killed and the others fled.

This battle was the exception to the rule. As well trained British, Ghurkha and Australian forces relentlessly hunted down the Chinese rebels, positive social and economic measures turned the rural population against the CTs, driving the insurgents into the inhospitable north of the Malayan peninsula. The British were not gentle. Any villages suspected of aiding the insurgents had collective punishments imposed upon them, and some were even burnt down.

In November 1957, 3 RAR (enjoying he nickname 'Old Faithful') took over the posting and continued to pursue the remaining communists deep into the Malayan jungle. Novel patrol tactics were used, such as 'tracker teams' consisting of an officer, a section of infantry, four Iban trackers from Borneo and one or two trained tracker dogs. These teams would chase the insurgents out of their jungle lairs. The patrols were in close radio contact and could rapidly call on each other for support. One notable victory occurred on 20 November, when several patrols managed to attack a communist camp and kill, among others, a district leader. Lieutenant Claude Ducker and his tracker team found foot signs leading to a small knoll that was occupied by a terrorist group. He left most of the party blocking the lower exit point from the knoll while he and two Iban's circled above the encampment. The lieutenant's party opened fire and the panicked terrorists fled straight into the blocking party's guns. Even though it was a small victory, it broke the CT's organisation in the region. The survivors surrendered soon after.

In 1957 Malaya was granted its independence. In 1958 the last guerrillas had either surrendered or fled into Thailand. The government declared an end to the state of emergency in July 1960. It is estimated that 6,700 guerrillas died, along with 1,800 Malayan and Commonwealth troops. Thirty-nine Australian soldiers died and 27 were wounded.

THE KONFRONTASI: AUSTRALIA'S SECRET WAR

IEDs (Improvised Explosive Devices) have become very much part of the modern vernacular. This is largely thanks to their common use in Afghanistan and Iraq, where they have frequently been used to attack coalition forces. In

1963 the Indonesians used very similar tactics in an effort to lower morale among Australian troops in Sarawak.

In 1963 Malaya, Sarawak, Sabah, and Singapore were united in the Federation of Malaysia. Just when it seemed the Australian military's role in the region was complete, a new threat emerged. President Sukarno had led the Indonesians in a long and bloody rebellion against the Dutch after World War II. The President, who was perceived to be a communist, saw the new state of Malaysia as a British puppet state. He also had designs on surrounding territories and sponsored a revived communist insurrection in Sarawak. The island of Borneo's largest provinces are Malaysian Sarawak and Indonesian Kalimantan. It was out of Kalimantan that most of the raids were launched.

Sukarno sought to unite the entire island of Borneo under his new Republic's rule. He ordered large raids of up to two hundred soldiers by land and sea into Sarawak to further his aim of 'crushing Malaysia.' His foreign minister, Dr Subandrio, came up with the term 'Konfrontasi' to describe his leader's policy of confronting Malaysia.

The raids launched into Sarawak and Sabah were at first made by militia or 'volunteers'. Some incursions were made into the Malay peninsula. The 3rd RAR was involved in encirclement movements to eradicate these clandestine attacks, but the Australian government was less willing to put troops into to Sarawak lest they be seen as aggressive by the pugnacious new regime in Jakarta.

The British needed the veteran Aussie jungle fighters and sent multiple requests to Canberra seeking troops for deployment. Finally, after the Malaysian government put in a request, 3 RAR was committed to Borneo, landing in March 1964. The Australians were teamed up with a British regiment and a Ghurkha battalion. The formation was known as the 99th Infantry Brigade; or West Brigade due to being given responsibility for securing the western border between Sarawak and Indonesia in the provinces of Bau and Lundu. It was an imposing task. Thirteen Commonwealth battalions were asked to secure almost 1,600 kilometres of jungle frontier.

Supported by artillery and engineers, 3 RAR was patrolling 56 kilometres of border between the two new nations. Small patrol bases were set up. These were supplied by helicopter and were used to launch foot patrols out to hunt down or ambush the opposition. The Australian's role was defensive and the most difficult part of the operation was detecting small parties of Indonesians, who would infiltrate across the border dressed as farmers or fishermen. When a confrontation did occur the superior training and weapons of the Australian battalions (the 4th RAR deployed in 1966) usually saw the Indonesians off.

Much more of a threat was the Indonesian deployment of mines and IEDs. Roads were few and far between and narrow tracks were necessary for transport. This gave the Indonesians plenty of opportunities to lay booby traps and deploy mines. Several days after arriving (on 23 March 1964) an anti-personnel mine was detonated, killing a sergeant of 3 RAR and a native guide. On 17 May two Australians were killed when a patrol was approaching a suspected path between Kalimantan and Sarawak. Private Larry downs of Toowoomba stepped off the track and detonated a mine. The blast killed Downs and his sergeant, Vince Vella.

It was during this period that the British and Australian governments decided to begin a clandestine war: Operation Claret. From June 1964 to early 1966 elite formations took the fight to the Indonesian aggressors.

Realising that it was almost impossible to police every possible infiltration point, the Commonwealth forces took the fight into Indonesian territory. The British SAS (Special Air Service) and the Australian and New Zealand Special Air Services, as well as regular troops and Ghurkhas, began to cross the border into Kalimantan. The process began with 'hot pursuits'. Indonesians contacted in a border clash weren't allowed to escape into friendly territory without the Commonwealth troops following them up until they were eliminated. By July, patrols were penetrating many kilometres across the border to set up platoon and company size ambush positions. All troops were sworn to secrecy; 'plausible deniability' was the cornerstone of Claret. The dense jungle allowed them to operate without detection and, if by some chance proof was obtained by the Indonesian government, the incursion could be put down to faulty map reading.

The Australian government acknowledged its involvement in Claret in 1996. Before this participants were forbidden from mentioning their involvement in the campaign, even to friends and family.

While the Indonesian armed forces were being denied the tactical initiative on the northern borders, Sukarno's increasingly bizarre behaviour was alienating his supporters. Crazy economic policies led to rampant inflation and parts of Kalimantan were in open rebellion as the domestic economy collapsed. Suharto seized the reins of power and, seeing the futility of the Konfrontation, he signed a peace treaty with Malaysia in August 1966.

3rd RAR and 4th RAR, along with support services, served in Borneo. Twelve RAN vessels, including HMAS *Melbourne*, patrolled the Strait of Malacca and the South China Sea, preventing seaborne incursions. No 78 Wing of the RAAF and its Sabres operated out of Labuan in Borneo in support of operations.

Fifteen Australians died on active service in the two years of the conflict.

Even now Australia has military assets in Malaysia. Given the ongoing tension in the area, even after the confrontation, a Five Power Defence Arrangement was signed between Australia, Great Britain, Malaysia, New Zealand and Singapore. Their headquarters was at RAAF base Butterworth, located at the northwest side of Malaya, and even now Australian RAAF assets are there, protected by company sized rotations from the RAR.

CHAPTER 11

VICTORY IN VIETNAM

The colonial French got a bloody nose in 1954. At the battle of Dien Bien Phu the forces of the North Vietnamese Army (NVA) proved that they could take on the best that France had to offer and pound them into humiliating surrender. The NVA was the fighting arm of the Communist Party of Vietnam (CPV), led by Ho Chi Minh. The CPV had, like the communists in Malaya, received initial support from the American government during World War II.

When the war ended the French sought to reimpose colonial rule but the NVA, under the talented leadership of Vo Nguyen Gap, isolated the French military from the population and expelled them with the effective guerrilla forces of the Viet Cong (VC).

The 1954 Geneva Accords were a face saving measure for the French, that allowed them to maintain the myth that their military had successfully held the communists out of South Vietnam. The country was divided into the Democratic Republic of Vietnam (DRV) in the north, and the Republic of Vietnam (RV) in the south. Free and fair elections were to be held in 1956 to ascertain if the country would be united, but concerns that the CPV would triumph forced their cancellation.

The Cold War had spread to Indo China. America wanted to avoid a massive communist bloc extending from China down to South Vietnam and, in 1955, huge amounts of American dollars began pouring into the Republic. In 1956 a US Military Assistance Advisory Group (MAAG) was formed to train South Vietnamese forces. Likewise, the communists began rebuilding their insurgent cells in the Republic of Vietnam and infiltrating regular troops, often disguised as peasants, across the 17th parallel that divided the two nations.

The reasons for Australian involvement in the Vietnam War are varied and complex. Two main threads emerge. Firstly, Prime Minister Robert Menzies had a Churchillian suspicion of a new communist Iron Curtain descending across the Asia-Pacific, and secondly the Americans wanted international support for their decision to back the government of South Vietnam.

Australia's commitment escalated along similar lines to the American commitment. The war was fought almost like a lovechild between the Korean War and the Malayan Emergency. There were conventional defensive and offensive battles where regular forces went head to head, just like in Korea. Then there were the seemingly endless, slow burning fights where long range patrols would spend weeks in rugged terrain seeking to outwit wily Vietnamese insurgents.

The Australian Army's experience in the earlier conflicts had prepared them well. By the end of the conflict there were few commands who could report that the province they were responsible for had been cleared of any real opposition, but the NVA (North Vietnam Army) and the VC (Viet Cong) had decided that Australians were too tough an opponent to eject and instead moved their resources on to more vulnerable prey.

One American general was reputed to have said: 'The British have the Ghurkhas; we have the Australians.' While patronising, it does reflect the respect the Australians earned in South Vietnam.

FIRST IN, LAST OUT – THE AUSTRALIAN TRAINING TEAM

The Australian military's doctrine can often be termed 'forward defence', best understood as fighting any threats to our north well before they get close to

Australia's shores. Thus the decision to fight communism in South Vietnam was part of Australian strategic theory. The first detachment sent to Vietnam was intended to train the ARVN (Army of the Republic of Vietnam) troops, but the realities of the insurgency led to the first Australian soldiers putting boots on the ground to find themselves in the line of fire.

On 1 July 1962 a plane set down into the tropical heat at Son Nhut Airport, Saigon. Colonel Ted Sarong, commander of the Australian Army Training Team Vietnam (AATTV), alighted; three days later the rest of his crew arrived. Composed of 29 officers and NCOs, this detachment represented the longest serving unit in any theatre of war and was active in the conflict for over 10 years. The men represented the cream of the Australian Army and all were veterans of conflicts ranging through the Pacific, in the Second World War, Korea and Malaysia.

They were well suited to the multiplicity of the AATTV's duties.

The Australian personnel were spread across the south. Some were responsible for training regulars of the ARVN, while others taught the local militias – made up of the Regional Force (RF) and the Popular Force (PF) – military techniques from scratch. This latter work was difficult and dangerous. Initially all instructions had to be given through local translators, and something as simple as teaching recruits how to lob a grenade was fraught with danger. Lessons that should have taken perhaps an hour were dragged out for several hours while each of the different parties tried to make themselves understood in the sweltering tropical conditions. Many of the teams were long miles from 'civilisation' and had to make do with the most basic resources in enclosed villages, or up in the mountainous highlands training the Montagnard tribesmen. Being attacked on all sides by bugs and fighting jungle rot was an exhausting and debilitating process.

But the theatre had many more dangers – dangers of aimed ordinance launched by an implacable foe.

While the first troops were meant to be there in an advisory role, this soon proved unrealistic. This was recognised in June 1964 when their role was changed from passive advisers to operational advisers: the Australians were playing crucial roles in ARVN operations and their personnel increased from 30 to 100 by 1965. They were included in the whole gamut of warfare in South Vietnam.

Sometimes the Australians were involved in patrols where ARVN platoons sought to ambush their enemies. At the other end of the scale the Australians were involved in brigade sized attacks and were crucial in coordinating assets such as artillery stonks, jet fighter passes and helicopter attacks. Often the heavy support for the ARVN came from American units and it was an advantage for them to have backup from the highly trained, English speaking Australians, who could be trusted to bring in a strike on exact coordinates to avoid friendly fire.

It was during this time that Australia suffered its first battle casualty. On 6 July 1964, Warrant Officer Kevin Conway fell in action at Nam Dong.

One of the most dangerous jobs given to the advisors was at an outpost near the DMZ (Demilitarised Zone) near the border between the two countries. These were established to allow patrols to disrupt NVA communications and the infiltration of resources into the south. These bases were usually just a peak or hill ringed with fortifications and packed with semi reliable ARVN forces. One or two liaison officers, usually American or Australian, had the responsibility of calling in fire support whenever NVA regiments decided to hit these isolated fortresses. The NVA often attacked several targets at once and the AATTV member needed to be able to convince the central command that his base really needed the assistance.

The experienced troops of the AATTV knew that to win the war their ARVN allies would need to maintain ownership of the land beyond the perimeters of their forts through constant patrolling. It was their function to introduce patrolling, ambushing and intelligence gathering techniques to the South Vietnamese soldiers. To meet this goal, the Mobile Strike force (Mike Force) was created. This unit, led by American and Australian specialists, helped to wrest the initiative from the VC in many areas of Vietnam.

However, Mike Force was neither trained nor equipped to hold large pieces of territory or to take the fight up to NVA or VC main force regiments.

That would be the task of the 1st Australian Task Force (1 ATF), a state-of-the-art crack combat outfit, which would write another chapter in Australia's military success. The South Vietnamese Government 'invited' the Australians to send a significant detachment of soldiers.

In April 1965 the Menzies government agreed to send combat formations. The 1 RAR served from May 1965 to May 1966 in Bien Hoa, just outside Saigon. Under the command of Lieutenant Colonel Brumfield, the battalion provided the blueprint for later operations. Once a solid defensive camp was established, patrols were sent out to patrol the surrounding area, denying freedom of movement to the enemy. Their equipment, developed over the years in Malaya, was more suited to the hot climate than the American kit. Green shorts and bush hats (known as giggle hats) made the diggers more comfortable as they worked than the Americans were in their full army fatigues, complete with helmets and flak jackets.

In March 1966 the Holt government increased the Australian commitment to a brigade sized force of two battalions.

THE 1ST AUSTRALIAN TASK FORCE ARRIVES

Recognising that Australian and American combat methods were different, the Menzies government requested that Australian forces be given their own Tactical Area of Responsibility. They were assigned Phuoc Tuy Province and began building a self-sufficient task force. This force would include a range of formations so as to be able to handle all combat missions independently. It was originally envisaged that the task force would include two full battalions (5 RAR and 6 RAR), as well as supporting troops such as artillery assets, Armoured Personnel Carriers (APCs) and engineers. It would amount to approximately 6,000 men.

Phuoc Tuy was chosen as it could easily be supplied by the sea and because it was seeing a significant amount of insurgent activity. The Australians were to be allowed to improve upon the counterinsurgency techniques they had developed during the Malayan Emergency. Continuing the ANZAC tradition, the Kiwis contributed the 161st New Zealand Artillery Battery.

1 ATF was given the task of eliminating VC activity in the province and securing communication along Route 15 to the port at Vung Tau. This was the logistic support base for the Australians; the aircraft carrier HMAS *Sydney* was soon named the 'Vung Tau Express' as it brought in all of the necessary equipment and supplies. Nui Dat (small hill) was chosen by the task force commander. It was an elevated position (perfect for a firebase), it sat astride some vital communist supply lines and it was fairly near to main population centres.

The Australians first had to establish their base, supplies and communications, before extending patrols through the rest of the province. Vung Tau was secured in April 1966, and soon after the base at Nui Dat was established. All Vietnamese within a 4,000 metre radius around the base were ejected and a free fire zone declared: anything that moved within the cleared area was fair game, 24/7. In another departure from American practice, no Vietnamese civilians were allowed in the base to perform domestic chores such as laundry. The Australians well knew that in an insurgency situation, no locals could be trusted.

The 1 ATF was initially composed of 5 RAR, 6 RAR, 1st APC Squadron, 3 batteries of artillery with eighteen 105mm L5 Pack Howitzers, 3rd SAS Squadron, and signals, recon and logistics support. Six 155mm M109 self-propelled howitzers from an American battery were also on permanent fire readiness to support the Australians.

The largest Australian field formation since World War II was determined to clear their province of hostile forces.

The VC were equally determined to stop them. They needed to destroy an Australian formation to score a propaganda victory. A trap was laid near Nui Dat at a rubber plantation called Long Tan. More than 2,000 well armed men from the 275th Viet Cong Main Force Regiment, as well as approximately 400 men from the D445 Provincial Mobile Battalion, were poised to wipe out a company of the newly arrived Australians. The 275 was a crack formation and had already inflicted significant losses on both ARVN and US forces in the past year.

THE BATTLE OF LONG TAN

First the trap had to be laid.

During the early hours of 17 August 1966 communist mortar and recoilless rifle shells crashed into the new base. They came from the east of the position, near the large rubber plantation of Long Tan. Shells landed near the SAS entrenchments and some of the artillery assets. Brigadier Oliver Jackson, the task force commander, was aware of the potential for a full scale attack and sent B Company 6 RAR to locate the firing positions. B Company secured the recently abandoned fire pits and was replaced by D Company, which continued to follow up the retreating communists. They moved through the rubber plantation towards the abandoned village of Long Tan.

D Company was moving in the usual triangular formation; two platoons up and one in reserve, with the command elements in the middle. Four kilometres east of Nui Dat 11th Platoon, commanded by Lieutenant Gordon Sharp, ran into a small group of VC, who they saw off in a brief firefight. The 11th Platoon pursued the VC into a major concentration of the 275 Regiment. Just after 4p.m. Sharp's platoon ran into a wall of fire, forcing them to take cover behind any fallen logs or other obstacles. Lieutenant Geoff Kendall with 10th Platoon was ordered to their assistance, but they too were soon pinned down.

The 275th had been lying in wait just out of artillery range, and were now coming in for the kill.

This was no minor firefight. The chatter of heavy machine guns combined with the bark of AK 47s as hundreds of bullets whistled around the prone Australians. Rocket Propelled Grenades (RPGs) and mortar shells added to the racket. The company commander, Major Harry Smith with 12th Platoon, gave what fire support he could and sent requests to Nui Dat for artillery.

A new element entered the battle: a tremendous tropical downpour reduced visibility under the thick rubber canopy and threw up a mud mist. Monsoonal rain splashed cloying mud up to 50cm into the air, coating men and equipment. Both 10th and 11th Platoons lost their coms, and when 12th Platoon was ordered up in support it too was halted by VC gunfire.

To the Australians on the ground it seemed each was fighting their own small battle. The 11th Platoon was in the greatest danger. In the first 20 minutes Sharp's command had lost half of their 28 men, dead or wounded. Through the mud and rain it was obvious that large units of VC were massing to assault and overrun the Australians.

Fortunately, there were three Forward Observers (FOs) embedded with the command platoon. Artillery from the two Australian and one Kiwi batteries was soon smashing into the Vietnamese. The experienced NVA veterans were using their tactic of 'hanging on to the enemy's belt', meaning that Smith almost had to bring the artillery onto his own positions. VC began infiltrating between the platoons and soon many of D Company were running out of ammunition. The situation became so dire that some diggers grabbed their entrenching tool in one hand and their grenades in the other ready to fight to the death in vicious hand-to-hand combat. Fortunately, two Hueys from 9 RAAF Squadron managed to drop blanket-wrapped boxes of ammo right where the Australians needed them.

Later in the afternoon things were turning in favour of the beleaguered company. Smashing into the VC concentration were aggressive 155mm howitzer shells. Ten APCs carrying A Company were dispatched to support D Company, and B Company was also ordered into the fray. The APCs, all with pintle mounted .50 Cal machine guns, smashed into and scattered a party of the 275 that was seeking to outflank D Company.

By 6p.m. the surviving members of 11th Platoon managed to pull back and consolidate on 12th Platoon, before both withdrew to a new firing line with the rest of D Company. Here they fought off human wave attacks of the 275, who continued to attack regardless of casualties. Finally, at 7p.m. the APCs appeared and used their massed heavy machine gun fire to tear into the communist formations. B Company appeared, after retracing their tracks, and completed the discomfiture of the enemy, forcing them to retreat.

The Australians had fought off a formation at least ten times its own size. More than 250 VC were killed and at least as many wounded. The American Commander-in-Chief, General Westmoreland, noted that it was one of the most significant victories in the theatre to date. Most importantly, the North Vietnamese had been denied a crucial propaganda victory against America's ally.

The Australians had not come out of the battle unscathed. The task force lost the most casualties of any other day in Vietnam, with 18 killed and 24 wounded. Shortcomings were revealed with some of the equipment. The APC .50 Cal machine guns were not shielded, meaning the commanders were vulnerable to enemy fire. Shields and turrets were soon installed. The pack howitzers proved to be too light for sustained fire and it was decided to replace them as soon as possible with American 105s.

Most importantly though, the battle established 1 ATF's dominance over the VC in Phuoc Tuy. They would be able to pacify the entire province in the following years.

DOMINATING PHUOC TUY

Once the base at Nui Dat was secure the task force began its mission to pacify Phuoc Tuy and clear out any enemy troops.

Operations were divided into four main categories: search and clear, search and destroy, cordon and search, and ambushing.

The multiplicity of threats meant that the Viet Cong could not operate with confidence in their jungle lairs. At any one time only enough men to secure the base remained at Nui Dat; the majority of the Australian troops were out in the field, hunting the enemy.

SEARCH AND DESTROY

Search and destroy missions were taxing on the soldiers and they could last for days and weeks. In a typical operation a company would be inserted into an area where the Viet Cong were likely to be operating. The insertion could happen at night and decoy operations would deflect attention away from the bases. The three rifle platoons would then patrol a zone methodically during the day and set up ambushes or laagers at night. The headquarters platoon would remain in a secure central position, coordinating the platoons and calling in support or resupplies as needed.

After deployment in a Huey the unit was on its own, as men were expected to hump 8 days rations. Unlike the Americans, who were supplied by choppers daily, the Australians chose to remain hidden from their foe.

The Australians were more like beasts of burden than trained killers. As well as their eight day rations, they carried slung from the basic harness or in their pack the following: weapon and ammunition clips, shell dressing, entrenching tool, machete, two M26 grenades, ten litres of water in one litre water bottles, stove with ignition tablets, shaving gear, mug, plate, blanket, spare socks with jocks, rain shelter quarter, one or two 100 round belts for the M60 machine gun, claymore mines, two smoke grenades and a single shot 66 rocket launcher. This could easily amount to 45 kilos of weight for each soldier.

The day was spent moving slowly through the bush. Paths were avoided, as that is where most casualties were likely to occur. Squads fanned out, searching for the elusive enemy. Hand signals were used for communication and, unlike the American line formations, smoking was forbidden. Australians never left empty bully-beef tins behind as they could be fashioned into deadly weapons by the enemy. The point man of a patrol would be on the lookout for signs of the enemy and only when a zone was declared clear would the troops, camouflaged with green and black face paint, move slowly onwards.

If the enemy was encountered it was likely to be a brief, savage firefight. The VC became increasingly well equipped as the Australian commitment continued. Increasingly large numbers of North Vietnamese Regulars were inserted into the battlefield. Just as the Australians remained active in the field, the VC training emphasised continuous movement, and it was rare that one unit would remain in the same location for more than two days.

The greatest danger for the diggers was the ever present threat of booby traps.

The Viet Cong used a range of booby traps designed to kill, mutilate and terrify their opponents. Whether they actually caused damage was often beside the point. The range of devices ensured that soldiers patrolling in hostile territory could never be comfortable in Vietnam, but were in a constant state of hyper alertness. The Australians ensured that whenever possible their routes avoided tracks and choke points. Nevertheless, this VC strategy of psychological warfare led to dire consequences even after the war. More than any other conflict, the veterans of the Vietnam War had problems with PTSD long after they returned home.

Some booby traps used Stone Age technology. At its most basic, the Viet Cong would tether small vipers along the side of pathways, in foliage or in tunnels where their opponents were expected. These angular green reptiles were nicknamed 'two step snakes' by the allied forces, as any soldier who was bitten by them would take another two steps before dropping down dead. Punji stakes were inserted into holes in tracks and covered with a thin screen. Any soldier unfortunate enough to crash through the screen would find one, two or several stakes piercing their combat boots and impaling their feet. The punji stakes were covered with rotted excrement and all sorts of nasty noxious elements, ensuring catastrophic infection. One concoction, called 'elephant trunk' by the VC, was reputed to kill within 20 minutes of entering the bloodstream.

Sometimes the Viet Cong dug tiger trap pits; if a squaddie fell into one he would become impaled on several stakes. One version had stakes buried in the wall of the pit but facing downwards, making the extraction of the foot painful and difficult. There was even a bear trap made out of poisoned punji sticks or metal spikes. The victim stepping onto this would hit two boards or steel plates with the wooden or metal spikes attached. The boards would then pivot and slam shut, burying the barbs into the leg just above the area protected by the boot. Another infernal device consisted of a bamboo whip with a large fish hook, set up at face level. When tripped the device would gash the unsuspecting soldier's face, perhaps taking out an eye or two.

More sophisticated was the use of crossbows, that were embedded in tree forks or pits and shot a bolt when a trip wire, often made of natural-looking tree roots, was tripped by an unsuspecting trooper. A heavy mud ball with spiked bamboo stakes sticking out of it was attached to a tree by a vine. Once a unit tripped the wire, the deadly device would soar down in a wide arc, and anybody standing below it would come to a painful end.

Another device relying on local materials was the coconut mine. This involved a hollowed out nut packed with explosive powder salvaged from unexploded ordinance. It was covered with rocks, and a simple detonating device would throw a shower of sub lethal, but frightening, missiles into the air. The bamboo mine operated on similar principles but was more deadly. It consisted of a large bamboo joint filled with nuts, bolts, scrap metal and explosive. Once detonated by a simple trip wire it could take out several soldiers at once.

The guerrillas relied on the allied forces for most of their explosives. During the Vietnam War a greater tonnage of explosive was dropped by the Americans than all of the belligerent forces of World War II. The Viet Cong employed specially trained ordinance spotters who would observe bombardments and chart the likely location of unexploded shells and bombs. Recovery teams then set out to retrieve any live shells and, using fairly primitive methods, sought to extract the explosive material. The shells were usually opened with a hack saw. One of the team did this while another poured cold water out of a teapot onto the breach, to ensure that it did not overheat and explode.

Sometimes shells were used whole. Recovered shells were dug into the ground and pressure detonated by a man's body weight. Any soldier who stepped on a primed 155mm shell was vaporised. Single bullets could be placed along a track, with a piece of sharpened bamboo acting as a firing pin. While not lethal, a bullet through the foot would require immediate evacuation and slow down any patrolling column.

The most common communist booby trap was the wired grenade used in tunnels and along paths. In the early days of the war the grenades were homemade, with wooden handles or using salvaged coke cans. On jungle tracks and paths, a favourite tactic was to place the grenade, with the safety pin removed, inside an appropriate tin can or length of bamboo. A pull on the trip wire extracted the grenade from its container, which allowed it to prime itself before exploding.

A CATASTROPHIC COCK UP

Australians got a nasty surprise when fighting in North Africa against Rommel's Africa Corp. For many diggers the first inkling that they had wandered into a 'Gerry' minefield was when a small cylindrical can leapt in the air and detonated, spreading a hail of ball bearings that could maim and kill. The was the infamous S-Mine, or Bouncing Betty.

This ingenious device consisted of a cylinder dug into the ground. At its base was a smaller tube filled with shrapnel and ball bearings. Below this tube was an explosive charge that was triggered when something brushed against filaments sticking out of the top of the mine. The explosive charge propelled the shot laden tube a meter or so into the air, where it detonated, spreading its lethal payload in a 360 degree arc. Like all good anti-personnel devices, the S- Mine could also be set off by trip wires or configured as a booby trap.

The technology was copied by the Allies and an almost identical device was built, called the M16 'Jumping Jack' land mine. This mine was lethal in a 25 metre radius, but was known to kill up to 75 metres away and could inflict wounds as far as of 200 metres.

In what was perhaps the greatest miscalculation in Australian military history, 20,000 of these lethal devices were made available to insurgents in Phuoc Tuy Province.

The first commanders of the First Australian Task Force came into the province perhaps lacking an understanding of the nature of insurgent warfare. They presumed that the densely populated villages in the southwest part of the province were not sympathetic to the communists, and he erected an 11 kilometre minefield to separate these villages from the north and northeast of the province; at the time held by regular units of the NLF (national liberation front). The barrier was sandwiched on both sides by extensive barbed wire entanglements, and within the mined zone were 20,000 Jumping Jacks.

The barrier was begun in early May 1967, but things started to go sideways almost immediately. Much of the ordinance was faulty and 13 sappers were killed or maimed. Heat, enemy action and time pressure led to fatal mistakes. Sometimes little kids would send a dog into the fields just to see what would happen.

The mines were fitted with anti-lift devices that would detonate if anybody tampered with the mine. It is possible that up to 30 NLF sappers and soldiers were killed before they worked out how to disarm this safeguard. Once this was accomplished, hundreds of the VC were instructed in safe lifting techniques. The extensive minefields were not patrolled at night, giving access to almost unlimited mines to Australia's enemies in Phuoc Toy. Of course, the planners' belief was fundamentally wrong: Vietnamese from both sides of the province lifted mines, and the NLF was dominant in the whole province.

By mid-1967, only months after the field was laid, at least 2,000 mines were in enemy hands. They used them to fortify the approaches to jungle strongholds, laid them in patterns to funnel diggers into the fire zones from bunkers and tunnel systems, or else laid them in the paths emanating from Nui Dat, making the very action of moving from the main firebase hazardous. The VC were past masters in laying the mines for maximum effect. Often laid in clusters of three or four, a digger would detonate one, and as his mates came to his aid they would trigger others. Even the arrival of a chopper as a medevac could be dangerous; in many instances the downdraught from the chopper blades triggered the sensitive devices, causing more carnage.

221

The Australian commanders had intended a passive defensive barrier. By using informers and intelligence, the insurgents used the mines as an offensive weapon. When informed that a patrol was setting out, they sought to predict the course of the patrol and move mines to interdict the Australians. They could be repositioned time after time until they scored a hit.

An example of the carnage that was visited on the Australians occurred on 21 July 1969. Lieutenant Peter Hines of A Company 6 RAR stepped on a mine just outside his command post. His legs were blown off and 18 other men of 3 Platoon were wounded as the balls ripped through their stomachs and legs. The men may have been bunched together, as Hines was telling them of the momentous events of the moon landing. Two more mines were set off soon after, killing another soldier and wounding five more, including the battalion CO. Three mines killed two soldiers and wounded twenty-three others.

Between 1967 and 1971 it seems that at least 55 soldiers were killed by M16 mines, and 250 were seriously wounded. More importantly, it gave the defenders of Phuoc Toy Province a strategic asset that denied Australian soldiers free movement in the area of operations.

AN EXHAUSTING BUSINESS

As night approached it was the task of the patrol commander to select a night harbour. These were ideally areas with few points of access, removed from paths and inhabited areas. The perimeter was established, with heavy weapons set up to cover likely approaches and ammunition laid nearby. The squad was rotated in two hour shifts. The first shift might be spent alert on the perimeter, while the next shift was given to kit maintenance. The next shift allowed the soldier to eat and catch about an hour's shuteye before the rotation began again. A soldier considered himself fortunate if he caught four hours of sleep. With patrols lasting up to five weeks, sleep deprivation became a real issue.

The land itself seemed determined to eject the Australians. Each man had up to ten canteens suspended from their webbing and each canteen contained a litre, but drinking the warm water gave little relief. From dawn as soon as the sun rose above the horizon the heat became intolerable. Diggers could set their watches to the monsoon. At 2p.m. every day an unimaginable downpour began that lasted for two hours. Once it stopped the entire countryside became a steam bath as humidity rose to what seemed like 100%. In these conditions clothes soon began to fall apart. Thread was the first to rot, leading seams to break open. Socks and jocks seldom lasted more than two days and it was often easier to leave them back at base camp. Pants began to tear, leaving gaps for leeches to colonise groins and buttocks and thighs, where they would set up shop for hours at a time.

Insects were a constant irritant, even more frustrating at night. When a soldier managed to lie down for an hour's shut eye it seemed that every bug, grub and worm in the area would make a beeline to the unfortunate digger. If it was not pouring rain, they could even hear them approaching.

Snakes too welcomed the warmth of sleeping bodies, and often curled up in packs, shoes or giggle hats to sleep. One member of 7 RAR was bivouacking on a small knoll in the middle of a swamp. He and his companion spent the whole night fending off snakes with the butts of their rifles. The snakes weren't aggressive; they just wanted some shut eye too.

The constant humidity led to all sorts of skin problems. Chafing turned to blisters which transformed into nasty ulcers. Rashes and tinea were common in the groin, under arms and in any fold of skin. Agonisingly itchy tinea set in between the toes and soon degenerated into foot rot and skin rot.

When on patrol, especially on ambush, itches which would have driven any man insane had to be ignored: any untoward movement could give the game away.

At least the Australians were prepared for this ordeal, to an extent at least.

Recruits began their training with 12 weeks basic infantry training at Kapooka Barracks, south west of Wagga Wagga in New South Wales. All army recruits were trained in basic drill and weapons handling as well as army law. Riflemen who were to find themselves on the front line then did 12 weeks infantry specialist training at Ingleburn, also in New South Wales. Those earmarked for service in Vietnam spent three weeks in jungle combat training. While learning jungle craft from experienced instructors, who had done their time in Malaya and later Vietnam, the recruits were also acclimatised for the conditions they could expect to experience in Nui Dat.

By the time diggers were dispatched for their first tour they might have as much as ten months training and experience in large scale manoeuvres. They were usually ready, willing and able. Contrary to the view that 'nashos' were forced to serve in Vietnam, it was common practice for battalion COs to parade the troops before shipping and give any who wanted to stay behind the opportunity to do so. Few did. Most wanted to 'do right by their mates.'

Even when the new troops rotated into Vietnam they were rarely thrown into the thick of things without some extra acclimatisation.

A section from 7 RAR went out on their first patrol straight after arriving at Nui Dat. The whole squad was filled with rookies except for their sergeant, who had seen service in Malaysia. After hours of moving through difficult terrain they set up an ambush position overlooking a gully filled with bamboo. In the dead of night, when their senses were dulled with fatigue, the patrol heard what seemed like a platoon of VC crashing through the bamboo. All hell broke loose when the sergeant hurled his grenade at the source of the sound, only for the American made M15 to hit a bamboo stalk and bounce straight into the heart of their position. Fortunately, no-one was hurt, and when the patrol retuned at dawn they realised that in fact they had only been 400 metres from the base and they had been ordered to set up an ambush in a path frequented by a local herd of pigs!

Another squaddie from 7 RAR had a somewhat more unnerving introduction to the jungle. While lying prone in a monsoonal downpour in the middle of the night he felt a heavy weight move onto his leg. The 21-year-old slowly turned and saw a king cobra making its way over his legs through the ambush position.

The SAS squadron took jungle patrolling to another level. Several squadrons rotated through Nui Dat and small groups would be airlifted to remote locations. Here the members engaged in information gathering, and it was crucial that they be extracted before the VC even had a whiff of their presence. This was in comparison to the RAR patrols which would 'track squat' on a likely VC infiltration point or set up an ambush on a suspected campsite.

CORDON AND SEARCH

While search and destroy or search and clear missions were aimed at depriving the VC of free movement in the countryside, cordon and search operations were mounted to deprive them of civilian support.

Whole villages were uprooted from traditional locations and relocated. Access to these new hamlets could only be gained with government issued identity cards. Road blocks would be set up to monitor all traffic and any suspects detained and sent to intelligence units for interrogation. Another tactic was when in the dead of night Australian companies would encircle villages, and at dawn move in and collect all villagers for screening. An exhaustive search was then mounted for firearms, explosives and hidden caches of food. Often single VC soldiers would be found hidden in walls, wells or bunkers built under huts. Black Labrador tracking dogs were introduced and there were few VC who could escape their attentions.

ESCALATION

1967 saw a third infantry battalion arrive, 3 RAR. Continued successes saw the VC reduced to almost a rump presence in Phuoc Tuy. The Tet Offensive in 1968 led the Australians to step up their pressure, and most of the settled farmlands passed into allied control. Some areas remained as VC strongpoints and the task force moved into the inaccessible, bunker ridden Long Hai Hills. APCs were too fragile for this environment and the government decided to add a squadron of Centurion Main Battle Tanks to the task force.

THE CENTURION – BATTLE WINNER IN THE JUNGLE

The M113 APCs proved too light for many combat situations encountered in Phuoc Toy Province. In dense jungle they tended to become stuck. Mines placed on roads took a heavy toll on crews, who had to choose between sitting on the top of the APC and being exposed to sniper fire, or sitting within the M113 and getting blown to pieces. A well placed RPG round from the Viet Cong and the NVA could destroy a vehicle, and the armour was not even proof against heavy machine gun rounds from the Russian built 12.7mm DShK machine gun.

To meet the needs of the Australian task force, C Squadron, 1st Armoured Regiment arrived in South Vietnam on 24 February 1968, and proceeded to Nui Dat. C Squadron was armed with the Centurion Tank.

The Centurion was armed with a state-of-the-art 20 pounder cannon, able to fire armour piercing rounds, smoke shells, high explosive shells and canister. Its turret had armour plating up to 152mm thick, while the glacis plate on the front of the chassis had 118mm of well sloped armour. The sides and rear had more than 50mm armour.

The Centurion was the culmination of decades of British tank design. During World War II, British tanks were either designated cruiser tanks, designed for speed with poor armament and thin armour, or else they were heavily armoured but too slow for the modern battlefield, with the designation of infantry tanks. The Centurion was classified as a MBT (Main Battle Tank) and was one of the best tanks of the era.

The Centurion arrived too late to take on the German Panthers and Tigers that it had been designed to fight, but it proved to be a brilliant design with a fine balance of speed, armour, armament and reliability. It became an excellent jungle fighter.

C Squadron was a remarkably powerful formation equipped with two tanks in the command platoon supported by two Centurion ARVs (Armoured Recovery Vehicles), two bridge layer tanks and three combat troops, which could each muster three or four vehicles for a mission. In May 1968 two tank dozers were added to the establishment, and by September the squadron was brought up to its full strength of four troops, each with four operational Centurions.

The Australians fielded Mark 5 Centurions which had been delivered in 1960. Before being shipped to South East Asia several modifications were made. Additional armour plating was welded to the hull front to give extra protection against mine blasts, an additional 450 litre fuel tank was added, a .30 calibre machine gun was mounted above the commander's cupola and a ranging .50 calibre machine gun was mounted next to the main gun. This normally fired tracer bullets and was an invaluable aid to aiming when the Centurions were engaging VC bunkers in poor tropical light.

Once in Vietnam, crews stripped the track guards from the side of the hull; mud and vegetation would build up there, impeding progress and even leading to track shedding. Racks were built on the back of most tanks to carry jerry cans filled with water and fuel. When each crew mounted for battle their vehicle was loaded up with 62 rounds for the 20 pounder main armament, 4,000 rounds of .50 cal and 9,000 rounds for the .30 cal mounted on the cupola's pintle and the two coaxial MGs. The attachment of an ARV and a dozer tank allowed a troop to master most of the difficult terrain encountered in South Vietnam.

In countless actions, both small and large, the Centurions were valuable assets. They were invulnerable to small arms fire and RPGs could only inflict superficial damage in most cases. The biggest danger was the standard Chinese anti-tank mine, which could knock out the tank's suspension and tracks. The tanks were often called upon to clear out anti-personnel minefields – by driving straight over them. Another threat came from the Viet Cong arming artillery shells or dud aircraft bombs and rigging them as IEDs (Improvised Explosive Devices). Sometimes Viet Cong stayed with these large shells and detonated them when the tanks drew near.

BATTLE OF FIREBASES BALMORAL AND CORAL

The Centurions soon proved their worth. The Americans requested the Australian task force set up firebases north of Saigon to interdict major communication routes used by the VC and NVA. In early May 1968 Australian infantry from 3 RAR, supported by several artillery batteries and a mortar company, established Coral and Balmoral, 60 kilometres north west of the Nui Dat task force base.

The North Vietnamese did not take kindly to this.

Some material was airlifted to Coral on 13 May, while the majority of the infantry and artillery arrived by road. The day was spent furiously digging fortifications for headquarters sections and weapon posts for the six 105mm artillery pieces. The function of a firebase was to support aggressive allied patrols in interdicting supplies and breaking up enemy concentrations. Since the artillery pieces provided the justification for the firebases they were the first to be dug in, with multiple machine gun positions surrounding the fire pits. Once the artillery and magazines were entrenched individuals could begin to work on their own 'scrapes' (foxholes).

Later in the afternoon rain began to bucket down, making it difficult for any worthwhile scrapes to be dug. Soldiers had to content themselves with meagre cover as shallow as one foot deep. Some of the more experienced squaddies noticed something else. As night fell, seemingly random shots from beyond the perimeter could be heard. They didn't do any damage, but were recognised as ranging shots for a battle to come. The communists also laid out the lines of assault and used green tracer to highlight their objectives.

At 2a.m. RPGs slammed into the canopy of some trees, still within the 2km wide perimeter of the firebase. One platoon suffered dreadfully with this attack; one man was killed and shrapnel wounded 11 others.

This was just an aperitif. At 3.30a.m. red and green flares howled over the base. NVA troops who had infiltrated to the edge of the perimeter stood and began to pour AK 47 fire into the incomplete Australian defences. RPGs and mortar rounds smashed into the base and two large thrusts overran much of the 1 RAR mortar position and one of the gun pits.

Fighting raged through the rest of the night and the NVA only began to withdraw at dawn when American artillery batteries, helicopters and fighters were called in to strafe the Vietnamese.

Superior fire power allowed the Australians to prevail. They suffered nine killed and 28 wounded in this set piece battle. Fifty-two enemy bodies were found around and within the perimeter, along with many blood trails indicating where corpses or wounded soldiers had been dragged away.

The NVA weren't finished and on the evening of the 16 May launched another powerful attack, with elements of a regiment of VC supporting the NVA regulars. Five more Aussies fell to this attack with another 19 wounded. Once again the NVA penetrated the wire and it was touch and go whether the base could survive.

This was enough as far as the commanders at Nui Dat were concerned. A convoy set out and soon the four tanks of 1st Troop C Squadron were within the Coral perimeter, and four from 2nd Troop were ensconced in Balmoral.

No doubt the VC commanders knew of this reinforcement, but nevertheless a battalion of NVA assaulted Balmoral. Coming in waves the regulars stormed up to the wire – directly in front of two Centurions armed with extra shells of canister shot. Shell after shell was fired into the oncoming NVA while the tanks' coaxial 30 cal machine guns fired thousands of rounds down the axis of attack. Aiding the defensive fire were two artillery batteries, one Kiwi and one Australian, who fired into the forming up areas of the attacking troops. This time the communists did not get close to penetrating the perimeter, as flares made them perfect targets for the fusillade of weaponry.

It wasn't over for the stricken NVA; the next day a troop of tanks with infantry from D Company 3 RAR sallied out of Balmoral to take the fight to the enemy. In the first example of tank-infantry cooperation since World War II, the Australians stormed a NVA bunker complex. The infantry would use flares or the phones mounted at the rear of the tank to indicate the location of the NVA bunkers and two or three tanks would concentrate their 20 pdrs on the target, pouring high explosive shells in to blow them to smithereens. Sometimes the bunkers were crushed under the 50 tonne tank's tracks. After three hours the bunker complex was all but destroyed.

The NVA were known for their determination and on 28 May another attack was launched straight at the Balmoral defences. This time it was an entire regiment, but no success was gained as they charged straight into the cannon fire of the Centurions. Even though they managed to carry off most of their dead, 42 North Vietnamese corpses were found in the perimeter the following morning. The Australians suffered one killed and eight wounded in this final attack.

The Centurions had proved themselves to be battle winners and life savers. This would become clear in one of the largest battles fought in Vietnam by the Australians: the Battle of Binh Ba.

FRAGGING

In Vietnam between 1969 and 1972 almost 1,000 fragging incidents occurred in the American Army. Eighty-six were fatal. The act of attacking one's own officers was called fragging after the weapon of choice: a fragmentation grenade lobbed at the overly keen officer in question.

Fragging was not only an American pastime.

On 10 December 1967 the Australian gunners of the 106 Field Battery 4th Field Regiment were resting after 17 days of almost continuous action supporting Australian infantry formations in Phuoc Tuy Province. At 8p.m., 15 minutes after the last fire mission of the day, a grenade was heard detonating within the perimeter of Fire Support

Base Bravo where the battery was situated. Some soldiers dived into their holes while others recognised it as a hand grenade and put it down to an accidental discharge.

Things took a serious turn for the worse when a 23-year-old Lieutenant was heard screaming for help from his dug in tent near the centre of the base. The young officer, the only son of a farming family in NSW, was found doubled up in pain and bleeding from multiple wounds. A chopper raced the wounded man to a field hospital, but after emergency surgery and multiple transfusions he died from blood loss and organ failure.

Just before he was evaced out the lieutenant had pointed to a nearby bunker and said the grenade had come from that direction. The next morning a grenade crater was found next to the officer's tent along with the M26 grenade striker lever. The evidence pointed to the bunker occupied by a disgruntled Gunner being the source of the grenade.

The two men had been in an altercation the very same day that the grenade was thrown. The gunner was, it seems, fond of the local beer and had been overindulging. His officer had threatened disciplinary action next time the gunner mucked up.

The suspect was firmly in the frame. He had earlier told his mates he would fix the lieutenant, who was obviously out to get him. He even told one of his gunner mates that he was going to lob a grenade at the officer, not to wound him but to kill.

It appears that the gunner, a nasho, was finding conditions in Vietnam difficult and particularly wanted to get leave so he could visit his newborn daughter. However, he seemed distressed as the severity of his officer's wounds were revealed.

On 15 January 1968 the gunner was tried by a General Court Martial. He was found guilty of manslaughter and sentenced to five years' imprisonment and a dishonourable discharge from the army.

Eight months later the conviction was quashed. It was argued that there was no proof that the accused ever had a M26 grenade in his possession and the evidence was purely circumstantial.

If that was the case, who fragged the artillery Lieutenant?

THE BATTLE OF BINH BA

Most people think of Vietnamese villages being built of flimsy materials such as bamboo, palm leaves and timber. While this is true of some provinces, the village of Binh Ba – very close to the main base at Nui Dat – was representative of many villages in Phuoc Tuy Province, built of brick and stone. Not only that but it was laid out in a planned grid formation with a large central square. The buildings were considerable structures and in the coming battle the Centurions often had to use their armour piercing shells to penetrate the VC defensive positions.

Binh Ba was only ten or so kilometres from the Australian base at Nui Dat. It was considered fairly secure; Route 2, the main road going past it, was classified at an amber threat level. This meant that an attack from the village was 'unlikely.'

'Unlikely' or not, on the morning of 6 June 1969 a Centurion and an accompanying ARV were shot at from the outskirts of the village. The RPG struck the Centurion's turret and wounded one of the crewman. Both vehicles sprayed the buildings with machine gun fire before moving out of range and calling in the incident.

It still remains unclear why the unidentified soldier fired the RPG. It may have been under orders. NVA regiments elsewhere were copping a hammering from the Australian Task Force and this may have been an attempt to divert resources from the northern battle. The local commander may have wanted to score a propaganda victory by getting the Australians to attack the now well-fortified village. Or else it may just have been an undisciplined soldier breaking fire discipline.

Whatever the reason, the single RPG round provoked a massive Australian response and the consequence was a singular Australian victory.

On the evening of 5 June elements of the 1st Battalion 33 NVA Regiment and the Viet Cong D440 Battalion had moved in and set up defence positions throughout the village.

Once alerted to the enemy presence the Australian Task Force Ready Reaction Force set off to eliminate the threat. D Company 5 RAR, a troop of Centurions and a troop of M113 APCs from the 3rd Cavalry Regiment were supported by the Australian 105 Battery as well as helicopter gunships from No 9 Squadron RAAF.

The great Australian general, Sir John Monash, who pioneered the use of combined arms on the Western Front, would have appreciated the well balanced force that was about to take on an entrenched, well armed foe. A perfect combination of mobility, firepower and communications overcame the one Australian weakness, a lack of infantry. D Company was at half strength, with just 65 men.

Major Murray Blake, the commander of the Ready Reaction Force, liaised with units of the ARVN to block some exit points and arrayed his forces to assault the town. The members of the 1st Battalion 33 NVA prepared to fight to the death.

By 11.30 the Australians formed up in an armoured phalanx to the south east of the village. The tanks were at the front of the formation while the mounted infantry were to their flanks and in support. The NVA began proceedings with a barrage of RPGs, but the Australians were well out of range at 300 metres.

Soon after, Operation Hammer began. The Australians moved to clear Binh Ba of hostiles.

The houses on the south east of Binh Ba received a volley of shellfire and machine gun fire from the advancing vehicles. As the armour penetrated into the village their turrets traversed left and right, firing high explosive and armour piercing rounds into the solid buildings. The NVA fought back desperately with RPGs and submachine gun fire. Behind the tanks came the APCs, firing thousands of rounds from their turret mounted machine guns. Helicopters flew overhead, targeting hostile troops seeking to reinforce the defences and radioing in the location of VC strongpoints.

As the task force penetrated into the town square it was realised that the opposition was at least at battalion strength. NVA troops seemed to swarm all around the Australian vehicles. Multiple rounds slammed against the Centurions, disabling kit and wounding crew men. After several hours in this maelstrom of fire, ammunition was running low.

With close range support from the Bushranger helicopter gunships armed with mini guns, the task force fought its way out of town to lick their wounds. Every Centurion had been hit with multiple rockets and one RPG had even penetrated a tank's armoured hull. One vehicle had its traverse mechanism knocked out. Many crewmen were wounded and had to be medivaced out, their places taken by reserve tank crewmen. One tank commander had a remarkable escape. He felt rather than saw the discharge of an RPG and ducked into his hatch. He was only just quick enough – the rocket's fins grazed his back as it passed.

No Australians were killed but the force spent an hour replenishing ammunition and replacing wounded crewmen. B Company 5 RAR was dispatched as reinforcements, as were tanks from 4 Troop.

The second assault went in. This time the infantry dismounted from their APCs and, in close liaison with the tanks and M113s, began to clear each house within the village. Teams of two to three men would wait until a 20 pounder was fired into a building or until the doors had been blown in. The tanks would put a canister round into the defences. The infantry threw in grenades to clear the rooms and then went in with all guns blazing to kill any remaining enemy soldiers. It was during this phase of the battle that Private Wayne Teeling received a mortal shot in the neck. Teeling's comrade climbed onto the hatch of a nearby tank and pointed out the building where the deadly fire had come from. A high explosive round slammed into the building, killing the six NVA soldiers defending the position.

As the infantry moved through the town, grenades were thrown into bunkers while air assets brought artillery onto suspected NVA strong points. The Australians had an edge as they had been trained for MOUT (Military Operations in Urban Terrain), even if they had not had cause to use these skills in Vietnam.

This second assault cleared most of the village. Dead NVA and VC bodies were hauled into the central square and placed in gruesome lines to be searched for documentation. At least 107 enemies were killed, with many more wounded or captured. The Australians lost one killed and nine wounded. Sweeps and interdiction movements in the following days ensured that Binh Ba was finally cleared and, on 8 June, Operation Hammer was finally concluded as an exceptional victory for the task force.

There is no doubt that without the heavy armour and firepower supplied by the Centurion tanks, the Australian casualties would have been a lot heavier.

The Centurions became a vital part of the Australian operation in Vietnam. By 1971 all three squadrons of the 1st Armoured Regiment had rotated one or more times through Vietnam. After the original deployment of 26 tanks, 58 vehicles had served in the battle zone. Forty-two had been damaged, with six declared total write offs. Only two crewmen were killed, testifying to the resilience and strength of the Centurion as well as the superior training of the crews.

VICTORY AND RETREAT

By 1969 the 1 ATF was at its strongest. More than 8,000 men and women from the three services were making life in Phuoc Tuy intolerable for the NVA and VC. By 1970 search and cordon missions were no longer undertaken, as the villages were all but clear of insurgent influence. New firebases were regularly set up and the infantry would sally out on patrols to ambush or capture the few remaining VC. All Main Force Units were withdrawn and remnants of D445 preferred by and large to stay out of the way of the Australians.

The insurgents did have one other reason to avoid combat: in 1969 Nixon had made it clear that the Americans would begin withdrawing their half a million men from Vietnam, and planned to hand over responsibility for defence to the ARVN. Australia too, under Prime Minister Gorton, announced that troops would not be replaced when they were rotated home.

By November 1971, Nui Dat was handed over to the ARVN. Soon after that the last Australians were shipped out of Vung Tau. With the allied withdrawal, the professional NVA soon overran the south.

In the course of the conflict, 15,381 Australians served in Vietnam; 495 soldiers died, along with 17 from the RAAF and eight from the RAAN. Just over 3,000 were wounded.

Despite the cost, physically and mentally, the Australian military had etched another proud chapter into its history. Three years after 1 ATF's deployment there was at least one province which the American high command did not have to worry about. Phuoc Tuy.

CHOPPERS IN THE 'NAM

On 8 March 1966 Prime Minister Harold Holt announced that a helicopter squadron of the RAAF would be sent to South Vietnam.

Two months later eight Bell UH-1B Iroquois, or 'Huey', helicopters of 9 Squadron RAAF were shipped to Vietnam in HMAS *Sydney*.

To the disappointment of many diggers, immediate support was not given by choppers. The Australian base at Nui Dat was too small and was continually subject to incoming mortar or rocket fire from VC raiding parties. To minimise the effect of these attacks, 'the Dat' was subject to an evening blackout. Choppers being choppers, they needed around the clock maintenance, so the squadron was based at the more secure base at Vung Tan on the coast.

The commander knew that to chuck his choppers straight into the fray would decimate his small unit. While the Yanks were able to commit large numbers on an operation, the equipment of the 9 needed modification. It took a while for the crews to acquire belly armour for their mounts, and flak jackets had to be scrounged from American depots.

The Battle of Long Tan on 18 August 1966 saw things begin to look up for the Australian pilots. While shots, shell, rockets and pouring rain swamped the desperate diggers of D Company, 6 RAR, they began to run out of ammunition. As night fell the commander called for an urgent resupply. Two choppers were loaded with more than half a ton of magazines and belts of ammo. The heavily laden helicopters flew in at tree top level and, in the howling rain, managed to pinpoint the company position and drop the cargo right where it was needed. D Company's commander was in no doubt that he owed the survival of his command to the pilots of 9 Squadron. His radio operator reported on the successful mission with these classic words: 'You bloody beaut. That was smack on.'

The unit also helped with evacuating wounded and dead from the battlefield. Two choppers were crewed and fuelled around the clock, waiting for a call for a medivac.

Until 1968 the Iroquois operated by the Australians were configured as what the Americans called a 'slick'; armed with one pintle mounted M60 machine gun on each side and crewed by two door gunners, a pilot and a co-pilot. The pilot flew the chopper and his co-pilot acted as a navigator, while the two door gunners kept their eyes out for any hostiles in the terrain below. They were able to ferry eight fully loaded infantry to and from the battlefield and were invaluable for dropping infantry squads into locations that lacked any infrastructure. Iron nerves and rapid decision making was required when called to insert or extract patrols from what were often 'hot' drop zones. They were also on call for supply runs and for medical evacuations called a 'dust-off'. Spreading defoliant over suspected VC hideouts was another task. Crews added firepower to their slicks in defiance of orders. Additional machine guns, M79 grenade launchers and various pieces of commandeered hardware were added to the helicopter arsenals.

SAS deep penetration raids posed a challenge for the helicopter crews. It was vital that these intelligence gathering missions remain undetected by the wily foe. When 'inserting' a patrol, helicopters crisscrossed the countryside as decoys. Identifications on choppers were swapped and zigzag flight patterns confounded the enemy. Under cover of these measures most insertions went smoothly, undetected by the enemy. Sometimes though, a hot landing was encountered where the mission would be aborted and gunships or jets were called up to pound the enemy. Extractions were challenging. Pilots had to use 'dead reckoning' to get in radio contact with the patrol, before being guided to the pickup point by a single shielded torch shone up to the sky.

One remarkable role was to operate American 'snoopy' equipment. This remarkable machine was operated from a Huey and was designed to detect sweat, human waste and smoke. The APD (Aerial Personnel Detector) could track VC units in dense jungle. The VC took countermeasures though; they would suspend bamboo filled with urine from trees and move to another location!

Platoon and squad search-and-destroy deployments were the bread and butter of 9 Squadron. On occasion they were involved in much larger operations. During Operation Bribie on 17 February 1967, seven Australian choppers cooperated with American compatriots to airlift a large number of infantry from 6 RAR into blockading positions, in an effort to corral and destroy several large enemy units. In the chaotic fighting involved in the operation, the choppers proved the battle winning difference. One chopper flew 28 missions in one day, ferrying troops and evacuating wounded.

During its stint in Vietnam, personnel of 9 Squadron won almost 30 Distinguished Flying Crosses.

The Bushmaster

In 1968 the RAAF in Vietnam were given a lethal new weapon. New model Huey's with increased lift capacity were purchased and armed with deadly array of weaponry. Firstly, two 7 tube rocket pods were strung from the side of the machine. Salvoes of these rockets could destroy bunkers and take out concentrations of enemy infantry. Added to the arsenal were two pod mounted 7.62 mini guns with a load of 9,600 rounds. They had a staggering rate of fire of 2,000-6,000 RPMs. Finally, each of the door gunners was equipped with dual mounted M60 machine guns with 4,000 rounds apiece.

Three bushrangers were all it took to turn many a firefight in favour of the Australians. The amount of lead they could pour into formed troops was truly staggering. When the VC saw them approaching they usually broke off the action and dispersed. In set piece battles such as Binh Bah, the 'Bushmasters' were used a tactical asset that could close off avenues of retreat or break up enemy concentrations.

CHAPTER 12

WINNING THE PEACE

After the Vietnam War, Australia has continued to play an active role in world affairs. However, while the country's commitment to satisfying treaty and alliance obligations has continued, our armed forces have not been deployed to the same extent as they were at the height of the Cold War.

The armed forces' role has been twofold: as a peacekeeping or observation force operating under the aegis of the United Nations (UN), and as an ally of America fighting in the Middle East.

PEACE KEEPING

The Golan Heights is one of the most contested regions in world history. For millennia the local peoples – including Babylonians, Palestinians, Assyrians, Greeks, European Crusaders, Ottomans and Jews – have been fighting over the strategic heights overlooking the Jordan Valley that dominate the approaches to modern day Israel. Most of the territory was seized by Isreal during the 1967 Six-Day War.

Since then UN observers, resplendent in their blue helmets, have sat perched upon the Heights, observing the two sides of the border and reporting on any worrying developments.

Australian military peacekeepers sent to keep an eye on the fractious neighbours may not know it, but there is a connection with their World War II forbears on top of the rocky hills bordering Syria and Israel. After World War II, Syria purchased surplus military equipment from the USSR as well as some reconditioned German panzers. Among these were several Panzer IV's, similar to the type which had been used by Rommel to try and capture Tobruk. During the Six-Day War, the Syrians had dug the panzers in and used them as armoured strong points. All were captured or destroyed by the IDF (Israel Defence Forces) in their successful offensives. By all accounts many of the rusting hulks of the once proud panzers are still atop the Heights, in the no-man's-land between the two states. No doubt many Australian Peace Keepers have observed them, whether they were aware of the provenance or not.

After the Second World War the newly formed UN (United Nations) took upon itself the role of monitoring and observing hostilities in an attempt to make sure that no major conflicts arose. While the UN's record is mixed, Australia, as a founding member of the UN, has played an important role in every major peacekeeping operation since 1947.

One of the longest deployments of the Australian military is their contribution to observing the ceasefire lines between Israel and her Moslem neighbours, and the monitoring of border violations by either side.

Since 1956 Australian military observers have been staking out the borders. Rotating in to isolated observation posts, accompanied by a representative from another nation, they have been tasked with watching the demarcation lines with binoculars, listening to radio chatter and interviewing the locals, before reporting back to the UN with reliable and impartial intelligence. This part of the UN is called the United Nations Truce Supervision Organisation (UNTSO).

Giving invaluable support to the troops on the ground are members of the RAAF. They use Iroquois helicopters to fly personnel and supplies to isolated observers in remote locations, such as the Sinai Desert, another historical flashpoint.

In fact, it was two Australians who first set up observation posts at these lethal flashpoints, just after the ceasefire between the warring parties. In June

1967, even while Egyptian forces were still exchanging shots with Israeli forces, who had occupied the Sinai desert up to the Suez Canal, Major Roy Skinner set up a control and observation centre at Qantara. His only protection was the UN flag flying proudly above his bullet-pocked building. Over the next several weeks Skinner set up a chain of observation posts and opened a dialogue between the commanders of the Israeli and Egyptian forces.

On the Golan Heights, a ceasefire was organised by the UNTSO's commander on 5 June 1967. Major Keith Howard led a detachment of UNTSO personnel up to the heights. Their first order of business was to mark out a 1 kilometre wide buffer zone and string a line of observation posts across them. Later, permanent structures would be built at these locations, but in 1967 they were more like shell scrapes. There were often exchanges of fire between the rival parties and it was always a danger that the UN personnel would be caught in the crossfire. Nevertheless, the UN presence became known and there are still Australian observers attached to UNTSO, doing their bit to maintain the peace. Their role is no doubt particularly dangerous at present, given the ongoing civil war in Syria.

It seems that Australians have been at the heart of countless flashpoints at the behest of the UN.

The UN came into being in 1945 and is an organisation dedicated to the maintenance of world peace and security. Australia was one of the founding members and was instrumental in the creation of the organisation's mandate. The UN has exercised military force on three occasions: the Korean War (1950-1953), the Sues Crisis (1956) and the first Gulf War (1991). Australia has contributed troops to the first and last of these crises.

In addition, the UN has set up various bodies to monitor flashpoints around the globe. Agencies that report directly to the Security Council, such as UNTSO, have operated all around the world. Australia has been involved in more than their fair share of assignments. These Australian postings have included Somalia, Cambodia, Rwanda, Iran, Iraq, The Middle East, Namibia, Indonesia, Papua New Guinea, the Solomon Islands, Bougainville, Somalia, and Zimbabwe.

These actions have not been of little consequence. More than 30,000 Australian military personnel have served in nearly 30 countries over the last six decades.

While this book cannot cover all the details of these operations, two are of particular note. The first is Rwanda, where Australian troops were exposed to the murderous activities of the Hutu and Tutsis. The second is East Timor, where the Australian government's rapid decision making turned a potentially catastrophic situation into the birth of a new nation state. The troops in Timor moved between peace keeping and peace enforcing.

HELL IN RWANDA

In April 1994 civil war broke out between the Tutsi minority and the Hutu majority in the tiny landlocked nation of Rwanda. This soon degenerated into a slaughter never seen in the modern world. The Hutus took to their Tutsi neighbours and moderate Hutus with the machete, massacring up to a million men, women and children. The slaughter continued until a Tutsi rebel army, the Rwandese Patriotic Front (RPF), seized power in July 1994. The UN had looked on helplessly. Only when the fighting died down did they send assistance under the UN Assistance Mission for Rwanda (UNAMIR).

The Australian government decided to send a contingent of medical personnel, accompanied by an infantry company for security purposes.

The first Australian component of UNAMIR landed in Rwanda in August 1994.

Its 308 members consisted of a medical company, an infantry company from 2/4 RAR, four armoured personnel carriers and a logistic support company. Two surgical teams were included and the medical unit was drawn from three services: 17 from the RAAF, seven from the RAN and the balance from the army. Twenty-six members of the medical team were women.

They landed in a hell on earth. Even though 'hostilities' had ceased, the country was still boiling with intense fear, anger and violence.

In addition to the one million killed, three million people had been internally displaced and two million had sought refuge in neighbouring countries such as Uganda. The economy was destroyed, infrastructure had collapsed and disease and infection from polluted waterways were in epidemic proportions.

When the Australians set down in Kigali's airport, plumes of smoke could be seen on the horizon. These showed where still smouldering villages had been 'cleansed'. Even in the airport things were no better. The floors, walls and luggage conveyers were covered in blood, while rotting corpses and body parts were strewn around the terminal. The unit was located at Kigali Central Hospital, but more decomposing bodies had to be cleared from the wards before medical procedures could begin. Attempts were made to count the numbers of victims who had perished while trying to take refuge in government buildings. As in the aftermath of Cambodia's experience with Pol Pot, the only way to do this was to line up the skulls of the deceased in rows of ten.

Random shootings, rapes and explosions continued to plague the medicos, and it was almost impossible to form routines with the variety of trauma cases experienced. Long shifts of 12 hours for the doctors and nurses and their guards were made more difficult by regular standoffs with RPF soldiers that could easily have degenerated into firefights.

Worse was to come for the second rotation, which replaced the first Australian contingent in February 1995. In April a detachment was sent to Kibeho, in the south of Rwanda, where more than 100,000 Internally Displaced Persons (IDPs) were taking shelter in a vast refugee camp. The RPF was determined to clear this and other camps as they saw them as a possible source of future Hutu resistance. They began clearing the civilians out, requiring them to run a gauntlet where surviving Tutsi's could identify any who had been involved in the horrific massacres. Those who were identified were hauled away and executed. Soon the Hutu's within the camp began to kill their compatriots to avoid being identified and the RPF began to shoot at the refugees. The Australians were powerless to prevent the massacres. Desperate civilians stampeded out of the compound and over the makeshift UN hospitals. Thousands died as machine guns, rifles and RPGs were fired into the fleeing masses.

For the first time since the Vietnam War, Australian infantrymen were given the order to fix bayonets, as they sought to fend off panicked civilians and armed militia. Despite this, restraint was called for. If the soldiers had returned fire they would have been wiped out, and the new Rwandan administration would have had an excuse to eject the UN from their strife ridden country. Most of the team was airlifted out in UN choppers.

On the following day, 23 April 1995, the Australians returned to Kibeho to look for wounded and count the dead. Within the immediate camp environs more than 4,000 corpses were counted. Blood trails where soldiers had dragged the dead off for disposal were everywhere. The unit patched up as many innocent casualties as they could and medivaced many back to Kigali.

During the next couple of years the medical teams concentrated on training up Rwandan personnel to perform many of their medical duties. The last detachment was withdrawn in 1996. While no casualties were inflicted on the Australians, many returned home with deep psychological scarring from the horrors they were forced to witness.

EAST TIMOR

The Australian deployment in East Timor proved that the Australian Army are still masters of intensive patrolling in a jungle setting.

East Timor was a Portuguese colony until granted independence in 1975. The former colonial power had done little to bring the country of almost a million inhabitants out of a primitive state of subsistence agriculture. The Indonesian military annexed the country as its 27th Province in December 1975. What followed were 25 years of harsh repression that saw a brutal crackdown on independence movements and an estimated 200,000 Timorese losing their lives to violence, starvation and disease.

In 1999 the newly elected Indonesian government allowed the citizens of East Timor a democratic vote to determine their future. The impoverished inhabitants could vote for complete independence, or to become an autonomous province remaining part of Indonesia but with some aspects of self-rule.

On 30 August 1999 a UN supervised referendum delivered an overwhelming vote to become an independent nation.

The TNI (Indonesian Army) and militias loyal to Jakarta did not respond positively to this development. Australians were shocked to see news footage of militia men chasing civilians and hacking them down with machetes. The military took to burning down large swathes of housing and destroying infrastructure.

A crisis had erupted on Australia's doorstep. The campaign of violence, rape, murder, looting and arson led to many deaths. Almost half a million Timorese fled their homes to take refuge in nearby hills.

The UN did not stand idly by. On 15 September 1999 the United Nations Security Council passed Resolution 1264, calling for a multinational force to 'enforce' the peace, to allow a peacekeeping force to arrive and 'maintain' the peace.

Under international pressure Indonesia agreed to allow the International Force in East Timor (INTERFET) to land and restore order. At its peak there would be 11,000 personnel from 23 nations deployed to the new state. Australian troops formed the core of this multinational force – 5,500 Australians would serve.

Australian Major General Peter Cosgrove was placed in charge of INTERFET. In the combined operation that followed, the RAAF, RAN and the Army all played crucial roles in the rapid deployment of forces within the troubled country.

The RAAF deployed F/A 18 Hornets and F111 fighter bombers to Tindal in the Northern Territory to provide close support of the coming landings. In addition, C130 Hercules and DHC4 Caribou loaded up with the personnel and equipment of the first landing elements. Fourteen ships were provided, including the frigates *Adelaide, Anzac, Darwin, Sydney, Newcastle* and *Melbourne*. Of particular use was the fast transport catamaran *Jervis Bay*.

On 20 September the lead elements of the 3 RAR, supported by special forces troops, landed in five aircraft to secure Dili Airport. The 3rd is something of a crack outfit and was the only fully air capable battalion in the Royal Australian Regiment. Membership required full training to earn a parachutist's badge. Cosgrove would later recognise the battalion as the 'backbone' of the operation. As the troops landed they immediately cleared any potential hostile personnel from the zone and secured a safe perimeter. Elements of the 2 RAR secured Dili Port, and the remainder of 3 RAR Group, with 108 Field Battery and B Squadron of the 3rd/4th Cavalry Regiment, steamed in to land from HMAS *Jervis Bay* and HMAS *Tobruk*. Thirty-three sorties from Hercules transports brought in supplies and defence works, and by the 24 hour mark 1,500 troops had landed. One day later, 3,000 boots were on the ground.

Into the fraught situation came the well armed and trained infantry. As Cosgrove opened communications with local Indonesian commanders, the RAR personnel fanned out in small patrols to disarm the militia. Using rigid protocols, the Australians were able defuse potentially lethal situations without the need to engage in heavy firefights. There was one major notable exception to this: when a recce party of the SAS were set upon by 20 militia. They were pulled out by Black Hawk helicopters after inflicting up to five casualties.

Seeing the destruction and devastation all around them, many diggers would have welcomed an opportunity to engage the militia, but training and good sense overcame these urges. The Indonesian military withdrew by sea, although one unit used the difficult roads into West Timor.

With Dili secure, the amalgamated 5/7 RAR Battalion group arrived on 10 October. Even at this later date Dili was largely deserted, as the population was still hiding in the hills. At night time the soldiers could see cooking fires surrounding the town as the locals cooked their dinners. The advantage that the 5/7 had was that it was fully equipped with M113 APCs. They were able to drive out into the surrounding countryside at platoon strength and set up a mobile platoon base in the small villages that dotted the countryside. Here they gathered information and brought in much needed medical and food supplies for the civilians.

In an accident of history, there is a small enclave on the northern shore of West Timor which is part of the original Portuguese Timor. This tiny bit of land is called Oecussi and a small detachment of the 5/7, along with four APCs, a troop of SAS and a platoon of Ghurkhas, was dispatched to seize the town. Once again the population had disappeared but, hearing of the Australian arrival, within 24 hours 10,000 people had returned.

3 RAR was posted to the Oecussi enclave, and it is here that the well trained infantrymen spent many long hours patrolling the border with West Timor – just as in Vietnam section sized patrols would set out to secure the terrain around the central firebase. Even though there was no threat as lethal as the VC, few chances were taken and the patrols moved through the bush using all their skills to ensure that they were not ambushed or attacked.

Each man knew his role. At each stop the unit would assume defensive positions and follow hand signals before going into bivouac. The greatest challenge was the harsh, mountainous terrain that the rifle companies had to patrol.

While 3 RAR had secured Oecussi, 5/7 RAR was responsible for securing coastal towns such as Liquica and hill towns such as Balibo. All around them was the debris of the post-election violence. The unit then relieved 2 RAR, which had used counterinsurgency tactics to secure the border. The APCs steadied the local population and night vision equipment allowed the troops to patrol the border.

There was still a threat. The militias had been largely ejected from East Timor but some groups bent on revenge sought to cross the border to destroy crops or attack villages. They proved to be an elusive foe and members of 5/7 often found themselves under attack from random sprays of automatic fire.

By day thirty, Cosgrove declared that 80% of the country was secure and that most of the population could begin to go about their business in a peaceful environment. On 21 February 2000 the 5/7 was given blue berets, becoming the first Australian infantry battalion to be permanently assigned to the UN since the Korean War. INTERFET's task was declared complete in late February 2000 and the UN peacekeeping force assumed responsibility for the new nation.

Despite this the border region was still seen as a hazardous posting. In 2001 the crack formation battalion was posted to the strategically important towns of Bobonaro, Maliano and Balibo. Here the 3 RAR was engaged in a remarkable process called 'Green' bush patrolling and 'Blue' village patrolling. As sections moved through the mountainous border countryside, they performed as if engaged in counterinsurgency operations with the requisite precautions developed during the Vietnam War. Upon approaching a village, a forward scout would ensure that there were no hostile forces there. Once the village seemed safe, the patrol would take off their green 'bush hats' and don the blue headgear that marked them out as UN peacekeepers. They would then enter the village in open formation. There was usually a steady store of sweets and lollies to dole out to the local children, as it was from this source that much of the best intel was gained.

The Australians found themselves in a world where belief in superstition, magic and witchcraft still ruled. Stifling tropical heat was a constant challenge, as was the inhospitable terrain. Troops detached to collect supplies from Dili always felt they were taking their life in their hands when they had to drive the high wheelbase Unimog over the rough mountain roads to the supply depots, despite the excellent off-road characteristics of the 4WD vehicle.

In May 2002 Timor became a fully independent nation state, and in 2005 the last Australian troops were withdrawn. During 2006 political disturbances in Dili saw Australian troops dispatched to the country.

Four Australian soldiers died during the Timor operations, although the casualties were not due to enemy action.

MIDDLE EASTERN CONFLICTS

Australia is one of America's keenest allies and has made a large contribution to that nation's conflicts in the Middle East. These conflicts are still not entirely resolved and even today there are Australian troops operating in the greater Middle East region, notably in Afghanistan and Iraq.

AUSTRALIA'S LONGEST WAR: AFGHANISTAN

Australian troops in the multinational base Tarin Kot in Uruzgan, Afghanistan were given a rude awakening. The silence of the night air was shattered with the tremendous discharge of a barrage of 155mm rounds from a Dutch Panzerhaubitze 2000. This mammoth, state-of-the-art field piece was able to perform the function that would have previously have required a four-piece battery to perform.

Within nine seconds, three 155mm rounds weighing up to 50 kilos each were winging their way towards Taliban forces. The insurgents had ventured out into the open and been spotted by alliance forces. Soon the first swarm of three shells would smash into their ranks, before a longer 50 second barrage of nine shells would finish them off.

Any hostile movements within 40 kilometres of the Australian base were guaranteed a warm reception.

As in Vietnam, the Australian contingents were assigned fortified bases from which they would sally out to fight the Taliban.

While the Australian contingent in Afghanistan has never reached brigade level, the professionalism, superior equipment and superior training make it a formidable foe for even the most wily, hard-line foe.

Australia's involvement in Afghanistan has been a long and difficult experience.

The Australian deployment began in late 2001. In response to the attacks on the World Trade Centre in New York, the American president declared his War on Terror. One of the first targets was the Taliban regime in Afghanistan, which had sponsored and hidden Al-Qaeda, the terrorist organisation of Osama Bin Laden. After intensive air operations, coalition forces were committed to a ground war to remove the Taliban.

Operation Slipper saw an Australian Special Forces Task Group with air support establishing a Forward Operating Base (Camp Rhino) south west of Kandahar. Bases such as these formed the foundation of American and coalition operations in Afghanistan, allowing armed forces to sally out and dispute terrain with the Taliban foe. Unlike the firebases in Vietnam, these were garrisoned by troops from various nations, not just Australians.

The Task Force was instrumental in the seizure of Kandahar International Airport in December 2001. A year later they were pulled out when Australia's initial commitment was wound down.

Phase two of Australia's commitment to the war came in September 2005. The resurgent Taliban was causing casualties with a new form of warfare: the IED, or Improvised Explosive Device. These had caused horrendous casualties to troops in the lightly armed Humvees utilised by the American Army. To counter this threat, the Special Forces Task Force employed the Australian-built Bushmaster. This tough, all-terrain vehicle drew on experience in the African Bush Wars and utilised a V shaped lower chassis to deflect the explosive blast from roadside bombs. Many a member of the SAS Regiment, the Incident Response Regiment and 4 Battalion RAR owe their life to this vehicle. RAAF Chinook helicopters provided heavy lift to the Task Force.

In 2006 the role shifted away from search and destroy missions and the Special Task Force was withdrawn. In their place was the first of four reconstruction task forces tasked with repairing infrastructure in Uruzgan Province. The Dutch-led reconstruction efforts required protection and elements of 5 and 7 Battalions as well as APCs from 2 Cavalry Regiment continued with active patrolling against insurgents. Their chief base was the Forward Operating Base Ripley, outside of Tarin Kot.

Despite the mission statement focussing on reconstruction, the hostile Taliban was always ready to take the fight to the coalition forces. With an uncanny ability to merge with the general population, they proved an elusive but ever present foe. Many Afghans realised that once the coalition forces left, the Taliban would be ready to fill any power vacuum.

As a result of the ongoing conflict, the Reconstruction Task Force was again reinforced with commandoes: a squadron of the SAS, and comms, intel and security assets. By 2007 there were 1,000 Australian personnel; by 2009 this had grown to 1,550.

In 2009 Australian specialists were inserted into Afghan National Army Battalions in Uruzgan Province. The two armies liaise on many operations and this has led to some of the most tragic incidents in Australian military history. As if fighting the Taliban was not enough, a new threat has emerged: the so-called 'green-on-blue' attacks. In May 2011, an Afghan National Army soldier turned his gun on an Australian soldier with fatal consequences, while they were on guard duty at a patrol base in the Chora Valley. In October 2011 three Australians and their Afghan interpreter were gunned down in a similar incident. One day in late August 2012 the Australian Army suffered its worst day of combat losses since the Vietnam War. In another green-on-blue attack, a man in an Afghan Army uniform killed three Australians in an attack at a base at Uruzgan Province. Two more were wounded. On the same day, two special forces men were killed when their chopper crashed while on operations in Helmand Province.

Nevertheless, there have been great examples of heroism in this difficult war. The first Victoria Cross since the Vietnam War was awarded to Corporal Mark Donaldson of 3 Squadron SAS. On 2 September 2008 a convoy was returning from a morning patrol in Uruzgan Province. Mark and his patrol heard a crack and suddenly the convoy was inundated with machine gun fire and rocket propelled grenades. Fire was returned and Corporal Donaldson saw that some of his comrades were wounded. He stepped out of cover and drew enemy fire upon himself until they were drawn to safety. As the convoy moved off, Donaldson saw that their seriously wounded Afghan interpreter had been left behind. The SAS trooper sprinted 80 metres back to save the man and returned safely with him through the enemy fire.

During 2012 and 2013 the Australians pulled out of Uruzgan Province, handing over security to the Afghan troops they had trained. By December 2013 the last Australian formations had left the country, although military personnel continue to train and support the Afghan Army in Kabul and Kandahar. Eleven Australians died on operations in Afghanistan from 2002 to the end of 2009, ten died in 2010, and eleven in 2011. A total of 41 have died during the war.

IRAQ

On 11 April 2003 Australian SAS troops seized Al Asad airbase in western Iraq. One of the key air defence installations of Saddam Hussein's brutal regime, it had to be secured to guarantee the security of the coalition forces in the area. Approximately 500 SAS troops were operating in western Iraq and many of them were present for the assault.

Emerging from the desert in heavily camouflaged vehicles, the elite Australian infantrymen surrounded the base, calling in support from their old friends of 75 Squadron RAAF in FA-18 Hornets. After pounding the militia defending the base, the SAS squadron moved in to take it – and found an Aladdin's cave of ordinance and equipment. What appeared to be gentle dunes or mounds of sand turned out to be heavily camouflaged, Soviet-built MIGs (Russian fighter jets) and attack helicopters. At least 57 MIGs, including the MIG 21 Foxbat Interceptor and several dozen attack helicopters, were part of the haul, along with whole batteries of anti-aircraft guns, machine guns and 7.9 million kilograms of munitions and ordinance.

The allied forces which invaded Iraq on 20 March 2003 numbered over 170,000 men. Approximately 2,000 Australians fought in the operation, but as usual their contribution far outstripped their small numbers.

Conflict with Iraq had begun a decade earlier when Saddam Hussein invaded Kuwait on 2 August 1990. In the First Gulf War which followed, Australian ships joined the multinational naval fleet maintaining order in the Persian Gulf. HMAS *Darwin* and HMAS *Adelaide* made valuable contributions, blockading the Iraq coast and enforcing maritime sanctions. The Australian tanker HMAS *Success* refuelled many coalition vessels while RAAF planes and choppers provided overhead cover.

Hussein and his army were bundled out of Kuwait. His military had suffered huge losses, but such was the strength of his dictatorial hold over Iraq that he survived and began to re-arm.

It was only a matter of time before the USA under the Bush dynasty would move to oust Hussein. A campaign was mounted alleging that Iraq possessed WMD (Weapons of Mass Destruction). While these may have been spurious, Hussein did not help his cause when he publicly inflated the capabilities of his array of SCUD missiles.

When American forces invaded Iraq in 2003, Australian forces marched alongside their allies. Three Hercules aircraft operated by the RAAF provided logistic support, and Hornets from 75 RAAF Squadron gave valuable close support to the advancing ground forces. Two navy AP-3C Orion maritime patrol aircraft operated over the gulf and helped alert HMAS *Darwin* and HMAS *Anzac* as they cleared hazards such as mines from the major Iraqi seaports. These two fighting boats also gave support to seaborne landings of coalition ground troops. HMAS *Kanimbla* played an active role in boarding suspect vessels to look for contraband and hidden weapons.

The major contribution came from the SAS (Special Air Services) Regiment. Several squadrons infiltrated across the borders from neighbouring countries into the vast barren expanses of western Iraq. This small group of men were a decisive strategic factor as they dominated vast swathes of country, denying its use to the enemy. They moved in two days before the main invasion, on 18 March, and may have fired the first shots of the war.

It was here in this hostile region that Hussein had hidden many of his mobile SCUD missiles, which he threatened would be used to rain a hail of destruction on other states, Israel in particular. Guarding these dangerous assets were mobile groups of elite Iraqi Republican Guard mounted on heavily armed four-wheel-drives. These mobile groups were trained to hunt down any special forces detachments, using a variety of tactics. Some would pretend to surrender and, when approached by coalition forces, other dug in elements would launch an ambush. Other units disguised themselves as nomadic Bedouins, with the intention of lulling the SAS into a false sense of security before opening up with automatic weapons.

These tactics all came to naught. The SAS origins were of ranging deep behind Axis lines in the desert during World War II. While their forbears originally used cut down jeeps and Chevrolet trucks, the modern SAS were equipped with long wheel base, triple axis Land Rovers purpose built for long range penetration activities. Designated as the LRPV (Long Range Patrol Vehicle) these tough vehicles were ideally suited for the desert conditions of western Iraq. Each vehicle carried a patrol of four or five men and was armed with several machine guns, including Browning 50 calibre and MAG 58 general service machine guns. They were also armed with grenade launchers and the lethal, shoulder mounted Javelin anti-tank rocket that was designed to reduce any target to its constituent particles. Of course the most lethal tools employed by the SAS were their radios. By moving stealthily at night the units were able to identify and call down destructive fire on any Iraqi formations. These patrols split from the main body and operated individually to sow terror and confusion behind the Iraqi lines.

Within one hour of crossing into Iraq the squadron was engaged in its first firefight. In the next 48 hours, two more large battles took place. In the following days the SAS initiated numerous contacts, using superior training and weapons to take down their Iraqi foes. They also targeted suspected weapon sites and mobile SCUD batteries, destroying many in the first two weeks. The SAS's superior mobility threw confusion into the Iraqi ranks – they were convinced that a much larger force was operating. By the third week of the war the patrols intercepted a number of convoys packed with fleeing Iraqis and even some Arab fighters, entering the country to answer Hussein's call for Jihad. They also established a cordon to prevent SCUDs leaving Baghdad for the west to place them in range of Israel.

The SAS patrols coalesced for the attack on Al Asad airfield and soon after capturing it were joined by elements of 4 RAR. Within a matter of hours the base was operational, and Australian Hercules aircraft brought in much needed supplies.

The special forces garrisoned the base until they were pulled out of the country when victory was declared. However, Iraq soon degenerated into civil war. In 2003 Australian troops were redeployed into Iraq to train Iraqi troops and provide security. They remained there until a phased withdrawal began in June 2008.

No Australian Defence Personnel died due to enemy action in the Gulf Wars.

However, there was one great tragedy in the Iraq War. American forces, grateful to their Australian allies, offered to ship some of the captured Iraqi material back to Australia for display in the National War Museum. This booty included a MIG Foxbat. Sadly, the generous offer was refused.

SELECT BIBLIOGRAPHY

BOOKS

Barnard, Simon. *A-Z of Convicts in Van Diemen's Land* (Text Publishing, Melbourne, 2014)

Bishop, Chris (editor). *WWII: The Directory of Weapons* (Greenwhich Editions, London, 2000)

Fitzsimmons, Peter. *Kokoda* (Hachette Australia, 2006)

Foster, Jason K (editor). *A Century of Anzacs* (New Holland Publishers, Sydney, 2014)

Haythornthwaite, Phillip J. *The Armies of Wellington* (Arms and Armour, London, 1994)

Hocking, Geoff. *The Eureka Stocakde* (Waverton Press)

Lincoln, William. *Uniforms and Accoutrements of the British Army, 1854 Eureka Stockade* (self-published, 2013)

Matthews, T. *Crosses: Australian soldiers in the First War 1914-19* (Boolarong Publications, Brisbane, 1987)

McKay, Gary and Stewart. *Elizabeth Vietnam Shots: a Photographic Account of Australians at War* (Allen and Unwin, Sydney, 2002)

Moore, John. *The First Fleet Marines* 1786-1792 (UQP, Queensland, 1987)

Morgan, Reverend John. *The Life and Adventures of William Buckley* (1854)

Odgers, George. *Army Australia: the Australian Defence Force Series* (National Book distributors, Brookvale, 1993)

Odgers, George. *Air Force Australia: the Australian Defence Force Series* (National Book distributors, Brookvale, 1993)

Odgers, George. *The Royal Australian Navy: An Illustrated History* (Child and Henry, Brookvale, 1985)

Pitt-Purnell, Barrie and sons (editors). *History of the Second World War* (London, 1967)

Simmelhaig, Helen and Spenceley, GFR. *For Australia's Sake* (Thomas Nelson, Australia, 1984).

Stanley, Peter. *The Remote Garrison: the British Army in Australia* (Kangaroo Press, NSW, 1986)

Tench, Watkin. *A Narrative of the Expedition to Botany Bay* (1788)

Convict Life in Australia: An Illustrated History (Summit Books, Dee Why West, 1977)

MAGAZINES

Wartime: Official Magazine of the Australian War Museum (including issues 4, 19, 21,22,24)

WEBSITES

http://www.gunplot.net

First published in 2018 by New Holland Publishers
London • Sydney • Auckland

131-151 Great Titchfield Street, London WIW 5BB, United Kingdom
1/66 Gibbes Street, Chatswood, NSW 2067, Australia
5/39 Woodside Ave, Northcote, Auckland 0627, New Zealand

newhollandpublishers.com

Copyright © 2018 New Holland Publishers
Copyright © 2018 in text: Jonathan J. Moore
Copyright © 2018 in images: New Holland Publishers

A record of this book is held at the British Library and the National Library of Australia.

ISBN 9781760790479

Group Managing Director: Fiona Schultz
Publisher: Alan Whiticker
Project Editor: Rebecca Sutherland
Designer: Sara Lindberg
Production Director: James Mills-Hicks
Printer: Times Printing, Malaysia

10 9 8 7 6 5 4 3 2 1

Keep up with New Holland Publishers on Facebook
facebook.com/NewHollandPublishers